LIFESTYLE SURVEY

Church of Scotland
Board of Social Responsibility

Academic Consultant
Dr Alex Robertson, Department of Social Administration,
Edinburgh University

Published by the Church of Scotland Board of
Social Responsibility and distributed by
Quorum Press, Church of Scotland,
121 George Street, Edinburgh EH2 4YN

First published by the Church of Scotland
Board of Social Responsibility, 1987
and distributed under the imprint of Quorum Press
Church of Scotland, 121 George Street, Edinburgh EH2 4YN.

Robertson, Alexander
    Lifestyle survey.
    1. Scotland—Social life and customs—20th century
    I. Title   II. Church of Scotland, *Board of Social Responsibility*
    941.1085'8   DA826

    ISBN 0-86153-090-X

Typeset by Swanston Graphics Limited, Derby, England

Printed and Bound by W.M. Bett Limited, Tillicoultry, Scotland

LIFESTYLE SURVEY

CONTENTS

This Volume is Dedicated to

Colin Wood Robertson

18.4.41 – 10.12.85

May it be worthy of his memory.

'In thee was wit, fredome, and hardiness;
In thee was truth, manheid, and nobleness;
In thee was rule, in thee was governance;
In thee was virtue withouten variance.'

'Wallace's Lament for
the Graham'.

From

The Wallace (1490)

by

Henry the Minstrel

INTRODUCTION

The Board of Social Responsibility of the Church of Scotland commissioned the Lifestyle Survey and, on its publication, would like to thank the members of the original Working Party for the work which they did in formulating the questionnaire (see Appendix 1 pp 199-209) and overseeing the collation of the results.

The Board would like to express its appreciation of the original idea to the Churches of Sweden which undertook a similar Lifestyle Survey, and to Mr Gunno Armyr, a Sociologist with the Ansvar Insurance Company which sponsored the Swedish survey, and who contributes the chapter, 'A Swedish Comparison'.

After the survey had been completed, the Working Party sought the personal perspectives and comments on the findings from the Very Rev Dr James G Matheson, a former Moderator of the Church of Scotland General Assembly; Dr Jonathan Chick, Consultant Psychiatrist with the Alcohol Problems Clinic of the Royal Edinburgh Hospital; Miss Morag Faulds, former Head of the Social Work Department of Paisley Technical College and a Regional Director of Social Work. The Board is appreciative of the help given by these contributors who have given freely of their knowledge and experience in reflecting their personal insights of the Survey's conclusions.

No words can express the indebtedness of the Board to Dr Alex Robertson of the Department of Social Administration of the University of Edinburgh, for his untiring commitment as primary author of the report on the Survey, and his willingness at all times, even at times of personal difficulty, to use his academic knowledge and skills so that this report can be a significant tool in the hands of the Church in arranging its priorities and in understanding itself better. Dr Robertson was ably supported by his colleagues in the University who helped with the computer processing of the analysis. The dedication of this book to Colin Wood Robertson is made with the Board's full accord. Colin Wood Robertson was the brother of Dr Alex Robertson. He was an active participant in the Church and community in which he lived, and was tragically killed in a road accident in December 1985. Those of us involved in the compilation of this Survey would wish their work to be an offering of thanksgiving for a life in the service of others.

The Board of Social Responsibility trusts that this publication will enable the Church both nationally and locally to reassess its situation and re-establish priority in its work and witness in the future. It would not only be a betrayal of the findings of the report, but the betrayal of the folk that the Church is called to serve, if its significant facts and conclusions were merely noted. It is the Board's prayerful hope that the report will be a base for action because it reveals that there are areas of the Church's life, and the society in which it is set, about which we all ought to be gravely concerned. The witness of the Church through its lifestyle ought to be a way by which the Church, in the name of Christ, makes impact on our society today in Scotland.

In all of this we seek to remember what Jesus said: 'as you do to the least of these My brothers, you do to Me.'

FRANK S. GIBSON
November 1986.

I. THE SURVEY

CHAPTER ONE

INTRODUCTORY MATTERS

Like all meaningful notions in the human sciences, the concept of 'lifestyle' is marked by an intricacy and a degree of ambiguity which make it difficult to construct a definition that is sufficiently precise to ensure complete uniformity of usage in different contexts. Credit for first coining the term is, however, generally accorded to Alfred Adler (see, for example, Munroe 1957, pp.340–3; Eckstein 1984, p.309) who, in rejecting the idea that human behaviour is determined by instinctual drives or simple responses to environmental stimuli, predicated his theory of personality upon the view that the conduct of human beings is guided by certain personally-significant goals which give meaning, purpose and coherence to their actions. Adler's implied emphasis upon those cognitive elements which help shape people's perceptions of the world and the influence such perceptions have upon behaviour continues to be the hallmark of work in this area (Ansbacher 1967). Recent studies have, for example, analysed the effects of ageing (Abrams 1978, 1980; Abrams and O'Brian 1981; Age Concern (England) 1977), and work environment and aspirations (De Luca 1982) upon individuals' ways of adjusting to the world in which they live, as well as the way in which such adjustments may themselves influence such factors as a person's health (Ford and Ford 1980) and family life (Sekaran 1982). From such precedents, and without wishing to enter into semantic or conceptual debate, we may therefore for present purposes view 'lifestyle' as a loose amalgam of attitudes, social circumstances, values and beliefs, and the patterns of behaviour to which these give rise in individuals and social groupings.

The present document reports the methodology and findings of a lifestyle survey carried out by the Board of Social Responsibility in 1984, as a means to learning something of the involvement and influence of Church of Scotland members in the life of the whole community. Religion has of course been shown to be a potent factor in shaping people's views and the ways that they typically behave in a wide variety of settings (see, for example, Lenski 1963). In conjunction with information gained from other surveys (see, for example, Brierley and Macdonald, 1985), a comparison of the attitudes, beliefs and habits of members of the Church of Scotland with those of members of other Churches and of the general public may not only reveal how distinctive Presbyterians and other Christians are in facing contemporary issues in the light of their faith and beliefs, but also provide strategic information to assist with future policy and planning.

The survey was to some extent based on a similar investigation carried out in 1979 by the Swedish Free Churches (Frikyrkosverige 1979). The Scottish survey was planned by a committee convened by the Reverend Frank Gibson and in addition comprising Miss Isobel Grigor, the Reverend John Stevenson, the Reverend Campbell Robertson and Dr Alex Robertson, of the

Department of Social Administration of Edinburgh University, who acted as academic adviser to the investigation. The questionnaire developed by this group covered issues relating to political and religious affiliation and degree of participation or commitment in political and religious affairs, together with opinions on a number of religious, moral and social matters, and the extent to which respondents agreed with statements covering a wide range of personal values, attitudes and forms of behaviour. The questionnaire is replicated in Appendix 1 pp.199ff) and the analysis and discussion in Chapters 2–6 are organised around the responses offered by different groups to the various questions it contains.

Sampling and Administration of the Survey

A sample of 1500 individuals were approached to complete the survey questionnaire. These comprised a random group of 500 drawn from congregations which had themselves been selected at random, to give a sample representative of Church membership distribution throughout Scotland, taking into account the varying sizes of Presbyteries and congregations and their geographic spread, and a group of 1000 people drawn from the Electoral Register.

The Ministers of the congregations drawn at random to provide individuals for the Church-member portion of the sample were approached in March 1984, with a request to provide the names and addresses of three individuals within their congregations, to be drawn from the congregational register by a prescribed procedure, to avoid the possibility of bias in the selection process. Of the 171 Ministers initially approached with this request, 11 refused to provide details of members of their congregations and another 11 failed to reply. An approach was therefore made to a further group of Ministers, also selected at random, to replace those lost in the first request for co-operation.

At this point, it was decided to increase the number of names required from three to five to allow for 'drop-outs', and those Ministers who had initially provided three names were approached again with a request to provide an additional two names from the Communion Roll, also to provide cover for drop-outs. In all, 203 Ministers were approached: 172 responded by providing the details required for the survey, while 11 refused to do so and 20 failed to reply. Ministers' response was sufficient to provide a Church-member sample of 500, plus a 'reserve pool' — also representative of Church membership across the country — to cover for refusals and other forms of non-response in the survey itself.

These were matched against a group of 1000 individuals taken from the Electoral Register, two to correspond to every Church member. An attempt was made to ensure broad comparability between the sample of Church members and that drawn from the Electoral Register by identifying the two individuals whose names appeared a fixed number of places on the Electoral Register (usually 20, though in smaller communities this obviously had to be reduced) before and after that of the congregational member. Because of the method of selecting members of the general public, a proportion of them would clearly also be expected to be members of the Church of Scotland and other churches. From analysis of the results, we then may consider and compare the beliefs, attitudes, and other aspects of the lifestyle of members of different Churches with each other, and with members of the community at large. By basing the sample upon congregations that were varied in terms of geography, size and urban/rural composition, it was also hoped that the survey would provide a picture broadly representative of Scotland as a whole.

In order to achieve a standardised means of delivery which would have greater impact and acceptance than a postal request (and so, it was hoped, elicit a higher response rate) an approach was made to Presbyterial Council Conveners of the Social Responsibility Women's Council to enlist the help of Women's Council delegates in delivering the forms to members of the Church and the general public within their area. The conveners agreed to assist the Board in this exercise and to inform their delegates of the Department's request. Accordingly, in April, Women's Council delegates were sent parcels containing sealed envelopes addressed to those approached to participate in the survey, together with a letter of request for their co-operation and instructions for delivering the questionnaires, and also a card to be returned to the Department when delivery was completed. In those congregations for which no Social Responsibility delegate was recorded, the agreement of the Women's Council was given for the Board to approach the Guild Secretary of each of the congregations in question, with a request for her to deliver the forms instead. In congregations where there was no branch of the Guild, the Minister was invited to nominate a female member of the congregation to assist by delivering forms.

Through these procedures, 510 Church members and 1226 members of the general public had received forms for completion. In addition to the survey questionnaire, the envelope they received contained a letter asking them to participate in the *Lifestyle Survey*. It presented the option of refusal by returning the form, so that a replacement could be found. They were also provided with an envelope for the return of the form, stamped and addressed to Dr Robertson at Edinburgh University, where the analysis of the responses was undertaken. Notice was also given that a reminder and an additional form would be sent out after a specified time lapse. This approach resulted in the response outlined in Table 1.1.

During the months of May and June, this was followed by a mailing of 856 reminders and an additional 647 forms to provide replacements for individuals who had failed to respond following a reminder, or who had indicated their desire not to participate in the survey. The final aggregate response is presented in Table 1.2.

Of the 997 completed forms returned, 746 were from individuals approached through the original request. Mailing to 647 replacements elicited 251 additional responses. The response rate of 997 from a total of 2195 individuals approached was thus 45%. Given the Church of Scotland affiliations specified on the questionnaire and the letter requesting co-

Table 1.1

	Completed	Unreturned	Refused	Form returned	No reply	Not available	Total
Church members	236	208	28	17	8	13	510
General public	292	528	35	24	55	92	1026
Total	528	736	63	41	63	105	1536

Table 1.2

	Completed	Refusals	Uncompleted forms returned	Not known/gone away	Deceased	No response
Church members	408	84	27	32	7	147
General public	589	173	48	123	17	549
Total	997	257	75	155	24	696

operation, it is not perhaps surprising that proportionately more members of the 'Church' than of the 'general public' sample agreed to participate in the survey. It is, however, interesting that the response to those requests delivered in person by members of the Women's Council was so much better than that elicited through the postal approach.

In the text that follows, it may be helpful to some readers to have a definition of the meaning of 'Significance Level' and 'Statistical significance'. These terms are explained briefly here:

Significance level
An arbitrary value used as a criterion for determining whether a given data set departs sufficiently from what would be expected, were only chance factors operating, so that it can evaluate and classify those data as statistically significant. The normal level adopted in the Social Sciences, is 5% of 0, as it is usually denoted p 0.05, where 'p is the probability of the observed results or the probability of the more extreme results occurring by chance alone.'

Statistical significance
The degree to which an obtained result was sufficiently unlikely to have occurred under the assumption that only chance factors were operating, and therefore the degree to which it may be attributed to systematic manipulations. The degree itself is typically specified and denoted as a probability; e.g. $p < 0.05$ means that the results obtained or those more extreme could only have occurred by chance in fewer than 5 cases in 100. The smaller the p-value, the more significant the results; that is, the less likely that they occurred by chance.

REFERENCES

Abrams, M (1979) *Beyond Three-score and Ten: A First Report on a Survey of the Elderly, 1978.* Mitcham, Surrey: Age Concern Research Publications.

Abrams, M (1980) *Beyond Three-score and Ten: A Second Report on a Survey of the Elderly.* Mitcham, Surrey: Age Concern Research Publications.

Abrams, M and O'Brien, J (1981) *Political Attitudes and Ageing in Britain.* Mitcham, Surrey: Age Concern Research Publications.

Age Concern, England (1977) *Profiles of the Elderly, Volume L.* Mitcham, Surrey: Age Concern Research Publications.

Ansbacher, H L L (1967) Lifestyle: a historical and systematic review, *Journal of Individual Psychology*, **23**, pp.191–212.

Brierley, P and Macdonald, F (1985) *Prospects for Scotland: Report of the 1984 Census of the Churches.* Edinburgh: National Bible Society of Scotland.

De Luca, R C (1982) Quotidianita e Aspirazioni Tra Giovani Operai. Una Ricerca Sul Campo Nel Contesto Urbano Torinese, *Sociologia del Lavoro*, **5**, 15–16, pp.191–221.

Eckstein, D G (1984) Lifestyle assessment, in R J Corsini (ed) *Encyclopedia of Psychology*, **2**, pp.309–10. New York: John Wiley and Sons, Inc.

Ford, A S and Ford, W S (1980) The good life: who's practising healthy lifestyles? *Journal of Sociology and Social Welfare*, **7**, pp.440–63.

Frikyrkosverige (1979) *En Livsstilsstudie*, Stockholm: Moderna Lasare.

5

Lenski, R (1963) *The Religious Factor: A Sociological Study of Religion's Impact on Politics, Economics, and Family Life.* New York: Doubleday and Co.

Munroe, R (1957) *Schools of Psychoanalytic Thought.* London: Hutchinson.

Sekaran, V (1982) An investigation of the career salience of men and women in dual-career families. *Journal of Vocational Behaviour*, **20**, pp.111–19.

CHAPTER TWO

CHURCH MEMBERSHIP, BEHAVIOUR AND BELIEFS

Various forms of analysis have been undertaken on the data of the survey. There is of course no way of accurately gauging how the study's results may be biased by the non-responses; although some inferences may be made in the light of associations emerging in the data.

Comparisons between groups naturally tend to focus one's attention on those areas where divergencies exist. Comment will be made upon such differences where they emerge in this analysis. But equal interest attaches where variations fail to appear in domains of attitude, behaviour or belief where one might reasonably expect members of various Churches to operate on a different basis of assumptions from each other and from non-churchgoing members of the general population.

The following discussion will consider convergencies and dissimilarities of response under the three broad rubrics of (i) general background factors; (ii) religion and the Church; (iii) social and moral issues; (iv) Lifestyle and (v) Alcohol. For the purposes of this analysis, those people from the 'general' sample who identified themselves as members of the Church of Scotland have been added to the sample of Church members drawn specifically from the Congregational Rolls. This gave a total of 605 Church of Scotland members. In addition, 47 people identified themselves as members of the Roman Catholic Church and a further 56 individuals claimed affiliation to other Churches. This latter group included Baptists, Congregationalists, Methodists, members of the Episcopal Church and the United and Presbyterian Free Churches; but none of these were present in sufficient numbers to make it possible to conduct a separate analysis for any one of these groups. Whilst obviously less than satisfactory from a theological point of view, the members of these denominations therefore had, for purposes of statistical analysis, to be aggregated into a single group of 'other' churches, comprising 56 persons. In addition, 286 individuals claimed no affiliation to any church at all, and these were treated as a single group of non-church members. In the ensuing analysis, comparisons will initially be drawn betweeen Church of Scotland members and other members of the sample, although where appropriate reference will also be made to significant variations on the part of the three remaining groups.

The Statistical Analysis and Interpretation of Results

The emphasis within this first half of the report will be on the presentation and analysis of the statistical trends obtained from the postal survey. Frequent reference will be made in the course of this analysis to the concept of statistical significance, and it may therefore be helpful to provide a brief explanation of how this term will be used throughout this section of the report.

In many places, the data will be presented in a purely descriptive fashion: to outline, for example, the proportion of people within the sample professing a certain belief or point of view, and to highlight trends that seem of particular interest. Given, however, the survey's primary concern with identifying the extent to which members of the Church of Scotland and of other churches differ from each other — and from those who are not affiliated to any church — it is necessary to move beyond a simple descriptive presentation of the findings and subject them to some independent test in order to assess whether the differences one observes are both significant and meaningful. These criteria were in the first instance ensured through the application of standard significance tests derived from the laws of statistical probability.

Statistical significance

In any study that depends on observations of a sample drawn from a larger population, some differences between the sample and the population-universe from which it is drawn are bound to occur. With many samples it is difficult, or impossible, to calculate the probable magnitude of such errors. When, however, truly random samples are (as in the present case) employed, such calculations can be made with ease; and this fact has given rise to the widespread use by social scientists of what are known as test of 'significance'. Such tests are designed to determine how likely it is that a given percentage difference between two or more sub-groups in a sample (for example, Church of Scotland members, Roman Catholics and those who are not members of any Church) could be entirely due to sampling error. If the probability is 5% or less that the difference in question could be accounted for on the grounds of sampling error (or in other words, 95% or more that it could not be attributed to sampling error), most social scientists accept as valid the conclusion that the difference observed in the sample reflects a real difference in the population from which the sample itself is drawn.

The present study made use of appropriate tests to establish the statistical significance of such differences. Whilst the probability level initially used was the conventional one of 5%, the overwhelming majority of the differences identified far exceeded this level of statistical confidence, most of them in fact being significant at the 1% level (that is to say, that the probability was 99% that the difference in question could not be accounted for on the grounds of sampling error).

Throughout the course of this report, those findings which are labelled as 'statistically significant' will accordingly have satisfied the appropriate test at the 1% level of confidence; and specific attention will be drawn to those differences which lie between the 1% and 5% levels of statistical probability (see also page 5).

Tests of significance should, however, be viewed simply as one of the tools available to survey analysts to aid in any formation of judgements concerning the validity and 'generalisability' of findings based on the responses of a sample polulation. They help point to those areas where genuine differences probably exist; but must be supplemented by other techniques for the purposes of both confirmation and interpretation of results.

In ideal circumstances, for example, one might hope to point to trends evinced in related surveys, in order to confirm or explore further trends or differences within one's own survey-data. The general dearth of relevant material makes this a rather difficult requirement to fulfil; but where appropriate, contrasts and parallels will be drawn with relevant survey-material gained from other contexts.

Within one's own survey-data it may, however, also be possible to elicit reasonably consistent patterns in the trends and differences that are established across groups. Thus, if one attempts to trace connections between various significant individual findings, one may establish to what extent patterns emerge within the data that resonate with the demands of either theory or intuitive commonsense; consequently one can begin to interpret the human (as opposed to the statistical) significance of these relationships. Consideration of the findings within a larger context may also help one to highlight other trends within the data which, though not statistically significant, may be significant in social or psychological terms because they form part of a consistent pattern of findings.

Bearing these considerations in mind, let us now examine and attempt to interpret the survey's findings, focusing in the first instance upon the similarities and differences between Church of Scotland members and other groups within the sample.

(i) General background factors

Information was sought on the age, income, marital status, occupation, type of housing and length of residence at present address, and the educational background of the people completing the questionnaire. A break-down of the age-composition of the sample is contained in Table 2.1.

Section (a) of Table 2.1 compares the age-structure of the present sample with the age-distribution for Scotland as a whole, as revealed by the 1981 Census (Registrar General for Scotland 1982). This shows the age-distribution of the study sample to vary significantly from the figures for the general Census, with proportionately many fewer members in the age-group 16–24 and rather more in those age groups aged 45 and over being found within the population covered by the present survey. These differences obviously say something about the age-composition of the sectors of society from which the Church of Scotland draws the bulk of its membership. They also severely undermine the hope that the data gathered for this survey would be reasonably representative of the (adult) Scottish population.

Section (b) of Table 2.1 examines the relationship between age and

9

Table 2.1

Age-distributions

(a) Survey population compared with 1981 census

Age-group	Present survey	1981 census
16–24	11.9	19.4
25–44	32.0	33.3
45–64	32.5	28.8
65–74	14.2	11.5
75+	9.3	6.9
	100	100

(b) Comparisons between survey sub-groups

Age-group	C of S	R C	Other Churches	Non-members
16–24	6.2	6.7	16.7	26.1
25–44	29.1	31.1	40.7	37.4
45–64	35.8	33.3	31.5	24.4
65–74	18.0	15.6	7.4	6.3
75+	10.9	13.3	3.7	5.9
	100	100	100	100

(c) Comparison between 1981 census and non-Church of Scotland groups

Age-group	Non-C of S groups	1981 census
16–24	22.0	19.4
25–44	37.1	33.3
45–64	26.7	28.8
65–74	7.7	11.5
75+	6.5	6.9

(There is no statistically significant difference between these two sets of figures.)

religious affiliation. It shows the Church of Scotland and the Roman Catholic Church to be extremely similar in age distribution, whilst members of other Churches and individuals who are not members of any Church prove to be much younger, with more than 50% of these latter groups being aged less than 45. By contrast, particularly few individuals between the ages of 16 and 24 are found among Roman Catholics and members of the Church of Scotland. Finally, Section (c) of Table 2.1 shows that when Church of Scotland members are removed from the study-population, the remaining sample is much closer to the age-structure for the country as a whole; there in fact being no significant difference between the proportions of people in the different age groups within the two populations. This underlines the unrepresentativeness of the Church of Scotland in age terms; and any analysis of differences existing between the sample's basic sub-groups will obviously need to take these statistically-significant age-differences into account.

A similar analysis is undertaken in Table 2.2, in respect of sex differences. Broadly similar findings emerge for this Table as for Table 2.1, with Section (a) showing a significantly higher proportion of females in the population covered by the present survey than are found in the population of Scotland as a whole. Section (b) shows the Church of Scotland sample to comprise 61% females; although the trends for the other groups vary somewhat from those for age, in that the Roman Catholic Church is much closer in its ratio of males to females to that for the non-church population, whilst the ratio for 'other' churches is identical to that for the Church of Scotland. And as for age, Section (c) of Table 2.2 also shows that, when Church of Scotland members are removed from the sample, the proportion of males to females among the remaining members is virtually the same as that for Scotland as a whole.

Table 2.3 shows that the survey sample also deviates significantly from the overall population of Scotland in the distribution of its members between the Registrar General's social-class groupings, with substantially higher propor-

Table 2.2

Sex differences

(a) Survey population compared with 1981 census

	Present survey	*1981 census*
Female	57.5%	52.7%
Male	42.5%	47.3%

(b) Comparisons between survey sub-groups

	C of S	*R C*	*Other churches*	*Non-members*
Female	60.9	51.1	60.7	49.6
Male	39.1	48.9	39.3	50.4

(c) Comparisons between 1981 census and non-Church of Scotland groups

	Non-C of S groups	*1981 census*
Female	51.6%	52.7%
Male	48.4%	47.3%

(There is no significant difference between the distribution of the sexes in the 1981 census.)

Table 2.3

Social class of survey population, compared with 1981 Census

	Survey population	1981 Census*
Social class 1 (professional and higher managerial)	7.48	5.3
Social class 2 (lower managerial and non-manual)	27.10	19.0
Social class 3 (skilled manual)	49.07	49.7
Social class 4 (semi-skilled manual)	15.65	18.2
Social class 5 (unskilled manual)	0.70	7.8

(* Adapted from Table 49 of the *Scottish Summary*, **Vol.2** (economically active persons), Edinburgh: HMSO.)

tions in social classes 1 and (especially) 2, considerably fewer in social classes 4 and 5; and virtually the same in the groups of skilled manual workers who constitute social class 3 in the Registrar General's classification. Perhaps not unexpectedly, therefore, we may conclude that the survey-sample is somewhat biased towards middle-class occupations (social classes 1 and 2) and away from the semi- and unskilled working classes (4 and 5).

As with age and sex we must accordingly conclude that, in terms of its social class composition, the present sample cannot be regarded as representative of the general population of Scotland. An analysis of the social class composition of the various sample sub-groups failed, however, to evince any statistically-significant difference. This suggests that the social class bias is consistent across all three Church groups and that, in those areas from which the Church of Scotland draws the bulk of its members, people who do not go to church are no more or less working- (or middle-) class than their church-going neighbours. Consistent with the age-differences noted in Table 2.1 is the indication that many more of the Church of Scotland and Roman Catholic members described themselves as pensioners. These were significantly under-represented among non-church goers; while significantly more non-churchgoers described themselves as either unemployed, self-employed or students, this last group comprising 1.4% of Church of Scotland members, as opposed to 10.4% of the non-churchgoing sample. And probably again related to the differences in the age-structure of the samples, rather more of the Church members were either married or widowed, whilst very many more of the other groups were single (31% of non-church members, as compared with 13% of members of the Church of Scotland).

A picture is therefore beginning to emerge of a Church of Scotland group who are rather older and possibly more settled in their social position (though not significantly different in social class standing) from their brothers and sisters in the general polulation. The picture of a socially settled group is further confirmed by answers to a question as to how long respondents had lived at their present address. Whilst some 44% of non-Church of Scotland members had been resident at the same address for 11 years or more, this fell some way short of the (statistically-significant) 56% of members of the Church of Scotland who had lived at the same address for this length of time, with some 31% having lived in the same house for over 20 years. By contrast, 36.6% of people outwith the Church of Scotland had resided at their present address for 5 years or less, as compared to the 24% of Church of Scotland members who fell into this category. These differences, outlined in Table 2.3, again yield a statistically significant difference. Also of some interest in the Table is the high porportion of Roman Catholics (virtually identical to that for members of the Church of Scotland) who had been resident at the same address for twenty or more years.

Table 2.4

Length of residence at present address

Years	C of S	R C	Other churches	Non-members
Less than 2	7.9	6.4	14.3	15.9
2–5	16.4	19.1	14.3	24.8
6–10	20.0	27.7	21.4	16.7
11–20	24.8	17.0	30.4	25.2
20+	30.8	29.8	19.6	17.5

Church of Scotland members had also tended to spend a shorter period of their life in full-time education, although this almost certainly reflects the older average age of this group and the earlier school-leaving age which was the norm in their youth. This difference is reflected in the different proportions of the four groups in the sample who had attended University or College. Table 2.5 shows that members of the Church of Scotland and the Roman Catholic Church were significantly less likely to have entered the tertiary education sector than were non-church members or those in the group of 'other' churches.

Table 2.5

Attendance at University or College

	C of S	R C	Other churches	Non-members
Yes	29.8	21.7	37.5	46.6
No	70.2	78.3	62.5	53.4

The larger proportion (35.8 as opposed 29.1%) of Church of Scotland members with incomes of less than £5,000 per annum again almost certainly reflects the larger number of pensioners within their ranks. Overall, Church of Scotland members have rather lower annual incomes than their fellow-countrymen or women from other backgrounds. The trends in Table 2.6, however, fail to yield any significant difference between Church of Scotland members and others.

Table 2.6

Total annual income per household

£'s	C of S	R C	Other churches	Non-members
Under 5000	35.8	37.0	18.8	29.7
5000–7500	21.2	21.7	18.8	16.2
7501–10000	14.8	15.2	14.6	17.1
10001–15000	14.9	15.2	29.2	22.1
15001–20000	7.3	8.7	16.7	7.7
20001–25000	3.7	2.2	2.1	3.2
25001 plus	2.3	—	—	4.1

No differences emerged within the sample in the proportions of people with varying forms of housing tenure (owner occupation or renting of flat or house) or (perhaps surprisingly, in view of the high proportions of elderly people among Church members) in the number of people, including children, living in their household. Nor was there any significant difference in the proportions of individuals in the different groups who possessed one car or more. (In this connection, one matter that had been of some interest to the members of the survey planning team was the number of people who held car insurance with Ansvar — who offer insurance cover to total abstainers in particular — but since only three individuals in the samle were insured by that company, the question is obviously not worth pursuing here.)

Finally, questions 12 and 13 of the schedule enquired whether individuals held public office and with which political party they most identified. Although proportionately more members of the Church of Scotland held public office than was the case for all of the other groups combined, the overall numbers were rather low — seventeen members (2.8%), as opposed to three (0.86%). This difference was, however, statistically significant; and one may therefore conclude that, whilst only a very tiny minority of people do become involved in public office, Church of Scotland members are significantly more likely to undertake such duties than are people from other backgrounds. And when one compares the kind of office held, it is perhaps of some interest to note that virtually identical proportions of the two samples held political office in the regional or district council; whilst the preponderance of Church members holding public office was attributable to their greater involvement in non- (party) political activities on community, school and local health councils. (Given the differences in average age emphasised at several points above, this modest trend may in fact have some significance.)

In terms of political sympathy and affiliation, rather more Church members (45.1%, contrasted with 38.5% of other groups) reported themselves as Conservative; with 19.7% claiming an identification with the Liberal party, this proportion being half as many again as the 11.9% of the other groups who reported Liberal sympathies. Identical proportions (some 12.5%) place the Scottish National Party at the apex of their political sympathies, whilst non-Church of Scotland members were more likely to identify with Labour (28.8%, as opposed to 17.2%) or SDP (7.7%, compared with 5.7%). These differences are statistically significant and one may therefore conclude that, although the majority within the sample claimed allegiance to the Conservative party, this commitment was rather stronger within the Church of Scotland. Roman Catholics, by contrast, were overwhelmingly more likely to support Labour, with more than half their members expressing this preference.

These analyses have perhaps served mainly to confirm expectations that might have been formed on the basis of everyday experience and common-sense. That the Church is, however, so manifestly failing to attract younger members is a matter of some significance and potential concern for it. It seems likely, for example, that the greater average age of the Church of Scotland sample will affect responses to a number of the later questions, as possibly will its preponderance of female members. For the present investigation, this presents an essentially methodological problem. For the Church itself, the problem is the wider and more important one of sustaining a range of opinion and debate within its own ranks which ensures that its message touches on issues, and is at least tempered by attitudes and approaches, which reflect the concerns of the whole range of society.

(ii) Religion and the Church

This section of the schedule started with a number of Questions on people's degree of commitment to the church and frequency of attendance at church services, together with questions on Bible-reading and prayer. Not unexpectedly, non-church members reported themselves as significantly less committed to the church than did individuals who had a formal involvement with one or other of the three church groups within the sample. When, however, the former were excluded from the analysis, the trend depicted in Table 2.7 emerged. This shows that the Church of Scotland sample saw themselves as significantly less committed than did members of the two remaining church-groups. A higher proportion of individuals from other churches described themselves as 'highly' committed; although fully three-quarters of Roman Catholics perceived themselves to be either 'highly' or 'fairly' committed to the Church, as opposed to only 57% of other churchgoers. In contrast to these figures, however, rather fewer Church of

Scotland members reported themselves as having no commitment to the Church (the higher proportion of those outside the Church of Scotland falling into this category being almost entirely attributable to the members of 'other Churches'); although this figure is again outweighed by the 31% who see themselves as 'not very committed', a proportion which is some 10% greater than that for churchgoers outwith the Church of Scotland.

Table 2.7

What is your level of commitment to the Church?

	C of S	R C	Other	Non-church
Highly committed	17.8	25.5	32.1	3.7
Fairly committed	42.5	48.9	25.0	16.0
Not very committed	31.5	21.3	21.4	28.4
No commitment	8.2	4.3	21.4	52.3

The pattern is thus made complicated by some minor fluctuations in the trends for individual churches. Overall, however, these figures would appear to suggest that Church of Scotland members have a more lukewarm commitment to the Church than have the other two groups, with smaller proportions falling into the more extreme categories of high or no commitment.

As for church commitment, the analysis of the data for frequency of attendance at church services excluded non-church members since these — not unexpectedly — were significantly less assiduous in going to church than were official church members. Perhaps surprisingly, fully 45% of members of the Church of Scotland reported attending Church services either several times or once in a week. This proportion was, however, greatly exceeded by the 64.7% of people from the other two church groups who went to church at least once per week. Closer scrutiny of these figures reveals that the difference is entirely due to the very much higher percentage of Roman Catholics and other church members who attend services several times a week (23.5% as opposed to 4.7% of those in Church of Scotland congregations). These trends are consistent with (though somewhat lower than) the figures reported by the National Bible Society of Scotland survey (Brierley and Macdonald 1985, pp.52–3), which points to the decline between 1980 and 1984 in the number of Church of Scotland congregations holding evening services and shows a much higher proportion of other churches in Scotland retaining both morning and evening services. That the differences in Table 2.8 are not solely attributable to the availability of opportunities for worship is, however, suggested by the fact that 35.3% of the Church of Scotland sample attended services only once a month or once a quarter. As with the figures for church commitment, it would therefore appear that a high proportion of Church of Scotland members possess a rather lukewarm interest in religious and devotional activities; whilst communicants with other churches appear more enthusiastic and engaged in devotional matters. It should, however, perhaps also be stressed that a substantial number of Church of Scotland communicants have a strong commitment to their faith and its formal celebration — the largest single proportion in Table 2.8 do, after all, attend Church once a week. This proportion is, however, to some degree offset by the appreciable numbers who retain a more formal and perhaps empty commitment to churchgoing and church affairs.

Table 2.8

How often do you attend Church services?

	C of S	R C	Other	Non-church
Several times a week	4.7	19.1	27.3	0.8
Once a week	40.5	63.8	21.8	12.6
Approximately once a month	19.2	4.3	9.1	6.5
Once a quarter	16.1	4.3	7.3	10.9
Twice a year	6.7	2.1	7.3	6.5
Once a year	2.2	2.1	7.3	8.9
Baptisms, weddings and funerals only	8.5	2.1	14.5	44.1
Never	2.2	2.1	5.4	9.3

Asked whether they attended church more frequently in their earlier adult life than they do now, the largest single proportion (45.8%) of Church of Scotland members replied that their attendance had in fact been more frequent in the past. This contrasted with the rather smaller proportion of the other churches who fell into this category, with more than half of those attending other churches (including Roman Catholics) reporting their past to have been 'about the same' as their present level of attendance. (For obvious reasons, non-church members were excluded from the test of statistical significance of these trends; although the data for this group are presented in Table 2.8). It should also be noted that these differences are significant at the 2.5%, rather than the 1% level. In response to a subsidiary question, the vast majority of Church of Scotland (66.3%) and of Roman Catholic and other church members (71.8%) felt that, in five years' time, their pattern of attendance would remain at about the same level as at present. The members themselves would not therefore seem to anticipate any great change in their churchgoing. It may, however, be of some interest that somewhat fewer (55%) of non-church members felt able to predict that their pattern of church attendance would remain the same, with fully one-third of this group replying that it was 'difficult to know' what their pattern of behaviour was likely to be in this respect.

When non-church members are again excluded, answers to the question as to how often respondents read the Bible yielded a highly significant association with religious affiliation, this being entirely attributable to the much higher level of Bible-reading amongst the 'other' church group. Thus, almost a quarter of these people read the Bible every day; whereas 69% of the Church of Scotland and 83% of Roman Catholics replied that they 'seldom' or 'never' read their Bible and only tiny proportions (7.3 and 4.3%, respectively) did so every day.

Responses to the question as to how often individuals pray again showed Church of Scotland members to be rather less assiduous in this respect than the members of the two remaining church groups. Roman Catholic members proved most active in prayer, with 60% reporting that they prayed every day, as opposed to 36% of Church of Scotland communicants and 45% of those in other churches. Conversely, a mere 2% of Catholics 'never or hardly ever' prayed, as opposed to 16% of Church of Scotland and 18% of other church members. The association (significant at the 2.5% level) apparent in Table 2.9 between prayer and religious affiliation seems almost entirely attributable to the elements noted above. There is something of a reversal of positions between Catholics and other church members therefore over Bible-reading and prayer, which seems consistent with the differing emphases they place upon ritual and liturgy on the one hand and private devotion upon the other. In both cases, however, Church of Scotland members again emerge as rather tepid in their involvement in such activities. Replies to an enquiry as to whether members of their family prayed together were also consistent with the trends in Table 2.9, Catholics again proving to be more likely to pray together frequently than their Protestant colleagues. Even so, the commonest response (55% for Church of Scotland, 52% for Roman Catholic and 56% for other churches) was that church members 'never or hardly ever' prayed together in family units.

Table 2.9

About how often do you pray?

	C of S	R C	Other	Non-church
Every day	35.9	59.6	44.6	19.1
2–3 times per week	13.1	8.5	7.1	6.5
Once a week	10.8	12.8	7.1	6.1
Seldom	24.4	17.0	23.2	22.8
Never or hardly ever	15.8	2.1	17.9	45.5

And finally in this connection, no significant relationship existed between the church group to which individuals were affiliated and the extent to which they reported a devotional life (praying and Bible-reading) to have been the rule during their childhood. To the extent that current behaviour may be influenced by parental precept, it would thus seem that the differences noted so far in this section are due either to a regression on the part of Church of Scotland members from the customs that prevailed in their childhood home, or an increase beyond the level of childhood devotional and religious activity on the part of the two remaining church groups.

Moving on to consider the sources from which people obtain their information about church and other events, Table 2.10 shows that Church of Scotland members listen to or view religious broadcasts much more frequently than the other three groups. Not unexpectedly, a much higher proportion of non-churchgoers never sample religious programmes; but even in this group some 59% do so from time to time. Perhaps also of some note in Table 2.10 is the rather small proportion of Catholics who regularly tune in to religious broadcasts. These figures yield a highly-significant association.

Table 2.10

Do you listen to or view religious programmes on radio or TV?

	C of S	R C	Other	Non-church
Regularly	24.5	10.6	17.9	16.2
Sometimes	68.7	76.6	71.4	58.7
Never	6.8	12.8	10.7	25.1

Asked to specify what in their own experience were the most important sources of knowledge of church events, members of the three church groups generally gave remarkably similar patterns of response, the only major difference being that communicants of other churches cited newspapers and television as the main fonts of information, whereas members of the Church of Scotland and Catholics gave pride of place to the Minister or Priest (who was ranked fourth by those from other churches). TV was ranked second in importance by members of the Church of Scotland (fourth by Catholics), newspapers third (second for Catholics), 'other Church literature' fourth (third for both Catholics and other denominations), and the magazine *Life and Work* fifth (while sharing sixth place for both Catholics and other churches' members). Least important places were accorded to radio (sixth in the ranking of Church of Scotland communicants and fifth for both Catholics and others) and to a stated lack of interest in church events, which appeared seventh for both members of the Church of Scotland and Catholics and sixth for those from other churches. There was some slight deviation from this pattern on the part of non-church members, who ranked TV, newspapers and radio first, second and third, respectively, whilst giving clergymen, other church literature and *Life and Work* fifth, sixth and seventh position. It is perhaps of some note that the 'not interested' option was ranked only in fourth place by those expressing no formal religious affiliation. Also of some significance was the overwhelming primary importance attached by Roman Catholics to the role of the Priest in the dissemination of information about church events.

Table 2.11
Where do you gain your knowledge of Church events from?

	C of S	R C	Other	Non-church
Newspapers	3 (52%)	2 (61%)	1=(58%)	2 (61%)
Radio	6 (25%)	5 (16%)	5 (35%)	3 (40%)
Television	2 (54%)	4 (40%)	1=(58%)	1 (68%)
Life and Work magazine	5 (41%)	6 (8%)	6 (8%)	7 (12%)
Other Church literature	4 (50%)	3 (45%)	3 (53%)	6 (22%)
Minister or Priest	1 (63%)	1 (82%)	4 (48%)	5 (24%)
Not interested in Church events	7 (4%)	7 (5%)	6 (8%)	4 (27%)

* The single digits in each column show the order of importance ascribed to each item by the group in question, on a rank order from 1–7.

Although readership of daily newspapers was broadly similar across all four groups, rather more of the 'other church' members and of those with no formal religious affiliation read quality dailies; substantially more Catholics read popular dailies and proportionately larger numbers of Church of Scotland members read provincial daily newspapers. In addition, 11% of those belonging to other churches read no daily newspaper at all. These differences yielded a trend significant at the 5% level. A much more substantial variation appeared, however, in respect of the Sunday newspapers read by members of the sample. The main feature of note here is the staggering 53% of the total sample who read the *Sunday Post,* with substantially more Church of Scotland members (57.8% compared with 45.8%) reporting that they read this paper. And as in the case of daily newspapers, higher proportions of 'other' and non-church members read the 'quality' Sunday papers, whilst a much higher proportion of Catholics read the popular Sunday papers (51% of Catholics also read the *Sunday Post*). These trends are displayed in table 2.12.

Some 54% of members of the various churches reported reading no religious newspapers or magazines (as compared with 84% of non-church members). The largest single group of church members (some 70%) who do read religious publications took organs categorised by the survey team as 'denominational'.

Table 2.12

What daily newspaper(s) do you read?

	C of S	R C	Other	Non-church
Quality daily (*Scotsman, Glasgow Herald, Guardian, Times, Telegraph*)	25.0	19.6	24.5	29.0
Popular				
(a) *Record, Express, Mail, Mirror*	41.2	60.9	39.6	40.4
(b) *Daily Star, Sun*	3.2	2.2	1.9	7.3
Provincial (*Press and Journal, Dundee Courier, Greenock Telegraph etc.*)	21.4	13.0	18.9	15.5
Evening papers (*Evening Express, Evening Telegraph, Evening News, Evening Times*)	4.4	2.2	3.8	2.4
Other	—	—	—	—
None	4.9	2.2	11.3	5.3

With regard to these data, other church and non-church members appear to have significantly more 'intellectual' newspaper tastes. Catholics are clearly located at the more 'popular' end of the mass newspaper market. Whilst significant numbers of Church of Scotland members also read both 'quality' and 'popular' organs, considerable proportions seem also to be rooted in more local (not to say parochial) concerns, as expressed in their readership of provincial dailies and the *Sunday Post*. To some extent, these tastes may reflect the influence of the age and sex-differences noted earlier in this Chapter. It is, however, also at least interesting to speculate whether more theological aspects of belief have some bearing upon these trends. It is difficult, in this connection, to know what to make of the significant association that exists between religious affiliation and the weekly magazines read by people in the sample, a relationship that seems mainly attributable to the higher proportion of Church of Scotland readers who subscribe to women's magazines and the much lower proportions of Catholics and non-church members who do so.

Table 2.13

What are your three most important reasons for Church membership?

	C of S	R C	Other	Non-church
Wish to support Church and Christian values*	1 (77%)	1 (80%)	1 (61%)	1 (67%)
Opportunity for Baptism, Marriage, Funerals	4 (27%)	4 (27%)	4 (29%)	4 (31%)
Participation in services*	2 (63%)	2 (67%)	3 (47%)	2 (56%)
Fellowship and contact with others*	3 (52%)	3 (38%)	2 (51%)	3 (41%)
Support missionary work*	11 (3%)	7 (11%)	=9 (8%)	=11 (2%)
Support everday Christian life	5 (25%)	=5 (20%)	5 (28%)	6 (23%)
Want to strive for justice and Christian solidarity	9 (6%)	7 (11%)	12 (2%)	10 (3%)
Natural for me to be a member of the Church	6 (22%)	=5 (20%)	6 (18%)	5 (25%)
Family expectations*	8 (6%)	=11 (0%)	7 (14%)	7 (12%)
Don't want to upset a relative/friend by leaving	12 (1%)	=11 (0%)	11 (4%)	=11 (2%)
Never thought of leaving	7 (7%)	=9 (4%)	8 (12%)	8 (10%)
Nothing special	10 (4%)	=9 (4%)	=9 (8%)	9 (7%)

* a significant association between church group to which individuals belong and importance ascribed to item.

Responses as to the most important reasons for Church members remaining in Communion with the church show remarkable similarity as between the three different church groups. Table 2.13 shows a desire to support the church and Christian values, participation in services and Communion, fellowship and contact with others, as well as an opportunity for baptism and other celebrations as the four most common reasons offered by members of the three church groups (as well as those who do not belong to any church) for retaining church membership. With the obvious exception of the first, these might be labelled as social and instrumental reasons for continued church involvement. One gains little sense — even from other church members, with their greater interest and participation in devotional activities — of the church as a force for justice and social change. Indeed, 'striving for justice and solidarity' and 'missionary work' both occupy low positions within the three rank-orderings.

The comments on Table 2.13 have, however, so far referred only to the *relative* importance attached to these factors by members of the different church groups, in the sense that we have compared the extent to which particular reasons for retaining church membership are endorsed more or less frequently than other reasons by members of the same church group. This simple comparison of rank-ordering does not, however, necessarily detect differences in the *absolute* importance or priority attached to particular reasons by the four groups under scrutiny. A particular item might, for example, be at the top of the rank-ordering of all four groups; but be endorsed by 100% of one particular church group, whilst receiving, say, the endorsement of only 70% in each of the three remaining groups. That item would therefore occupy the same *relative* position in the rank orders of all four groups, but be seen as important by many more of the members of one group, thus indication that it occupies higher *absolute* priority in the minds and choices of its members.

Although none of the items in Table 2.13 show such extreme variation as the hypothetical example outlined in the previous paragraph, significant differences do appear between the church groups on five of them, these being indicated by an asterisk. These show Church of Scotland members attaching higher priority (along with Roman Catholics) than the members of 'other' churches to a desire to support the church and Christian values including participation in services, whilst Catholics give significantly higher priority to 'missionary work'. Roman Catholics also emerge as significantly less likely than Church of Scotland or other church members to proffer 'family expectations' and 'fellowship and contact with others' as reasons for remaining members of the church.

As indicated above, the trends in Table 2.13 suggest that none of the three sets of church members view the church as a force for justice or social change. But the Church of Scotland, perhaps in particular, is not seen (or desired) as a radically reforming force by its members, whilst the Roman Catholic Church emerges as slightly (though significantly) different in this respect.

The Woman's Guild (11.9%) and other women's organisations (4.5%)

were by far the most frequently mentioned Church of Scotland organisations of which respondents reported membership (including in a small number of cases, members from outwith the Church of Scotland itself). And small, but nonetheless appreciable, numbers of those replying held office of various kinds within the Church. Most frequently mentioned was membership of the Kirk Session, with 13.4% of Church of Scotland members holding office in this capacity. In addition 10.4% of Church of Scotland communicants were members of the Congregational Board.

Not unexpectedly, there were very significant differences between non-church members and the remainder of the sample in the extent to which they reported their mother and father as having been regular church attenders, with non-members in both cases significantly more likely to reply in the negative. It may be of some interest to note that the fathers' influence seemed the more crucial, with 55% of non-members reporting their fathers as not having been a regular attender at church, as opposed to 43% of non-members whose mothers had not attended church. No significant difference emerged between Church of Scotland members and the other two church groups in this respect. By contrast with the non-church members it is, however, interesting to report that among those formally affiliated to a church, mothers were very much more frequently reported as having been regular church attenders than were fathers.

Again not unexpectedly, churchgoers from all three denominational groups proved significantly more likely to regard themselves as Christian than did their non-churchgoing brethren. But when a separate analysis is conducted on the data for church members only, we find that Catholics are much firmer in their affirmation of their Christian identity, whilst rather more members of 'other' churches deny that they are Christians (see Table 2.14).

The overwhelming majority (94.4%) of the sample had been baptised;

Table 2.14

Do you regard yourself as a Christian?

	C of S	R C	Other	Non-church
Yes	86.9	97.9	81.0	57.9
No	3.6	0.0	10.4	18.2
Doubtful, don't know	9.4	2.1	8.6	23.9

Table 2.15

Do you believe that God controls our lives here and now?

	C of S	R C	Other	Non-church
Yes	71.5	84.8	62.5	40.7
No	10.3	13.0	17.9	30.9
Don't know what to believe	18.2	2.2	19.6	28.4

although among those not members of any church, this proportion falls to 83%.

The majority (54%) of Church of Scotland members never attend services in other denominations. As against this, some two-thirds of Catholics and 60% of other churches' members report themselves as visiting other denominations' services of worship, with a small proportion of the 'other' church group being particularly active in this regard. These trends make for a highly-significant association between church affiliation and willingness to attend the services of other denominations. By contrast, and again complying with one's expectation, 70% of non-churchgoers never attend services of any kind. Perhaps related to this, only a tiny proportion (2.7%) of Church of Scotland members of the sample belonged to an ecumenical group, whereas 9% of Catholics were so affiliated.

Asked 'Do you believe in God?', rather more Roman Catholics (93.6%) replied in the affirmative than did those in the other two church groups (86.7% and 83.9% for Church of Scotland and other, respectively); whilst conversely, a significant minority of Church of Scotland (11.6%) and 'others' (10.7%) replied that they 'don't know what to believe'. Fifty eight per cent of non-church members professed a belief in God, with 13% denying any belief and 28% professing agnosticism. A question as to whether they believe 'God controls our lives here and now' again revealed evidence of a more coherent set of beliefs on the part of Catholics than the other two groups of church-members. The greater degree of uncertainty among the non-Catholic groups is also reflected in the much higher proportions in Table 2.15 who endorse the 'don't know' response. These differences between the religious groups are statistically-significant. It seems unnecessary to conduct any statistical tests in order to demonstrate the significance of the enormous differences between non-church members and the remainder of the sample in this Table.

People's responses to a request to indicate which of a range of statements most closely corresponded to their view of God followed the pattern presented in Table 2.16. These complex trends yield interesting statistically-significant differences between groups within the sample.

In the first place, non-church members are obviously very different from the denominationally-defined groups, with the largest single proportion having 'no opinion' on the matter. Even so, the substantial proportion of this group who do profess to believe in God show rather varying views between God as a loving father and a distant, impersonal force. It need hardly be said that this group differs significantly in this respect from the remainder of the sample. The majority of Church of Scotland members choose alternatives that indicate a belief in God as a caring, succouring being ('He hears our prayers and controls our lives'; 'a father whose concern is to save and to help'), with very much smaller percentages seeing God in terms of power or impersonal forces. The succouring view of God is endorsed by just under half of the other church groups; and although the largest single proportion of Catholics perceive God as a loving father, the next most common view within

Table 2.16

Which one of the following most closely corresponds to your own opinion of God?

	C of S	R C	Other	Non-church
All powerful judge who sees and judges our sins and virtues	13.0	27.6	16.7	6.6
Loving. He hears our prayers and controls our lives	40.5	44.6	22.2	24.1
A father whose concern is to save and to help	20.3	21.3	29.6	12.4
A sort of distant, impersonal power or force	13.6	4.3	14.8	18.3
No opinion	12.6	2.1	16.7	38.6

this group is of God as an all-powerful judge. The apparent greater immediacy and potency of the religious views of Catholics (which we have already noted in certain places above) is perhaps also reflected in the tiny proportion who endorse the conception of God as a 'distant, impersonal power or force'. These divergencies between the three religious groups are also statistically significant at far beyond the 1% level.

This story is to some extent replicated in answers to the question as to whether respondents believed that Jesus died for their sins. Ninety-two per cent of Catholics responded in the affirmative, as opposed to 75% of Church of Scotland members and only 66% of the members of other churches. The bulk of the remaining Church of Scotland and other church members professed agnosticism over the issue, rather than direct rejection of the statement, with 17.7% of Church of Scotland and 21% of other church members preferring the 'don't know' alternative. These inter-denominational differences are again significant (though at the 5% level); nevertheless the major statistically-significant differences in answer to this question emerged from the replies of non-churchgoers who were much less likely to answer affirmatively (42%), whilst 35% were undecided and 23% rejected the statement. Answers to the question of whether Jesus is risen from the dead seem to be very closely related to those for the previous question, with virtually identical proportions in each of the four groups replying 'yes', 'no',

Table 2.17

Do you believe Jesus is risen from the dead?

	C of S	R C	Other	Non-church
Yes	73.6	91.5	64.3	41.1
No	6.8	2.1	10.7	26.8
Don't know what to believe	19.6	6.4	25.0	32.1

or 'don't know'. Thus, 92% of Catholics in Table 2.17 affirm a belief that Jesus is risen from the dead, a proportion which stands in marked contrast to the 74% of Church of Scotland members and 64% among those of other churches, who give the same response. As against this, 20 and 25% of the Church of Scotland and other church samples, respectively, indicated that they 'don't know what to believe' on this particular matter.

Some 14% of Church of Scotland members denied a belief in eternal life — a much higher proportion than the other two denominational groups — with an additional 27% professing not to know. Again, Catholics emerge as much more certain in this respect, with 87% endorsing the 'yes' answer, as opposed to 59% of both Church of Scotland and other church members. One-third of this latter group were agnostic over this question. These inter-denominational differences are again significant. Among non-church members, opinion was virtually evenly divided between the three possible answers to this question, each of which received the endorsement of roughly one-third of the members of this group. Members of the Church of Scotland proved rather less likely than Catholics, however, to believe in life after death, with 53% of the former and 70% of the latter answering this question positively. As Table 2.18 also suggests, Church of Scotland communicants are also rather more agnostic over this matter than their two groups of religious confreres; and indeed a comparison between Church of Scotland members and the two other church groups yields a statistically-significant difference.

Table 2.18
Do you believe in the individual's life after death?

	C of S	R C	Other	Non-church
Yes	52.6	71.7	62.5	34.8
No	14.4	10.9	12.5	32.8
Don't know what to believe	33.0	17.4	25.0	32.4

Question 43 of the schedule, concerned with individuals' opinions of the Bible evinced an interesting pattern of responses. The largest single proportion of all four groups saw it as 'written by men' and therefore requiring interpretation. Among other church members, however, this proportion (41%) only barely exceeded the number (37.5%) who construe the Bible as 'God's word — true in every detail'. Proportionately more non-church members (though still at 10%, a very small proportion of their total number) saw the Bible as 'normal book', whilst 20% professed to have no opinion on the matter. Once more, statistically-significant differences emerge from comparisons between the church groups themselves, as well as the comparison involving non-church members.

Table 2.19

Which one of the following most closely reflects your opinion of the Bible?

	C of S	R C	Other	Non-church
God's word — true in every detail	18.7	27.7	38.2	11.3
Written by men who were inspired by God and therefore must be interpreted	63.3	63.8	41.8	45.0
Contains much vision but God has not affected it specially	7.0	2.1	12.7	12.9
A normal book	2.2	—	—	10.4
No opinion	8.8	6.4	7.3	20.4

Table 2.20

Which one of the following is nearest to your own opinion of what happens after death?

	C of S	R C	Other	Non-church
After death man stands before God and his judgement	30.8	72.3	47.3	15.9
Man's soul lives forever without judgement	5.5	2.1	—	2.5
Man's soul goes to another existence	11.6	6.4	14.5	12.3
Death is the end — man ceases to exist	8.2	2.1	7.3	21.3
We don't know what happens after death	41.3	14.9	29.1	44.3
No opinion	2.7	2.1	1.8	3.7

Answers to the question of what happens after death again yielded substantial differences between the various groups. Once more, Roman Catholics stand out as confident in the sure and simple view that 'after death man stand before God and his judgement', whilst only a minority of members of the Church of Scotland subscribe to this view. Table 2.20 shows that the most commonly held view within the Church of Scotland sample is that 'we don't know what happens after death'; and in this respect, their views are virtually identical to those of non-church members. Indeed, Church of Scotland members' views on this matter seem remarkably heterogeneous and

Table 2.21

Which one of the following is nearest to your own opinion about heaven and hell?

	C of S	R C	Other	Non-church
Heaven and hell are places of eternal bliss or suffering where man must live after God's judgement	26.0	61.4	37.3	19.0
After death, man may live near or far from God, but otherwise there are no possibilities	23.2	20.5	23.5	11.9
As such, heaven and hell do not exist — everything is related to man's life here and now — the Manichean view	25.2	13.6	23.5	33.6
No heaven or hell now or in the future	4.2	—	2.0	13.7
No opinion	21.4	4.5	13.7	21.7

unfocused, standing in marked contrast to those of their Catholic brethren. A similarly-structured question concerning opinions on heaven and hell show trends similar to those apparent in Table 2.20, with a majority of Catholics apparently secure in the unvarnished belief that heaven and hell are places of eternal bliss or suffering, whilst almost as many members of the Church of Scotland (21.4%) felt unable to express an opinion as endorsed other responses. These trends, which are portrayed in Table 2.21, again yield statistically-significant differences between denominations and between church and non-church members.

Answers to Question 46 suggest that, in contemporary Scotland at any rate, people subscribe neither to the doctrine of Original Sin nor to the Calvinist distinction between the elect and the damned, with the overwhelming majority (91.6%) seeing humanity comprising good and bad elements. Nonetheless, a significant minority (12%) of Catholics saw man as 'basically good', whilst 6% of the other church sample saw humanity as basically bad; and these divergencies were sufficient to render a difference significant at the 5% level between the four sub-groups in the sample. It should perhaps also be said that non-church members were rather more ready to endorse the view that humanity contains good and bad elements (94%), while none of this group purported to see humanity as 'basically bad'. Finally, answers to Question 47 indicate that Church of Scotland members think rather less often about these issues than do the members of the other two denominational groups. Thus, only 52% of members of the Church of Scotland reported thinking 'often' about the matters covered in this section of the questionnaire, as opposed to 68% of Catholics and 63.5% of other churchgoers. This meant that 48% of Church of Scotland members seldom or never reflected on such issues, as opposed to only 31% of Catholics and some 36% of the members of other denominations. It is also interesting (and somewhat depressing) to note that only 38% of those claiming no church affiliation think 'often' of these matters. The remaining 62% seldom or never turn their minds to these significant questions of human existence.

Question 48 attempted to assess the degree of importance attached by respondents to various possible church developments and the results of this analysis are presented in Table 2.22. Perhaps the first point to note about this Table is that both Church of Scotland and Roman Catholic members give reasonably high priority to all of these items, in that all eight are endorsed by 60% or more of these two samples as being important or very important, with Catholics overall according a higher degree of priority to these items than their Church of Scotland counterparts: indeed, Roman Catholics show a significantly higher concern than other groups with the need to develop joint services between the Church of Scotland and other denominations, joint prayer groups, joint efforts such as information campaigns, a common view on Bible translation, improved co-operation with the Roman Catholic church and improved co-operation on inter-church marriage. Second, although the unaffiliated generally give less precedence to these factors than the two former groups (with joint communion and local Bible study receiving less than 50% of their votes) this general perception is apparently shared by the members of other churches, whose average priority rating — with the notable exception of local Bible study groups — is remarkably similar to that for non-church members.

Accepting, therefore, these divergencies in the absolute priority attached to these elements by the different groups, one may observe further that there is reasonable agreement across all four in ascribing high priority to joint information campaigns and inter-church marriage; a medium priority to joint services for the Church of Scotland and other denominations; and low priority to joint Communion between the churches.

This unanimity is broken by the (understandable) divergence of Roman Catholics from the importance accorded by the three remaining groups to improved co-operation with the Roman Catholic church; by the higher emphasis placed by the other churches upon local Bible study and by Church of Scotland members' greater stress upon the need for a common view between the Churches on Bible translation.

There was rather less apparent congruence between the four sub-samples, and also between the three church groups within the sample population, in their responses to the final question in this section, which asked people to rank a number of areas of potential social involvement, in the order of importance they felt these would have for the church's future. These trends are portrayed in Table 2.23, which shows the three church groups agreed in giving pride of place to 'Christian education' and 'spiritual leadership', with Catholics and members of the Church of Scotland also in accord in the

Table 2.22

What importance would you attach to each of the following?

	C of S	R C	Other	Non-church
Joint services for Church of Scotland and other denominations*	5 (73%)	4 (88%)	5 (60%)	4 (63%)
Improved co-operation between the Church of Scotland and other Protestant Churches*	1 (91%)	5 (83%)	2 (77%)	1 (77%)
Joint Communion for Church of Scotland and other denominations*	8 (60%)	8 (64%)	8 (46%)	8 (48%)
Local Bible Study and Prayer groups including Church of Scotland members and members of other Churches*	7 (66%)	6 (83%)	4 (62%)	7 (50%)
Joint effort (e.g. information campaigns about under-developed countries)*	2 (84%)	3 (93%)	1 (81%)	3 (74%)
Church of Scotland and other Churches should have a common view on Bible translation*	4 (74%)	7 (83%)	6 (59%)	6 (61%)
Improved co-operation with the Roman Catholic Church*	6 (69%)	1 (96%)	7 (51%)	5 (62%)
Improved co-operation on inter-Church marriage	3 (80%)	2 (95%)	2 (78%)	2 (76%)

* a significant association between church group to which individuals belong and importance ascribed to item.

priority they give to work with pensioners and the sick, whilst other churches give this a slightly lower (though still important) position. There is also agreement across all four groups in the uniformly low priority they accord to the position of women in the church and (with only minor variations) the (surprisingly) low importance they attach to 'political awareness'. These broad agreements on relative priorities do, however, mask considerable variation in the absolute importance attached to individual items in this list by the members of different churches. Thus, Catholics express much stronger support for Christian education as an area of concentration in the church's future work, whilst 'other' church communicants are significantly more committed to the need for more spiritual leadership, and Catholics again emerge as significantly more committed to political awareness and increased awareness of economic and social justice than are their counterparts in the two remaining church groups. Similarly, although all three groups place 'the position of women in the church' in lowest or second lowest position, members of the Church of Scotland accord greater *absolute* priority to this item than do members of the other two churches.

In other areas, however, we find variations in the relative importance ascribed by members of the three church groups to certain of these items, with Church of Scotland communicants departing significantly in both absolute and relative terms from the views of their fellow Christians on the importance of efficient organisation and good financial management (possibly reflecting their greater involvement in the governance of their Church). Catholics, by contrast, supplement their endorsement of increased awareness of economic and social justice as a priority for future church work with a concern for help to developing countries; and other church members show a proselytising concern for 'personal renewal' and 'evangelisation' on which they are markedly more insistent than either of the two remaining groups of church members. People unaffiliated to any church, on the other hand, emphasise pastoral concerns, with work with pensioners and the sick, social work and help to developing countries occupying the first three places in their

Table 2.23

*Which of the following activities do you think will be
most important for the church's future?*

	C of S	R C	Other	Non-church
Political awareness*	11 (8%)	8 (14%)	10 (9%)	8 (19%)
Evangelisation*	9 (19%)	10 (5%)	4 (38%)	11 (8%)
Social work	=4 (33%)	6 (30%)	6 (28%)	2 (44%)
Help to developing countries*	7 (26%)	=3 (39%)	7 (26%)	3 (40%)
Work with pensioners and the sick	3 (37%)	=3 (39%)	5 (34%)	1 (56%)
Personal renewal*	6 (27%)	7 (16%)	3 (40%)	9 (14%)
Increased awareness of economic and social justice*	8 (22%)	5 (32%)	8 (19%)	5 (31%)
The position of women in the church*	10 (11%)	11 (2%)	11 (2%)	10 (13%)
Efficient organisation and good financial management*	=4 (33%)	9 (11%)	9 (15%)	6 (26%)
More spiritual leadership*	2 (41%)	2 (46%)	1 (54%)	7 (26%)
Christian education*	1 (52%)	1 (71%)	2 (46%)	4 (38%)

* a significant association between church group to which individuals belong and importance ascribed to item.

ordering of preferences; whilst proselytising activities (evangelisation and personal renewal) attract little support from this group.

Overall, we may therefore conclude that people participating in formally organised religion place unanimous emphasis upon their churches' functions of moral leadership and education. Beyond that, Church of Scotland members construe the Church's primary future commitment in terms of pastoral concerns (social work, work with pensioners and the sick), along with efficient organisation and good money-management. Catholics, on the other hand, seem to tinge their commitment to work with pensioners and the sick with an emphasis upon social/global justice (help to developing countries and increased awareness of economic and social justice). In the case of other churches, a concern with spiritual leadership and Christian education is welded to a more evangelical commitment. And as already noted, unaffiliated members of the public see the most important issues for the churches as pastoral ones.

(iii) Social and moral issues

Members of the Church of Scotland and of the Roman Catholic Church were significantly more supportive (80 and 85%, respectively) of the idea that there should be greater control over the amount of sex and violence shown on television than were non-church members (57%) and the members of other churches (71%). It is, however, interesting to note that a majority of all groups claimed to be in favour of such a policy, with 74% of the entire sample endorsing the affirmative answer to the Question. There was also substantial support (78%) within the total sample for the classification of home videos; and a significant difference again emerged between the sub-samples, although in this case, the members of all three church groups were much more substantially in favour of such a policy than were non-church members. It is, however, perhaps also interesting to note that 12% of members of the Church of Scotland confessed to uncertainty on this matter — a very much higher proportion than for the other two church groups.

Asked to rank six professions in order of the importance that was felt to attach to their position in the community, over two-thirds of the sample placed the doctor at the top of their hierarchy of social utility, with no significant variation between groups in this regard. Significant differences did, however, emerge in the valuation placed on policemen, with Church of Scotland and non-church members ranking the policeman significantly higher than the other two groups. Church of Scotland members also ranked social workers significantly lower than did non-church and other church members, with Catholics occupying a rather equivocal position between these two extremes. One need not look far for an explanation of the significantly lower ranking ascribed to Ministers by non-church members as compared with their more religiously-active counterparts. The significantly lower position ascribed to schoolteachers by members of the Church of Scotland is, however, rather harder to explain, given Presbyterianism's historic commitment to education. Perhaps this difference reflects the higher average age of this group. All four groups were unanimously agreed in ranking lawyers lowest of all.

Looking only at those in employment, Church of Scotland communicants were significantly more likely to claim that they would never go on strike, diverging particularly in this respect from people who were not members of any church. The other church group showed a very similar pattern to that for the Church of Scotland sample. Catholics were, however, virtually identical in their responses to non-church members. Even so, it should be noted that less than 50% of any group endorsed the 'Yes' answer; whilst some 55% of Church of Scotland and other church members replied in the negative.

Sixty per cent of the sample as a whole saw the present level of unemployment as unacceptable, with a further 29% seeing it as necessary for economic regeneration. Other church members were rather more likely to endorse the latter option, whilst Catholics were much more likely to endorse the former; but answers to this Question were not significantly correlated with church membership.

Church of Scotland communicants proved much less likely to see nuclear weapons as morally unacceptable and more willing to endorse the notion that they constitute an effective deterrent (a position supported by 51% of Church of Scotland members).

Table 2.24

What is your opinion of nuclear weapons?

	C of S	R C	Other	Non-church
An effective deterrent against war	50.8	21.3	42.6	45.5
Morally unacceptable	36.2	66.0	37.0	45.1
No Opinion	13.0	12.7	20.4	9.3

In direct distinction to this was the position of Roman Catholics, 66% of whom saw nuclear weapons as morally unacceptable, with only 21% accepting the argument that they constitute an effective deterrent. The two remaining groups are more or less evenly divided between these two options, with a residual proportion of 'don't knows'. These trends yield a highly-significant statistical association.

Asked for their views at to whether membership of groups like the Orange Order and Freemasons are consistent with Christianity, the largest single group of respondents (53% and 45% respectively) replied in the negative, with a substantial proportion (38% and 36%) confessing to uncertainty on this matter. Whilst rather more Catholics (70%, as opposed to about 50% for the other three groups) saw affiliation to the Orange Order as inconsistent with Christianity, there was no statistically-significant difference between the groups in this regard. But a significant difference does emerge over the endorsement of Freemasonry, with 68% of Catholics opposing it, whilst only 42% of the remaining groups specifically saw membership of the Freemasons as inconsistent with Christian belief. Once again, a substantial proportion (36%) were uncertain about the validity of the match between these two factors. The third question in this group concerned membership of the Knights of St Columba (a fraternal benefit society of Roman Catholic men). There was apparently very substantial ignorance of the nature of this group, with 56% taking the 'don't know' category (though only 19% of Catholics). Whilst a majority (53%) answered in the negative, the fact that a quarter responded affirmatively and that, when the other three groups gave anything other than a 'don't know' response they tended to reply negatively, made for a difference significant at the 0.1% level between Catholics and others on this variable.

The majority (54%) of Church of Scotland members saw abortion as 'justifiable in certain circumstances', with an additional 35% seeing it as 'a matter entirely for the persons concerned'. Only 6% saw it as 'always wrong'. The figures for Roman Catholics showed a directly antithetical pattern, whilst non-church members were more or less evenly divided between the first two responses. The trends presented in Table 2.25 yield a highly-significant statistical association.

Table 2.25
Which of the following corresponds to your view of abortion?

	C of S	R C	Other	Non-church
A matter entirely for the persons concerned	35.2	13.0	35.7	43.3
Justified in certain circumstances	54.4	41.3	53.6	45.7
Always wrong	6.4	43.5	10.7	8.2
Don't know	4.0	2.2	0	2.9

Not unexpectedly, Christians are much more opposed than non-church members to the idea that sexual intercourse before marriage is justifiable. The proportions endorsing the different options within the three church groups are virtually identical (though Catholics seem much less likely to give a 'don't know' reply) and this pattern produces a highly-significant difference between church and non-church members.

The majority of respondents in all three church groups (56% in each case) viewed homosexuality as 'an unnatural act', as compared to 43% of those without church affiliations. Forty six per cent of this latter group saw such behaviour as a personal matter that should be left to the individual, a view that was endorsed by about a third of each of the church samples. Only a tiny proportion (3%) of the sample were prepared to endorse the statement that 'sexual love between members of the same sex is acceptable', but the differences already referred to were substantial enough to render a further statistically-significant difference between church-members and those with no formal religious connections.

Viewing these recently-considered findings as a whole, it seems possible to discern a relatively consistent pattern in the responses of the different groups. Thus, while church members are in general more conservative in matters of personal morality than non-church members, within the Christian group, Catholics emerge as more conservative than others on television, sex and violence, video classification and (for obvious reasons) abortion. They are, however, also more 'tender minded' on issues that have a more overtly political content — being, for instance, more likely to criticise unemployment as an unacceptable waste of human resources, to see nuclear weapons as morally unacceptable and to see help to developing countries and awareness of economic and social injustice as important aspects of the churches' future role. Communicants with the Church of Scotland and other churches tend by contrast to adopt a 'tougher' stance on these social and political issues and of course gave low priority to related concepts in the list of items presented as potentially significant for the church's future. It should of course also be remembered that there were significant differences in the political affiliations of Catholic and Church of Scotland members. Whether these divergencies in views concerning personal morality and social affairs reflect differences in the religious beliefs of the parties concerned, or are due (in the case of Roman Catholic/Church of Scotland comparisons) to the differences in the sex-composition of the sub-samples or (in the case of comparisons with the other groups) to age-differences can only be settled by a further analysis of the data which will be undertaken in later Chapters of this report.

Indeed, the caveat should perhaps more frequently have been entered throughout this analysis — given the higher average age of and bias towards the female sex within the Church of Scotland sample — that such differences as have emerged should be further tested for the differential influences of age, sex and religious belief upon the attitudes and behaviours reported. Such strictures, however, perhaps become particularly necessary in considering responses to the thirty-nine statements, covering various aspects of 'life-style', that were included in the Questionnaire. In this section of the schedule, people were asked to state whether they agreed or disagreed with each of a list of statements reporting behaviours or attitudes relating to a wide range of social, political, psychological and moral questions.

(iv) Lifestyle

As in the earlier sections of this Chapter, we shall search for the total range of individually-significant differences before attempting to detect patterns and interpret their meaning. However, for the sake of both clarity and economy, we shall consider only those fifteen statements which yielded significant trends within the data. These are all listed in Table 2.26.

The first item in this Table shows that, whilst a majority of all groups agreed with the statement that 'Our family do many things together', those from the Church of Scotland were very much more likely to endorse this statement than people in the three remaining groups. Indeed, a separate analysis comparing Church of Scotland members with all others increases the significance of this difference.

Item 2 again shows a majority of every group endorsing the statement that 'I have got pretty much what I expected out of life'. But in this case, Catholics and Church of Scotland members are significantly more likely than members of the other two sub-samples to agree with this statement. The third item, to the effect that individuals have the things that make life satisfying is again endorsed more frequently by Church of Scotland and Roman Catholic members than the two remaining groups; although as before, the great majority of all four groups agree with the assertion. And to complete this picture of apparent contentment, Church of Scotland members (above all) and Roman Catholics (though in this case closely followed by the members of other churches) proved much less likely to agree with the statement that 'My life could be happier than it is now'. By contrast, a bare majority of non-church members were in accord with this view. To this first set of items that obviously relate to personal life-satisfaction might be added the apparently greater readiness of Church of Scotland and other church members to agree with the assertion that 'I like simple things ...' which, although accepted by the very great majority of all groups, does yield a significant association with religious affiliation, as a result of these trends.

A second set of items — perhaps not entirely unrelated to the first cluster — appears to uncover differences in people's attitudes towards material objects. Thus, the sixth and seventh items in Table 2.26 show that members of the Church of Scotland believe that the only way to obtain things of value is to save for them and express a preference for paying cash for purchases. The pattern is somewhat complicated by the fact that the first statement is also endorsed by Catholics, whilst the second is supported more by other church members. The associations yielded are, however, both highly significant. Finally, members of the Church of Scotland and other church members prove significantly less likely than their counterparts in the other two groups to agree with the statement that it would be useful for them to reduce their material standards.

Members of the Church of Scotland and the Roman Catholic Church were also significantly less amenable to 'new exciting experiences even if they are a bit frightening or unconventional' and were more likely to believe it best to live in an area 'where all the neighbours have a similar standard'. The two statements concerning approval of a teenage son or daughter going on holiday with a partner of the opposite sex provide identical patterns, which are also entirely consistent with responses to the questions concerning personal

37

Table 2.26

Indicate your view on each of the following

			C of S	R C	Other	Non-church
(i)	Our family do many	Agree	81	72	70	66
	things together	Disagree	19	28	30	34
(ii)	I've got pretty much what	Agree	81	81	69	72
	I expected out of life	Disagree	19	19	31	28
(iii)	I have to a great extent the things that make life pleasant and satisfying	Agree	91	100	89	83
	for people of my age	Disagree	9	0	11	17
(iv)	My life could be happier	Agree	36	40	43	51
	than it is now	Disagree	64	60	57	49
(v)	I like simple things and	Agree	96	89	94	84
	a natural way of life	Disagree	4	11	6	16
(vi)	The only way to get something valuable is to	Agree	85	87	79	76
	save for it	Disagree	15	13	21	24
(vii)	I prefer to pay cash even if I have to wait for	Agree	81	62	80	68
	larger purchases	Disagree	19	28	20	22
(viii)	It would be useful for me to reduce my material	Agree	16	30	17	25
	standards	Disagree	84	70	83	75
(ix)	I like new experiences even if they are a bit frightening	Agree	40	41	48	57
	or unconventional	Disagree	60	59	52	43
(x)	It is best to live in areas where all the neighbours	Agree	56	63	44	48
	have a similar standard	Disagree	44	37	56	52
(xi)	If I had a teenage daughter I would let her go on	Agree	49	39	50	59
	holiday with her boyfriend	Disagree	51	61	50	41
(xii)	If I had a teenage son I would let him go on	Agree	52	40	56	67
	holiday with his girlfriend	Disagree	48	60	44	33
(xiii)	Religion is important	Agree	76	89	61	35
	in my life	Disagree	24	11	39	65
(xiv)	When I join a club or society I engage myself	Agree	58	48	57	46
	fully in its work	Disagree	42	52	43	54
(xv)	In an election I would always vote for a party with	Agree	49	42	43	37
	a strong defence policy	Disagree	51	58	57	63

morality earlier in the schedule. Thus, Roman Catholics are much less likely to agree with this assertion, whilst non-church members are most in favour of it, with the other two groups somewhere in between. It is possibly of some interest that the three other groups are more positive about such proposals in the case of sons, whilst Catholics appear unaffected by the sex of the child in question.

It is not at all surprising that Christians on the whole affirm that religion is important in their life whilst for non-church members this view is sustained by only a minority. Of greater interest, however, are the variations in the relative strength of this view as between the three denominational groups; with 89% of Catholics, 76% of Church of Scotland and only 61% of other church members supporting this affirmation. Moving to the next item on this list, the 59% of Church of Scotland members who report themselves as engaging themselves fully in the work of clubs or societies of which they are members echoes the earlier finding that significantly more Church of Scotland members hold offices of responsibility — particularly outside the political arena. Finally, and rather on its own, is the fact (again consistent with earlier findings) that Church of Scotland members report themselves as significantly more likely to vote for a party with a 'strong defence policy'.

On the whole, therefore, Catholics and members of the Church of Scotland report rather more satisfaction with their life situation than do other members of the sample. But given the fact that, in all cases, a majority of people report themselves as contented with their life, it is perhaps more reasonable to infer that most people seem to manage to attain a personally satisfying lifestyle or situation, but that membership of the two churches in question for some reason makes a person less vulnerable to feelings of dissatisfaction.

These differences could be attributed to complacency generated in the two church samples within the boundaries set by a rather conventional lifestyle. This interpretation would, for example, be consistent with church-attenders dislike of new experiences, and their desire to live in socially-homogeneous areas, as well as their cautious attitude towards cash transactions. Alternatively, it could reflect a lifestyle based on more integrated social networks and contacts, a view that might be supported by their affirmation that 'our family do many things together'. Alternatively, it might in the case of Church of Scotland members, simply reflect the greater average age of the members of this group.

Two additional questions concerning the individual's preferences over social contact and use of spare time tended to give further support to this analysis. Thus, Church of Scotland members were by far more likely to prefer to spend their spare time with their family, with this proportion being very much smaller among non-church members. Similarly, members of the Church of Scotland were significantly less likely to express a positive preference for being with people of different views (although this option was endorsed by a minority of all groups). In fairness, however, it should also be said that 68% of Church of Scotland members reported that they 'didn't mind' being with people of different ideas and values, with 13% preferring not to confront such experiences.

No group proved more likely to report feelings of loneliness. Nor was there any significant association between religious affiliation and the extent to which respondents described themselves as happy or unhappy.

(v) Alcohol

A final set of questions focused on attitudes and behaviours relating to the use of alcohol.

Whilst the majority in all four groups reported that they drank alcohol occasionally or very occasionally, a quarter of the members of other churches and 17% of Church of Scotland members never drink alcohol. By contrast, fully 66% of non-members drink alcohol either regularly or occasionally. These trends are outlined in Table 2.27.

Table 2.27

How would you describe your present consumption of alcohol?

	C of S	R C	Other	Non-church
Never drink alcohol	17.3	14.9	25.5	10.7
Very occasionally drink alcohol	37.4	34.0	41.8	23.0
Occasionally drink alcohol	35.1	34.0	18.2	42.6
Regularly drink alcohol	10.1	17.0	14.5	23.8

Looking at a detailed breakdown of the kinds of alcohol consumed, the differences noted in Table 2.27 seem almost entirely attributable to differential use as between church members (of the various denominations) and non-members, of beer, wine and spirits (with the latter group reporting significantly more frequent — though still relatively modest — intakes of all three of these). It is, however, interesting to note that significantly more Church of Scotland members indulge in the consumption of fortified wine, though the great majority 'seldom' or 'never' drink it. No substantial differences existed in the extent to which the different groups make their own wine or beer and no differences worthy of comment were evident in their putative reactions to being served with wine at a function.

As in other areas of the questionnaire, there was a very high degree of uniformity in the rankings offered by the four groups to a question concerning their main reasons for drinking. The items endorsed by all four groups as their top four reasons were 'to increase the value of a good meal ... easier to relax ... easier social contact'; and 'atmosphere is better with a little alcohol'.

It does, however, seem worthy of note that Roman Catholics and individuals who are not official members of any church place significantly

40

greater emphasis upon easier social contact and ease of relaxation as reasons for drinking; whereas members of the Church of Scotland and of other churches accord greater weight to increasing the value of a good meal as a motive for taking alcohol.

Those ranked as the bottom four of a total group of twelve items were 'difficult to be TT in my job ... abstinence is out of date ... want to use my Christian freedom ... and don't want to be different from my friends'. It thus appears that people view alcohol in primarily instrumental terms, as enhancing eating and the social atmosphere. It does, however, at least offer food for thought that the hoariest of all rationalisations for drinking ('medicinal purposes') is significantly more frequently proffered by Church of Scotland members as a justification — perhaps for drinking their fortified wine. These trends are displayed in Table 2.28.

Table 2.28

If you drink at all, what are your main reasons for drinking?

	C of S	R C	Other	Non-church
Easier social contact*	3 (42%)	2 (61%)	4 (36%)	2 (58%)
Easier to relax*	2 (54%)	1 (71%)	2 (45%)	1 (65%)
In order not to appear self-righteous*	8 (12%)	8=(8%)	6 (21%)	9 (6%)
Abstinence is out of date	11 (5%)	11 (3%)	12 (0%)	12 (1%)
Atmosphere better with a little alcohol	4 (35%)	3 (37%)	3 (40%)	4 (42%)
Increase value of a good meal*	1 (57%)	4 (34%)	1 (57%)	3 (46%)
Difficult to be TT in my job	12 (3%)	12 (0%)	9=(10%)	11 (2%)
Don't believe I'd be damaged	5 (25%)	6 (13%)	7 (14%)	5 (23%)
Want to use Christian freedom	10 (7%)	10 (5%)	9=(10%)	10 (5%)
Don't want to be different from friends	9 (10%)	8=(8%)	11 (5%)	8 (8%)
Medicinal*	7 (19%)	7 (11%)	9=(10%)	7 (10%)
Other reasons	6 (20%)	5 (21%)	5 (33%)	6 (20%)

* a significant association between church group to which individuals belong and importance attached to item.

A question asking drinkers why they did not drink more produced rather greater variance between the rank-orderings ascribed by the four groups. Thus, although 'damaging to my health' ... 'don't want to get drunk' and 'have seen what alcohol has done to others' are all accorded a uniformly high priority, Church of Scotland and non-church members accorded much higher priority to 'drinking and driving is dangerous and against the law' than did Catholics especially. Avoidance of a hangover was also fairly important for non-church members, whereas amongst Catholics and members of the Church of Scotland it was given relatively minor significance. Catholics and Church of Scotland members also accorded greater weight to 'setting an example for my children' than either of the other two groups. (It should of course be remembered that there are more single people outside the two major church groups). But despite these variations, one may again in general conclude that the structure of the attitudinal systems of the four groups is relatively similar over these matters.

Table 2.29

If you do drink, why do you not drink more?

	C of S	R C	Other	Non-church
Damaging to my health	1 (48%)	1=(43%)	2 (38%)	1 (48%)
Avoid a hangover	9 (15%)	10=(12%)	6=(16%)	7=(20%)
Resisting social pressure	17=(2%)	18=(0%)	15=(8%)	15 (4%)
Drinking in pregnancy damages foetus	15=(3%)	18=(0%)	18=(3%)	18=(2%)
Don't want to get drunk	3 (33%)	1=(43%)	3 (32%)	2 (36%)
Don't want to become dependent	7 (20%)	4 (31%)	6=(16%)	7=(20%)
Drank too much in earlier life	15=(3%)	18=(0%)	10=(11%)	13=(6%)
For sake of those damaged by alcohol	17=(2%)	14=(5%)	18=(3%)	18=(2%)
Drinking and driving against the law*	2 (36%)	8=(14%)	5 (22%)	3 (32%)
Don't want to be danger in traffic	12=(8%)	16 (2%)	15=(8%)	13=(6%)
Don't like the taste	10 (12%)	13 (7%)	10=(11%)	11=(8%)
Don't want to lose control	8 (16%)	6=(17%)	4 (30%)	7=(20%)
Don't want to gain weight*	14 (6%)	8=(14%)	1 (5%)	9=(9%)
Example for my children*	6 (23%)	5 (26%)	8 (14%)	9=(9%)
Example for others*	11 (9%)	10=(12%)	15=(8%)	16=(3%)
Can't afford it*	4=(27%)	6=(17%)	10=(11%)	4 (31%)
Seen what alcohol has done to others	4=(27%)	3 (35%)	1 (39%)	5 (28%)
Solidarity with friends	19 (1%)	14=(5%)	18=(3%)	16=(3%)
Other reasons	12=(8%)	10 (12%)	10=(11%)	11=(8%)

* a significant association between church group to which individuals belong and importance attached to item.

Some 12½% of the entire sample did not drink at all. The rather small numbers in the individual sub-samples made it difficult to draw valid comparisons between them. Scrutiny of the response does, however, again indicate a relatively high degree of congruence as to the reasons they offer for not drinking, with 'damage to health', 'Christian conviction', 'no need of alcohol' and 'for the sake of those damaged by alcohol' emerging as the most frequently-cited reasons. It would thus seem fair to infer that a combination of health concerns and personal conviction constitute the primary motivating factors for total abstainers. A dislike of the taste of alcohol was also pinpointed as an important motive for abstention.

The question 'Do you think a Christian should be a total abstainer?' received an overwhelmingly negative response from both church and non-church members; although it should be noted that those from other churches were rather more accepting of this notion, with only 70% responding in the negative as opposed to between 80-87% for the other groups; and although some 30% of the members of all churches felt that Communion wine should be non-alcoholic, a majority (54%) of church members reported that it 'doesn't matter' — this proportion being identical to that for the non-church group. There was thus no significant difference on this item.

As one might expect in these modern times, only a minority (29%) of the sample identified themselves as smokers. In none of the four groups were smokers in the majority. Nonetheless, 38% of non-church members smoked and this was significantly more than the proportion for any of the church groups. The final question in the schedule asked respondents whether they thought people should be allowed to use cannabis freely. Whilst overall the vast majority (83%) were opposed to such a move, members of the Church of Scotland were hostile to such a possibility; and although again a clear majority of all groups endorse the same opinion, the magnitude of the discrepancy between the proportions mentioned made for a statistically significant association between religious affiliation and attitudes towards the legalisation of cannabis.

Interpretation and Discussion

What, then, may we deem to be the social meaning and more human significance of the trends noted throughout this chapter? Clearly, given its age, sex and social-class deviations from the census data, the present sample (unfortunately) cannot be regarded as representative of the country as a whole. The large size and method of selection of the sample should, however, have ensured that it closely mirrors the membership of the Church of Scotland. The clearly-indicated Church of Scotland sponsorship of the survey may very possibly have introduced a bias into the pattern of responses obtained from groups outside Scotland's majority Church; although there is no easy way of tracing and isolating the effects of any potential bias within the current analysis. The schedule itself was attractively designed and printed; and arranged for ease and clarity of both reading and completion. The various written comments inserted by many respondents when they returned the completed form lead us further to believe that people found responding to it an interesting and enjoyable experience, and that the answers themselves therefore in general comply with the requirements of reliability and validity.

More substantively, both the number and the consistency of the statistically-significant trends recorded in the Chapter strongly support the contention that religious affiliation has an important bearing upon people's lifestyle and involvement in society. In common with long-established churches in other countries, members of the Church of Scotland are rather older than other sectors of the population (this also being true of Roman Catholics); and, as for most established Protestant churches, are predominantly female (this also being the case for 'other' churches). They are not, however, any more biased towards the middle class than are other groups drawn from the same areas of residence. The significantly greater likelihood that members of the Church of Scotland (and Catholics) will have an income of less than £5,000 per annum and have been resident at the same address for 11 years or more very probably reflect their higher average age and suggest that one should bear this age-factor in mind when interpreting other differences. The greater probability, for example, that members of the two major church groups will *not* have attended University or College is a possible testimony to the more restricted opportunities for higher education in an earlier generation; although it may also reflect a tendency for people with less formal education to be attracted to the church. But whatever the explanation of these trends, the interaction of these age, sex, education, and other factors will clearly have a more immediate influence upon the attitudes, preferences, activities and debates within the church itself and possibly reinforce certain tendencies within it.

In terms both of their stated commitment to the church and their involvement in devotional activities within and outside it, members of the Church of Scotland seem to carry a greater number of 'passengers' within their number than is the case for the two other denominational groups. A higher proportion of Church of Scotland members also reported a reduction in their frequency of church attendance since earlier adult life and if anything, they were more likely than other groups to see a devotional life as having been the rule in their childhood, with their mothers in particular having been regular church attenders. Nor did the majority anticipate any increase in their frequency of church attendance over future years, although 20% found it difficult to make any specific prediction over this matter.

Roman Catholics seem to possess a much more coherent system of religious beliefs than either Church of Scotland or other church members, being more likely to regard themselves as Christians, to affirm a belief in God, to believe that God controls our lives here and now, that Jesus died for our sins and is risen from the dead, and to endorse a belief in eternal life and life after death. This may be correlated with their greater tendency to view God as an all-powerful judge, as well as a loving being who controls our lives, whilst significant minorities of the other two denominational groups conceptualise God as a distant, impersonal force. Catholics also have a much more definite belief that 'after death man stands before God and his judgement' whilst the two Protestant sub-samples are more heterogeneously distributed over a range of responses. The same general pattern holds true for people's beliefs about heaven and hell, with a clear majority of Catholics seeing them as places of eternal bliss or suffering after God's judgement, whereas other Christians possess a less coherent view.

Conceptions of the importance of different possible courses of action for the future of the church seem linked in meaningful ways to people's lifestyle and attitudes to moral, social and political issues. The greater political Conservatism of Church of Scotland members may be a function of age (though it is difficult to equate this with Catholics' propensity to support Labour), but it almost certainly informs their support for strong defence policies, their acceptance of the deterrent value of nuclear weapons and their majority opposition to industrial strikes. By contrast with people who have no attachment to the church, Church of Scotland members are, with other denominations, more opposed to pre-marital intercourse and more inclined to view homosexuality as 'an unnatural act'. They are, however, generally supportive of abortion.

Church of Scotland members' tendency to do many things together with the family and their greater preference for local as opposed to national newspapers, together with the lower priority they attach to issues of social justice and help to developing countries in the work of the church perhaps suggest a membership rooted in rather narrow parochial concerns (an impression that is possibly further supported by their readership of the *Sunday Post*). It may be this combination which engenders their overall satisfaction or complacency with life; although the rather similar degree of satisfaction expressed by Catholics, with their rather different range of concerns with the world around them, suggests that one may need to look further for the proper explanation of this cluster of relationships.

Although members of all three denominational groups were much more abstemious in respect of alcohol (and particularly of beer), no very substantial difference appeared on the other variables in this section. In terms of the absolute value they placed upon alcohol, Church of Scotland members were significantly less likely to see alcohol as making for ease of social contact or relaxation; rather less likely to see abstinence as out of date; and more likely to use alcohol to improve a good meal or for 'medicinal purposes'. The relative importance attached to alcohol by the different groups is, however, very similar indeed. And looking again at *the absolute* importance people attach to reasons for not drinking more, those within the Church of Scotland proved more likely to cite the dangers of drink and driving and a desire to set an example for children and for other people as factors influencing them to control their drinking; whilst members of the other groups were more likely to avoid excessive drinking for fear of gaining weight. Clearly, moral precept and awareness of social responsibilities are important factors in restraining Church of Scotland members' drinking habits (these factors may also relate to their heavier involvement as office-bearers in organisations of which they are members); but the *relative* ranking ascribed to the various factors by the members of different groups again emerges as extremely similar.

Turning to that question which asked total abstainers the reasons why they do not drink at all, the only significant difference that emerged was on the Church of Scotland members' desire to avoid dependency. The relatively small number of responses to this particular question make it difficult to analyse the relative importance attached by the different groups to the various reasons specified, but scrutiny of the factors identified as most important by the four groups again suggests reasonable homogeneity between them.

We feel we have established a reasonable case for considering religion as an important influence over personal attitudes and behaviour. The next stage of the analysis will, however, require to focus mainly on those basic background elements (mainly age and sex) which distinguish these four groups from each other. It will then be fascinating to note whether the variations already noted disappear when those other factors are held constant; or whether the divergencies on political, moral and other issues reflect what are perhaps more interesting differences of underlying values and beliefs.

CHAPTER THREE

LIFESTYLE AND AGE

The previous Chapter has shown religious denomination to be strongly associated with a whole range of (self-reported) beliefs and patterns of behaviour. At the same time, it is also correlated with two attributes — sex and age — which may reasonably be expected to have some bearing upon those same behaviours and beliefs. The attributes in question may exercise their influence either independently of denominational affiliation or (as is perhaps more likely) through some complex interaction with particular religious beliefs. We must therefore take account of these possibilities; and this and the ensuing Chapters will accordingly test for the independent effects of sex, age and the intensity and content of religious commitment and belief, before examining certain of their combined effects. We shall start with an analysis of the age factor.

Age has both a potent and a pervasive influence upon human life-experience. Biologically, it shapes our mental and physical capacities in ways that impinge on our performance of social and individual tasks. Sociologically, progression through the various stages of the life-cycle from childhood to extreme old age is accompanied by changes in the patterns of obligations, rights and opportunities that confront us in our daily lives. Chronologically, individuals spending their formative years during particular periods in historical time will develop attitudes and expectations that tend to differ from those held by people born to earlier or later generations. And psychologically, the aggregate effect of these elements, as one moves into the later stages of the ageing process, is likely to be to increase one's awareness of the brute fact of mortality and thereby cause one to reflect upon the essential pathos of the human condition and the prospect of an after-life. All of these factors may in one way or another have had some bearing on the trends that were noted in the previous Chapter. We shall thus have recourse to at least certain of these notions in attempting to account for those results.

An analysis identical to that for denominational membership was undertaken on the data in respect of age. For this purpose, the sample was divided into three groups comprising those aged between 18 and 44 at the time of the survey (a 'young' group); those aged between 45 and 64 ('middle-aged'); and those aged 65 or over ('elderly'). As before, the strength of the association between age and other factors was tested by standard statistical procedures, and reference will in the main be made to those where the significance level exceeded 1%. And as before, this account will be organised around the three main areas contained within the survey questionnaire.

(i) General background factors

A test of the relationship showed no significant association between the variables of sex and age. This means that there is no preponderance of women over men among the elderly (or any other) age-group. Further reference will be made to this analysis in Chapter 4, but for present purposes, we can safely assume that any relationships that emerge within our analysis between age and other factors will not be complicated by the additional possibility of sex/gender influences.

Elderly people also tended to have significantly smaller incomes and to have been resident for longer periods at the same address. They were also more likely to be widowed or single than members of the other age-groups; to be living on their own or in a household with only one other person; to have left school at an earlier age; and less likely to have attended College or University.

None of these findings offends against expectation. In combination, however, they do present a picture which thus far corresponds remarkably closely to the profile that emerged in the last Chapter for Church of Scotland members. This finding is further reinforced by the data in Table 3.1, which show a very strong association between age and a propensity to vote Conservative. Also of some potential interest is (a) the rank order of degree of support for the various parties is consistent across all age groups, and (b) the fact that there is an apparent groundswell of support for the SDP among the young. With respect to another finding in Chapter 2, however, no association was found between age and involvement in public office.

Table 3.1

Age in relation to political loyalty

	Young	*Middle-aged*	*Elderly*
Conservative	35.8	42.4	52.6
Labour	24.3	22.7	18.5
Liberal	17.1	19.7	12.5
SNP	13.6	11.5	11.2
SDP	9.2	3.7	5.2

Table 3.2

Age in relation to degree of commitment to the Church

	Young	*Middle-aged*	*Elderly*
Highly committed	9.9	15.3	24.1
Fairly committed	24.5	39.3	46.2
Not very committed	36.6	30.7	19.0
Not at all committed	29.1	14.7	10.7

(ii) Religion and the Church

It is not surprising to discover that age correlates very strongly with frequency of church attendance, with older people attending very much more, and younger very much less often than would be expected in a chance distribution. And consistent with this, Table 3.2 shows that older people report themselves as significantly more committed to the church than do younger members of the sample.

For whatever reason, older people thus emerge as both more active in and more psychologically committed to church affairs. And given that the analysis in Chapter 2 showed Church of Scotland members as significantly lower in these attributes than members of other churches, it would seem that those differences are not attributable to the older average age of the Church of Scotland sample. These apparently contradictory results could, however, be explained in terms of a much lower level of commitment to church affairs and activities on the part of youthful Church of Scotland members than their age-peers in the two other denominational groups. This possibility will clearly require to be tested further in later stages of the analysis.

Responses to the question as to whether they had attended church more or less frequently in earlier adult life than they do currently, yielded no significant association with respondents' age, even when the very youngest group of respondents (aged between 18 and 25) were excluded from the analysis, on the grounds that their 'adult life' was too short for any appreciable change to have occured in their behaviour in this respect. Viewed in conjunction with the findings reported in the preceding paragraph, these data appear to suggest that elderly people have grown up in a context of fairly regular and frequent church-going and have retained this habit throughout their adult life. Similarly, people in younger age-groups have remained consistent in a pattern of less frequent church-going. Once more, therefore, it would appear that the difference reported between members of the Church of Scotland and other churches in this respect in Chapter 2 are not attributable to differences in age-structures between the denominations.

Responses to the subsidiary question as to how frequent they felt their attendance was likely to be in five years time showed a highly significant relationship with age; with a significant minority of older people reporting their attendance as likely to be less frequent, whilst an equivalent proportion

Table 3.3

Age in relation to expected frequency of future Church attendance

	Young	Middle-aged	Elderly
More frequent than at present	11.9	9.2	4.8
About the same	63.7	68.8	57.4
Less frequent	1.9	1.3	11.2
Difficult to know	22.5	20.7	26.5

of younger people saw their attendances as probably tending to become more frequent. When, however, people aged over 65 were excluded from this analysis (on the grounds that the responses of an appeciable proportion of them might be affected by doubts as to whether they would still be alive in five years time) the significant association between age and predicted frequency of future church attendance disappeared. For what they are worth, these differences are presented in Table 3.3.

Answers to the questions concerning the frequency with which people pray and read the Bible yield trends consistent with the notion that elderly people engage themselves more fully in religious activities. Thus, Table 3.4 shows a very substantial proportion of elderly people praying every day, whilst the great majority of those in the younger age-group seldom or never pray. Only about 40% of elderly people read their Bible at least once a week; this proportion is very much higher than that reported by either of the two remaining age-groups. Thirty-four per cent of elderly people sample religious programmes on radio or television, as opposed to 26% among the middle-aged and only 9% among the younger groups.

Table 3.4

Age in relation to frequency of prayer

	Young	Middle-aged	Elderly
Every day	18.9	36.1	53.6
Two to three times per week	11.2	10.9	10.4
Once a week	9.0	11.6	7.2
Seldom	28.9	22.5	16.4
Never or hardly ever	32.0	18.9	12.4

Table 3.5

Age in relation to extent to which devotional life was a rule in childhood

	Young	Middle-aged	Elderly
Yes	22.0	42.6	55.4
No	72.4	49.5	34.1
Doubtful/don't know	5.6	7.9	10.4

The relationship between age and answers to the question as to whether a devotional life had been the rule during respondents' childhood is presented in Table 3.5. This is consistent with the differences between the different age groups that were reported above in respect of their frequency of church attendance in earlier life. Thus, more than half of the elderly group report a devotional life as having been the rule in their childhood; whereas very much smaller proportions of middle-aged and younger people (42 and 22%, respectively) claim that religious devotion formed an important part of their childhood life. This gives further support to the idea that what we are observing is a generational difference, with religion having played a much more central role during the formative years of elderly people; and, it would seem, still exerting a much greater influence over their lives at the present time.

This view is further supported by the proportions in the three age-groups who reported themselves as having been baptised. Whilst fully 90% of the youngest age group had in fact been baptised, this was still some way short of the 98% of elderly people and 97% of middle-aged people who had received baptism. This difference was significant at the 0.1% level. Similarly, elderly (and middle-aged) people had attended Sunday School for a considerably greater number of years than had younger people (Table 3.6).

Table 3.6

Age in relation to attendance at Sunday School

	Young	*Middle-aged*	*Elderly*
Stopped by age 11	25.7	14.2	7.9
Stopped between 12 and 15	58.9	74.7	75.4
Stopped at 16 or over	9.1	6.5	10.8
Never attended	6.3	4.6	5.9

This picture of a decline in church-related activities over the generations represented within this sample is completed by the trends presented in Table 3.7. This shows rather more elderly people reporting that their mothers and far more, that their fathers, were regular church attenders than is the case for either of the other two groups — with the differences between the reported frequency of attendance between mothers and fathers echoing the tendency commented on in Chapter 2, for continuing church members to have had mothers who were frequent church attenders, with fathers' influence apparently being more negative in this regard. (In this connection, it is interesting to note that as many middle-aged as elderly people saw their mothers as having been regular church attenders, whilst the proportion of regular church attenders among the fathers of middle-aged people is substantially less than that for the elderly.)

There was no significant association between age and either, attendance at the services of other denominations, or membership of an ecumenical group. For whatever reasons, therefore, the apparently stronger religious habits and commitment of elderly people do not lead them to seek additional contact with the members of other churches.

In view of the differences noted in the preceding paragraphs, it is hardly surprising that substantially higher numbers of elderly people regarded

Table 3.7

(a) *Age in relation to regularity of mother's Church attendance*

	Young	Middle-aged	Elderly
Regular attender	59.6	70.6	70.8
Not regular	36.3	25.4	18.8
Don't know	4.1	4.0	10.4

(b) *Age in relation to regularity of father's Church attendance*

	Young	Middle-aged	Elderly
Regular attender	36.7	53.8	61.9
Not regular	57.4	39.3	26.7
Don't know	5.8	6.9	11.3

themselves as Christians than was the case for members of the youngest age-group (87%, as opposed to 73%, with 83% of middle-aged people responding in this way). Again, this difference is significant at the 1% level. And when we consider the proportion of people who profess a belief in God, the pattern of a more religiously-committed elderly population is supported yet further by the figures presented in Table 3.8, which reveal a much higher proportion of elderly people affirming a belief in God than is the case for their younger brethren, with middle-aged people falling somewhere between the two. The notion that elderly people have stronger religious beliefs is given further apparent confirmation by the fact that proportionately many more elderly (77.3%) than young (52.9%) people believe that God controls our lives here and now, with middle-aged people (67%) again coming somewhere between.

Table 3.8

Age and belief in God

	Young	Middle-aged	Elderly
Believe in God	73.3	81.9	86.5
Don't believe in God	7.8	3.6	1.2
Don't know	18.9	14.5	12.3

When we turn to consider the views of God endorsed by people in the three age-groups, we find the trends portrayed in Table 3.9, which yields an association between the two variables that is significant at the 0.1% level. Thus, although the most frequently-chosen response for all three groups is that which characterises God as a loving figure, this is chosen by almost half the elderly group, as opposed to only a little over a quarter of young people. Conversely, many more young people either have no opinion or construe God as an impersonal force; whilst 22% of this group see Him as a father whose concern is to save and help. Also of some possible interest is the fact that the only response in which middle-aged people are in the majority is that which conceptualises God as an all-powerful judge.

Table 3.9

Age and conception of God

	Young	Middle-aged	Elderly
All powerful judge who sees and judges our sins and virtues	9.1	17.1	12.0
Loving, he hears our prayers and controls our lives	27.2	37.8	45.6
A father whose concern is to save and to help	22.3	16.7	16.4
A sort of distant, impersonal power or force	19.1	10.4	11.6
No opinion	22.3	18.1	14.4

The same pattern appears in answers to the enquiries concerning respondents' belief as to whether Jesus died for our sins and is risen from the dead. In both cases, elderly people showed a much higher propensity to reply in the affirmative, whereas very substantial numbers of young people replied either in the negative or that they did not know what to believe, with members of the middle-aged sample occupying their usual position between these two extremes. Table 3.10 portrays the trends for the association between age and belief that Jesus died for our sins. The related question concerning belief that Jesus is risen from the dead gave a virtually identical pattern of responses. With regard to this chapter's primary concern with the extent to which the trends reported for Church of Scotland members in the previous Chapter may be attributed to the higher average age of that group, the findings in the current set of Tables lend little support to this argument. Although there are certain parallels between these trends and those reported for Catholics in the previous Chapter, there are still too many inconsistencies for one to be able reasonably to conclude that the association between denominational affiliation and the varying aspects of belief reported here may be accounted for in terms of the higher average age of Church of Scotland and Roman Catholic communicants. If age is a factor in explaining these trends for Church of Scotland members, then we must probably seek it in the apparently declining strength of belief among the Church's younger members.

Table 3.10

Age and belief that Jesus died for our sins

	Young	*Middle-aged*	*Elderly*
Believe Jesus died for our sins	58.5	69.6	76.2
Don't believe	15.5	10.9	5.2
Don't know	26.0	19.5	18.7

Table 3.11 depicts the relationship between age and belief in eternal life. This shows the familiar pattern of a significantly (at the 0.1% level) stronger system of belief among elderly people, with a steadily declining acceptance of this notion in the other two groups, to the point where less than half of young people affirm such a belief. The large proportion of don't knows across all three groups does, however, appear worthy of note.

Table 3.11

Age and belief in eternal life

	Young	*Middle-aged*	*Elderly*
Believe in eternal life	48.5	55.8	60.5
Don't believe	24.8	15.2	9.5
Don't know	26.7	29.0	30.0

By contrast, however, no significant association exists between age and individuals' belief in life after death. Although rather more young than elderly people (23.1, as opposed to 13.9%) reject such a belief, the proportions accepting this belief are relatively similar (47% and 52%, with middle-aged people occupying their now-customary intermediate position).

Answers to the question of what happens after death did, however, yield a significant (though only at the 5% level of confidence) association with age. Although Table 3.12 shows interesting divergencies between the three groups, it is difficult to interpret these. Why, in particular, should middle-aged people apparently have more definite ideas about what happens after death, with a smaller proportion opting for the don't know response and a significantly higher proportion affirming that after death man stands before God and his judgement? And why, given their much stronger commitment to organised religion and their apparently firmer religious beliefs, should such a high proportion of elderly people endorse the agnostic option?

Table 3.12

Age and belief in what happens after death

	Young	Middle-aged	Elderly
After death man stands before God and his judgement	26.3	36.6	27.4
Man's soul lives forever without judgement	5.1	3.3	3.6
Man's soul goes to another existence	13.7	9.6	10.5
Death is the end — man ceases to exist	12.9	11.9	8.1
We don't know what happens after death	40.0	35.6	46.4
No opinion	2.0	3.0	4.0

A highly-significant association exists (at the 0.1% level) between age and opinions of heaven and hell. Table 3.13 shows that, consistent with their belief that after death man stands before God and His judgement, the largest single proportion of middle-aged people opt for heaven and hell as places where man must live after God's judgement — closely followed in this case by the proportion of elderly people who select this statement. It should, however, also be noted that the majority in all age groups either opt for statements that in varying degrees deny the existence of heaven and hell, or are unwilling to

Table 3.13

Age and opinions of heaven and hell

	Young	Middle-aged	Elderly
Heaven and hell are places with eternal bliss or suffering where man must live after God's judgement	22.9	30.2	28.0
After death man may live near or far from God, but otherwise there are no possibilities	23.9	18.1	15.9
Heaven and hell do not exist – everything is related to man's life here and now	29.8	24.6	24.2
No heaven or hell now or in the future	9.0	4.3	4.3
No opinion	14.4	22.8	27.5

express an opinion on the matter. By contrast with the other two groups, young people are more willing to deny the existence of heaven and hell altogether.

Question 43, which concerned people's opinions of the Bible, failed to yield any significant association with age, the great majority of all three age groups seeing the Bible as written by men who were inspired by God and therefore requiring interpretation. Nor was there any relationship between respondents' age and their opinion of whether human beings are basically good or basically bad. A highly significant association does, however, exist between age and respondents' reported frequency of thinking about the kinds of issues covered by this section of the questionnaire. Table 3.14 shows that elderly people think significantly more and young people significantly less often about these questions. Once more, middle-aged people occupy an intermediate position in this respect.

Table 3.14

Age and frequency with which respondents think of the above questions

	Young	Middle-aged	Elderly
Often	40.8	54.9	61.2
Seldom	51.2	40.1	34.0
Never	8.1	5.0	4.8

In summary, elderly people's greater acceptance of the fundamental tenets of Christian teaching is consistent with the apparently greater strength of their religious upbringing and current belief. This fact, however, seems to have no direct link with the content of more complex factors like what they believe to be the ultimate nature of God, their views of heaven and hell, and even their opinion of the Bible. The strength of their religious conviction seems likely to be due to their membership of a generation whose lives and upbringing were more centrally based upon the guiding tenets of the Christian faith. The greater frequency with which they reflect on these profound issues of belief and human existence may also be in large part attributable to their membership of a more religiously-backed generation, although greater awareness of the inevitable fact of death may also be exercising an influence here. The more subtle elements contained within this framework of belief are more difficult to account for within the simple fact of age itself.

To turn to rather more mundane matters, responses to the question concerning the relative importance of different sources of knowledge about Church events are detailed in Table 3.15. That Table shows very similar patterns between the three-age groups in the relative significance they ascribe to each of these sources, with perhaps the only notable differences being the higher importance accorded to newspapers by the younger age-group, together with the lesser importance they attach to *Life and Work*. But whilst the relative weighting attached to these sources is extremely similar across the three groups, significant differences emerge when one compares the absolute importance attached by them to all of these items, with the sole exception of other Church literature. Thus, many more young people place newspapers as their most important source of information; rather more (though still only a minority of) middle-aged people give pride of place to radio; and substantially more young and middle-aged people see TV as an important source of knowledge. By contrast, elderly people were more likely to cite *Life and Work*, the denominational magazine of the Church of Scotland, and the Priest or Minister as their most significant providers of information on these matters, though in the former case a sizeable proportion of middle-aged people also attributed importance to this organ.

Table 3.15

Age and importance of different sources of knowledge concerning Church events

	Young	*Middle-aged*	*Elderly*
Newspapers	1 (65%)	3 (52%)	3 (43%)
Radio	5 (28%)	6 (35%)	6 (24%)
TV	2 (62%)	1 (59%)	2 (46%)
Life and Work	6 (18%)	4 (36%)	4 (41%)
Other Church literature	4 (3%)	5 (35.5%)	5 (37%)
Minister/Priest	3 (47%)	2 (53%)	1 (62%)
Not interested in Church events	7 (15%)	7 (8%)	7 (5%)

These differences suggest that the associations reported in Chapter 2 between Church of Scotland membership and sources of information on church affairs are almost entirely attributable to age. It may be remembered that the two churches (Church of Scotland and Roman Catholic) with the oldest membership specified the Minister or Priest and TV as first and second, respectively, in their order of importance as sources of such knowledge. By contrast, other churches (with the youngest membership) cited newspapers as their most important source.

Readership of daily newspapers yielded an association with age that was significant at the 5% level. This finding seems largely attributable to the relatively small proportion of middle-aged people who read no daily newspaper and the rather larger numbers of young people who read popular dailies such as the *Sun* or *Star* as well as the proportionately smaller number of the same group who read provincial dailies. A significant association also appeared (this time at the 1% level) between age and readership of Sunday newspapers. Young people are rather more, and older people substantially less, likely to read a quality Sunday paper; whilst significantly fewer young and significantly more elderly people were readers of the *Sunday Post*. These patterns seem consistent in the case of Sunday, but only partially consistent in the case of daily newspapers, with the idea that the relationships reported between church membership and newspaper readership in Chapter 2 are attributable to variations in the age-composition of the different church samples.

In the case of religious newspapers and magazines, significantly higher proportions of young and middle-aged people — as opposed to very substantially smaller percentages of younger people — read denominational magazines; whilst a significantly higher percentage of young people read no religious organs of communication whatsoever.

It would thus seem possible to account in large part for the denominational differences in newspaper readership by reference to the factor of age. Like other church and non-church members, slightly higher proportions of young people appear to have more intellectual newspaper tastes, whilst elderly people seem rather more anchored to local concerns. The slight inconsistency in the case of daily newspapers does, however, perhaps suggest that other factors may also be operating here.

Table 3.16 presents the results of an analysis of the relationship between age and respondents' views of the importance of various possible church developments. There is considerable similarity in the relative importance attached to the first five elements by the three generational groups: but divergencies appear in the priorities they attach to the final three items. These show elderly people as attaching greater significance to the need for a common view on Bible translation; young people as giving rather more weight to improved co-operation with the Roman Catholic Church; and both young and middle-aged people attaching greater priority to the need for improved co-operation over inter-church marriage.

Scrutiny of Table 3.16 suggests that older people attach greater absolute importance than the other two groups to items 1, 2, 3, 4 and 6; whilst young people give more priority to items 5, 7, and 8. In all cases (with trifling exceptions on items 5 and 7) middle-aged people are in their usual position intermediate between the other two. Analysis of the significance of these differences does, however, yield significant results only for items 1, 2, 3, 4 and 6 — all of these being the items on which elderly people possess the strongest views. By contrast, none of the items accorded greatest priority by the youngest members of the sample give statistically-significant differences between the three groups. On the whole, therefore, it would appear that elderly people feel strongest about these matters, which would again fit with their apparently greater general commitment to and interest in church affairs.

Table 3.17, which shows the relative importance (on a scale from 1–3) attached by respondents to various areas of potential social involvement on the part of the church, reveals a high degree of similarity in the rank orders ascribed by all three groups to all of the areas mentioned; with the exception of help to developing countries, which is placed significantly higher by youthful members of the sample than by elderly and middle-aged people, and more spiritual leadership, which is ranked higher by elderly and middle-aged

Table 3.16

Age and importance attached to the following possible developments

	Young	Middle-aged	Elderly
Joint services for Church of Scotland and other denominations	5 (66%)	4 (73%)	4 (77%)
Improved co-operation between Church of Scotland and other Protestant Churches	2 (83%)	1 (88%)	1 (91%)
Joint Communion for Church of Scotland and other denominations	8 (50%)	8 (59%)	8 (63%)
Local Bible Study and prayer groups including Church of Scotland and other Churches' members	7 (57%)	7 (65%)	6 (70%)
Joint effort, e.g. information campaigns about the under-developed countries	1 (84%)	3 (79%)	2 (81%)
Church of Scotland and other Churches should have a common view on Bible translation	6 (65%)	5 (71%)	3 (80%)
Improved co-operation with Roman Catholic Church	4 (72%)	6 (68%)	7 (68%)
Improved co-operation on inter-Church marriage	3 (82%)	2 (81%)	5 (75%)

individuals. In both these cases, there is also a significant association between age and the absolute importance attached to these factors.

Whilst the lower significance attached by elderly people to giving help to developing countries is consistent with the pattern reported for Church of Scotland members in Chapter 2, it would not seem legitimate to explain that variation in terms of age alone, since Roman Catholics ascribed high priority to this item. Indeed, the same observation applies to the call for more spiritual leadership. The fact that personal renewal and evangelisation — both of which were endorsed more heavily by members of other churches, who were of course also younger than the two longer-established churches — would also seem to suggest that factors other than age are important here. The absence of any association between age and a commitment to increased awareness of social and economic justice makes one wary of concluding that younger people have a more idealistic commitment to social and political concerns. Similarly, the lack of any apparent concentration of the responses of older people on such factors as personal renewal and Christian education

Table 3.17*

Age and importance attached to various Church activities

	Young	*Middle-aged*	*Elderly*
Political awareness	11 (2.6)	11 (2.7)	11 (2.6)
Evangelisation	9 (2.2)	9 (2.2)	9 (2.1)
Social work	4 (1.8)	4 (1.8)	4 (1.8)
Help to developing countries	3 (1.7)	7 (2.0)	6 (1.9)
Work with pensioners and the sick	2 (1.7)	1 (1.6)	2 (1.7)
Personal renewal	7 (2.0)	6 (1.9)	7 (2.0)
Increased awareness of social and economic justice	8 (2.0)	8 (2.1)	8 (2.1)
Position of women in the Church	10 (2.5)	10 (2.3)	10 (2.3)
Efficient organisation and good financial management	5 (1.8)	5 (1.9)	5 (1.8)
More spiritual leadership	6 (1.9)	3 (1.7)	3 (1.7)
Christian education	1 (1.6)	2 (1.6)	1 (1.6)

* Numbers in parentheses specify the average scores obtained by each group on the item in question on a scale from 1 to 3.

also suggests that those in the more senior age groups are not more concerned with promoting spiritual and religious development in society.

(iii) Social and moral issues

Although a majority of all age-groups reported they would welcome greater control over the amount of sex and violence shown on television, the proportion for young people (56%) was very substantially less than that for either middle-aged (84%) or elderly (91%) members of the sample. The same was generally true of support for classification of home videos; although here the statistically significant association with age may be explained by the higher proportion of young than elderly people (18% compared with 4% respectively) who were opposed to such a measure, rather than by any variation in the numbers who supported it. As before, one should take special note of the fact that, for both questions, a majority of all age groups were in favour of some controlling measures.

A significant association does exist between age and the importance ascribed to different occupations. Thus, whilst doctors, policemen, social workers and lawyers all received similar evaluations (in both relative and absolute terms) from the three age groups, Ministers were ranked significantly lower and schoolteachers significantly higher by young people than by elderly people, with middle-aged members of the sample occupying their customary intermediate position. The propensity reported in Chapter 2 for Church of Scotland members to rank schoolteachers significantly lower than do the members of other denominations is thus perhaps attributable to the higher average age of Church of Scotland members. The higher significance accorded Ministers by elderly people may, on the other hand, possibly best be accounted for by the more central role that religion apparently occupies in the lives and thoughts of those belonging to older generations.

Taking into consideration — as in Chapter 2 — only those in employment, a very strong association appears to exist between age and willingness to claim that one would go on strike, with 41% of young and only 14% of elderly people claiming that they would do so; as opposed to 35% and 71%, respectively, who affirmed that they would never take such action.

There was of course no significant association between church membership and people's views concerning the present level of employment. This variable is, however, significantly correlated with age. Perhaps because their own generation are nearer to the strains and worries of the current situation, many more young (67.4%) than middle-aged (58%) or elderly people (52%) judged the present level of unemployment to be unacceptable because of its waste of human resources. By contrast with this, a small but significant proportion of elderly people (5%, as compared to 0.7% of young people) saw unemployment as helpful for putting the Unions in the right perspective; whilst 26% of young people and 33% of elderly people saw it as necessary for getting the country back on its feet economically.

If, therefore, we wish to explain tough-minded attitudes towards industrial affairs in terms of age-differences between denominational groups, we must somehow account for the fact that members of the Church of Scotland do not diverge in any significant way from other denominational groups in their attitudes towards current levels of unemployment. It would seem that an effective explanation of these differences must be sought in some other factor, with church affiliation still however, remaining a possibility.

Table 3.18

Age and attitudes to Nuclear Weapons

	Young	*Middle-aged*	*Elderly*
An effective deterrent against war	39.3	50.8	56.2
Morally unacceptable	48.0	37.7	30.1
No opinion	12.7	11.5	13.7

The same is probably also true for opinions about nuclear weapons. Although the 39% of young people, when measured against the 51% of middle-aged and 55.8% of elderly people, who see nuclear weapons as an effective deterrent against war show age to be a potent contributory factor in the possession of such views, one should also bear in mind that two-thirds of Catholic members of the sample saw nuclear weapons as morally unacceptable. There would thus appear to be an interaction between age and church membership in respect of such beliefs and it will accordingly be necessary to explore this at a later point.

No significant relationship exists between age and a perception of membership of the Orange Order as consistent with Christianity, with the great majority in all age-groups rejecting such a claim. A significant association does, however, exist between age and a perception of Freemasonry as consistent with Christianity, with 53% of young people denying this, as opposed to only 35% of elderly people and 48% of the middle-aged. Catholics' rejection of this statement can therefore not be attributed to age — a fact which endorses the fairly obvious likelihood that, in this particular case, religious belief is more important. To complete the trio of questions in this part of the schedule, the 46% of young people who saw membership of the Knights of St Columba as inconsistent with Christianity showed a significantly higher proportion of this age-group to be rejecting of this than was the case for elderly people, only 31% of whom shared this opinion, though this association was significant only at the 5% level of confidence. In direct contrast, however, to the questions over the Orange Order and Freemasons, the majority in all three age groups ticked the don't know response for this question. Young people would thus seem rather less accepting of closed societies than those in older age-groups; although whether the lack of an association between age and views about the Orange Order may be explained by the relatively low support such a statement received throughout the sample, or whether we must seek an explanation in some other factor, is still open to further exploration.

Answers to the three questions concerning abortion and sexual mores all showed the same consistent trend, with young people significantly more likely to see abortion as a matter entirely for the persons concerned; sexual intercourse before marriage as acceptable; and homosexuality as a personal matter that is up to the individual. That said, it should, however, also be noted that the commonest response across all age groups for the question on abortion was that it is justifiable in certain circumstances. An appreciable minority (41%) of young people also view homosexuality as an unnatural act; although in this, they are surpassed by the 57% of middle-aged and 66% of elderly people who reply in the same vein.

Viewed as a whole, it would therefore seem that a significant shift has taken place in people's attitudes towards such questions; and that as Church teaching has exerted a lesser influence upon the younger generation, so have the attitudes of younger people towards sexual matters undergone a transformation over time. Insofar as it can be said that there is a specifically Christian attitude towards sexual matters, that attitude has clearly become much less influential in shaping the views of young people over this area of human relationships.

(iv) Lifestyle

On turning to that section of the questionnaire which dealt with lifestyle, we find that 28 of the 39 statements yielded statistically significant differences between the three age-groups. It may therefore be worth prefacing our discussion and interpretation of these trends by saying that both in terms of the number of significant differences, and the magnitude of the differences themselves, age appears to be a more potent factor than religious affiliation in shaping the attitudes and reported behaviours of people in these more general areas of their life-experience. As before, we shall consider only those statements that gave statistically-significant differences; although for the sake of clarity we shall attempt to place the statements themselves into clusters that *prima facie* appeared to have some association with each other. The list of statements is presented in Table 3.19 (pp. 64–5).

A first group of statements seem to relate to a stoical or forbearing attitude to life, with elderly people emerging as much higher in this attribute than their younger counterparts in the sample. Thus, old people are more likely to cut down on social life and pleasure, to affirm a liking for simple things, and to prefer not to show their feelings at work. Probably also related to these, although perhaps tapping a slightly different aspect of this attitudinal dimension, is the preference of elderly people for paying cash, even if they have to wait for larger purchases; their feeling that the only way to get something valuable is to save for it; their wish (along with middle-aged people, who in this case are the largest group endorsing the statement) that society could be changed so that material things matter less; and their view that private motoring has more disadvantages than advantages.

One would like to make two basic points about this list. First, whilst a stoical attitude towards material possessions may in part be fostered by elderly people's current situation of dependence upon state benefits, one intuitively feels that these trends are better covered by a generational explanation. This is to say, the differences noted above are probably attributable to formative experiences undergone at a time when different (and perhaps more religiously-based) precepts governed the values that were communicated to an earlier generation. Young people, on the other hand, have been raised in a much more frankly 'consumerist' society, which has probably tended to foster more hedonistic goals and standards (Robertson, 1981). Second, it will probably not have escaped the reader's notice that many of the items that gave rise to these differences also distinguished Church of Scotland members from other groups in Chapter 2. It would thus seem that age, rather than religion, is the more likely explanation of those differences that were noted in the previous chapter.

A second set of items appears to centre on the varying degrees of life-satisfaction reported by the groups in question. These items themselves appear to fall into three (or possibly four) subsidiary though related clusters. First, is a range of statements concerned with an over-view and assessment of one's past experiences and current life-situation, and the degree of

Table 3.19

Age and lifestyle

			Young	Middle-aged	Elderly
(i)	In order to work more efficiently, I cut down on social life and pleasure	Agree Disagree	42.2 57.3	49.0 51.0	53.0 47.0
(ii)	One shouldn't show one's feelings at work	Agree Disagree	41.1 58.9	60.3 39.7	64.1 35.9
(iii)	I like simple things and a natural way of life	Agree Disagree	86.6 13.4	96.3 3.7	98.0 2.0
(iv)	The only way to get something valuable is to save for it	Agree Disagree	73.5 26.5	87.2 12.8	92.9 7.1
(v)	I prefer to pay cash even if I have to wait for larger purchases	Agree Disagree	65.0 35.0	80.3 19.7	91.4 8.6
(vi)	I think that private motoring has more disadvantages than advantages	Agree Disagree	14.9 85.1	19.5 80.5	27.4 72.6
(vii)	I would like to change society so that material things matter less	Agree Disagree	59.2 40.8	69.1 30.9	64.6 35.4
(viii)	Compared with other people of my age, I've made a lot of foolish decisions in my life	Agree Disagree	20.2 79.8	27.6 72.4	39.4 60.6
(ix)	When I think back over my life I didn't get most of the important things I wanted	Agree Disagree	17.9 82.1	26.5 73.5	41.4 58.6
(x)	I have to a great extent the things that make life really pleasant and satisfying for people of my age	Agree Disagree	86.5 13.5	90.5 9.5	94.0 6.0
(xi)	I've got pretty much what I expected out of life	Agree Disagree	73.9 26.1	83.5 16.5	78.4 21.6
(xii)	My life could be happier than it is now	Agree Disagree	45.8 54.2	38.0 62.0	36.6 63.4
(xiii)	These are the best years of my life	Agree Disagree	63.4 36.6	53.8 46.2	42.6 57.4
(xiv)	I never felt better in my life	Agree Disagree	52.2 47.8	48.1 51.9	31.6 68.4

			Young	Middle-aged	Elderly
(xv)	During the past few weeks I have felt particularly excited or interested in something	Agree	69.2	59.6	43.7
		Disagree	30.8	40.4	56.3
(xvi)	During the past few weeks I have felt pleased about having accomplished something	Agree	71.0	79.8	74.7
		Disagree	29.0	20.2	25.3
(xvii)	When I join a club or society I engage myself fully in its work	Agree	49.3	56.9	60.5
		Disagree	50.7	43.1	39.5
(xviii)	I like to discuss politics and community questions	Agree	39.5	46.4	52.2
		Disagree	60.5	53.6	47.8
(xix)	Solidarity with the weak is important to me	Agree	49.2	62.1	63.2
		Disagree	50.8	37.9	36.8
(xx)	In an election I would always vote for a party with a strong defence policy	Agree	29.6	50.0	67.7
		Disagree	70.4	50.0	32.3
(xxi)	Religion is important in my life	Agree	52.5	71.9	77.6
		Disagree	47.5	28.1	22.4
(xxii)	If I had a teenage daughter I would let her go on holiday with her boyfriend	Agree	63.1	44.2	39.4
		Disagree	36.9	55.8	60.6
(xxiii)	If I had a teenage son I would let him go on holiday with his girlfriend	Agree	68.6	49.0	59.3
		Disagree	31.4	51.0	40.7
(xxiv)	I like new exciting experiences even if they are a bit frightening or unconventional	Agree	57.9	38.8	32.3
		Disagree	42.1	61.2	67.7
(xxv)	It is best to live in an area where all the neighbours have a similar standard	Agree	40.2	61.4	70.9
		Disagree	59.8	39.6	29.1
(xxvi)	I am attracted by new religious groups outside the Christian Church	Agree	2.7	7.3	2.7
		Disagree	97.3	92.7	97.3
(xxvii)	Our family do many things together	Agree	71.0	79.0	80.4
		Disagree	29.0	21.0	19.6
(xxviii)	I restrict my circle of friends to a few	Agree	41.2	54.3	51.3
		Disagree	58.8	45.7	48.7

contentment this engenders. Thus, items (viii) and (ix) in Table 3.19 are essentially asking the individual to evaluate his or her activity over the span of life; and in both cases, elderly people emerge as more dissatisfied than the two younger groups. The next three items seem more concerned with the degree of contentment which the individual experiences in surveying his/her current life-situation. And by contrast with their regrets over frustrations and mistaken decisions, the elderly emerge as the most satisfied group, feeling that they have the things that make life really pleasant and satisfying; that they have got what they expected out of life (though here they take second place to the middle-aged); and denying that their life could be happier than it is now. Possibly also on this same dimension, though pointing to a higher degree of contentment among young people, is the tendency for younger members of the sample to affirm that 'these are the best years of my life'; and that they never felt better in their life.

A further dimension of life-satisfaction appears to centre on appraisal of more direct experiences. Under this rubric would fall the tendency of young people to have felt particularly excited or interested in something during the past few weeks; and middle-aged people's apparently greater likelihood of having felt pleased about having accomplished something within the same time-span.

Perhaps two comments in particular deserve to be made about these trends. First, elderly people are in general less likely to be satisfied with the results of retrospective appraisal of their life-experience; but to profess to greater satisfaction with their current circumstances. These trends are possibly best understood as inherent aspects of age itself. In the former case, elderly people will on average obviously have had more frustrating and embarrassing experiences in the course of their lifetime. Elderly people's apparently greater degree of contentment with current circumstances may be attributable to an ability to attune their expectations to a realistic level, so that their wants are always capable of achievement within the resources at their disposal (Morrison 1971). Whether this is something that is learned through experience or due to their more self-denying value system remains an interesting question that cannot be resolved within the present data. In this connection, the two items ('these are the best years of my life' and 'I never felt better in my life') on which young people score higher than the elderly seem more closely connected with physical prowess and enjoyment. Elderly people's lower rating on these items probably reflects the physical decline associated with old age.

Second, one is again struck by the affinity between a number of these items and those that distinguished Church of Scotland members from other denominational groups. This further reinforces the emerging likelihood that the differences noted in Chapter 2 with regard to this area of the questionnaire are most strongly attributable to the effects of age.

A third set of factors may be aggregated under the broad heading of social and political involvement. Again, elderly people emerge as highest on these; and again they resonate with trends identified in Chapter 2. Thus, elderly people were more likely to assert that they engage themselves fully in the work of clubs or societies of which they are members. They also more frequently describe themselves as liking to discuss politics and community questions.

A more mixed group (probably related to, though different from, those reported in the previous paragraph) covers a mixed range of political and religious issues. Thus, elderly people ascribe higher significance to solidarity with the weak; are more likely to vote for a party with a strong defence policy; and agree that religion is important in their lives.

The two questions concerning sexual mores show young people as more likely to permit a hypothetical teenage daughter to go on holiday with her boyfriend; whilst the same question posed in respect of a teenage son shows the middle-aged as most likely to reject such a possibility, with young and elderly people showing differing degrees of majority support for it.

A further set of items apparently concerned with amenability to new experiences shows the elderly to be more resistant to them. Thus, young people are very significantly more likely to welcome new exciting experiences, even if they are a bit frightening or unconventional; and elderly people think it best to live in an area where all the neighbours have a similar standard. Rather surprisingly, perhaps, a small but significant minority of the middle-aged claim to be attracted by new religious groups outside the Christian Church. And not unrelated to these, though probably tapping a slightly different dimension of experience, is a pair of statements concerned with the intimacy of one's social contacts. These show elderly people as endorsing the statement that our family do many things together along with their affirmation, together with members of the middle-aged sample, that they restrict their circle of friends to a few.

Throughout the recitation of this list, one has been struck by the number of items that appear in common between Table 3.19 and the parallel Table (2.25) in Chapter 2. It seems almost certain, on the basis of this evidence, that age is an extremely potent factor in shaping these responses; and that the differences noted on these particular items in Chapter 2 are attributable for the most part to age, rather than religious denomination.

A final group of questions on these matters establishes further significant associations between age and people's preferred ways of spending their spare time and feelings of happiness and integration. Scrutiny of Table 3.19 suggests, however, that the primary differences in respondents' preferences arise between young and middle-aged people. In particular, middle-aged people are much more likely to endorse the family option and significantly less likely than either of the two remaining groups to assert a preference for spending time with friends. It should of course also be said that the majority response in all three groups indicates overwhelming preference to spend spare time with the family. In this particular instance, elderly people depart from the pattern that has been established in almost every other area of the questionnaire, in that their responses tend to place them between the young and the middle-aged. These trends almost certainly reflect differences in the life-circumstances of the three groups concerned. Because of the stage at which their age would place them within the chronology of the normal adult life-cycle, the great majority of our middle-aged sample will be living in their own marital families, probably in the majority of cases with young or adolescent children; with the result that their use of free time will tend to be determined by the responsibilities of parenthood. Finally, whilst these trends fit in a general way with the findings concerning Church membership, this section of the Table contains patterns that make it difficult to account for inter-denominational differences entirely in terms of age.

Table 3.20

Age and preference for spending spare time

	Young	*Middle-aged*	*Elderly*
Alone	9.1	10.6	10.2
With the family	56.9	69.1	61.0
With friends	31.3	19.6	28.9
In a crowd	2.7	0.7	0

No association exists between age and the extent of people's reported preference for being with people whose ideas and values vary from their own. The possibility therefore remains that Church of Scotland members' greater dislike of being with people of different views is due to a specifically denominational factor.

Table 3.21 shows significant differences between the age-groups in the extent to which they report feeling lonely. On the whole, middle-aged people (very probably for reasons related to the figures reported in Table 3.20) appear rather less likely to experience such sentiments. Generally speaking (and again for entirely understandable reasons) elderly people emerge as rather more likely to experience feelings of loneliness.

Probably because of this, significantly fewer elderly people proved likely to report themselves as very happy. The main part of the remainder did, however, classify themselves as quite happy, with no apparent differences emerging between the three age-groups in the proportions who describe themselves as either not particularly or not at all happy. The figures presented in Table 3.22 provide a difference that is significant at the 1% level. And given that no statistically significant association was found between answers to this question and the religious affiliations of respondents, age would seem to be a primary factor in determining people's degree of happiness.

To summarise the results of this section, elderly people experience more retrospective dissatisfaction with their general experience of life. They are, however, more contented with current circumstances than their counterparts in younger groups, although they appear to experience less joy in their present activities and experience of life than do younger people. They are slightly more likely to experience feelings of loneliness and less likely to

Table 3.21

Age and frequency of feeling lonely

	Young	Middle-aged	Elderly
Often	5.6	8.6	10.4
Sometimes	37.9	28.5	34.0
Seldom	39.6	38.7	33.6
Never	17.0	24.2	22.0

Table 3.22

Age and perception of self as happy

	Young	Middle-aged	Elderly
Very happy	31.8	33.4	19.7
Quite happy	64.1	60.3	75.5
Not particularly happy	4.1	5.3	4.4
Not at all happy	0	1.0	0.4

perceive themselves as very happy. They also, however, appear to suffer a reduction only of degree in their happiness with their current lives, with proportionally more of them reporting themselves as 'quite' happy.

Their apparently more spartan attitude towards life may of course induce them to under-report the extent of their unhappiness; although a more plausible explanation may be that a reasoned appraisal of the situation at which they have arrived in life enables the cognitive satisfaction which this exercise gives to compensate for any reduction they experience in more transient feelings of pleasure with the processes of life itself. Their stoical attitudes and their less permissive views on sex seem very likely to be rooted in the values of a different generation, rather than factors that will themselves change with age. One's explanation of old people's apparent dislike of new experience must remain equivocal as between a chronological or generational account. Their apparently greater penchant for involvement in political disputation and active membership of the groups to which they are attached is a further interesting trend that awaits more detailed exploration. In sum, however, we may conclude that the influence of age upon these aspects of social behaviour and personal satisfaction and belief is much more potent than that of (formal) religious attachment.

(v) Alcohol

Table 3.23 shows that elderly people are much more abstemious over alcohol. This appears consistent with the greater reported strength of their religious upbringing and also with their apparently more self-denying values. Equally, however, one cannot rule out the possibility that these differences are due to the lower incomes which were demonstrated earlier in this Chapter to be the normal lot of the elderly.

When we turn to a more detailed analysis of the actual drinking-patterns of the three groups concerned, we find that young people drink beer significantly more frequently than do the elderly, with the middle-aged coming somewhere between. The same applies to the consumption of wine and (though with a small variation, in that a slightly greater number of middle-aged people report drinking them every day) of spirits. All three of these yield associations that are significant at the 0.1% level. Fortified wine is much less popular with young people, a very significant proportion of whom never drink it: and there is again an interesting fluctuation in that significantly more elderly people than would be expected by chance (though still a tiny proportion of the total) report drinking fortified wine every day. One again detects a close similarity between these data and those reported in Chapter 2.

Reactions to the question concerning how people would react if they were served with wine at a function are outlined in Table 3.24. This shows that, although the commonest single response in all three age groups is for people to assert that they would drink it, young people are very much more likely to reply in these terms than elderly people, especially. The elderly, by contrast, are much more likely to claim either that they would allow it to be poured and only sip it, or ask for a non-alcoholic alternative. The data reviewed so far for this section of the questionnaire would accordingly suggest the elderly to be much more hostile to the consumption of alcohol, with a significant minority of them claiming to be complete abstainers.

Table 3.23

Age and frequency of consumption of alcohol

	Young	Middle-aged	Elderly
Never	7.8	16.0	30.5
Very occasionally	29.9	35.7	38.2
Occasionally	43.9	34.3	23.7
Regularly	18.4	14.0	7.6

Table 3.25 summarises the responses to the enquiry made of those people within the sample who do drink, as to their main reasons for drinking. One is first struck by the extreme similarity of the rankings ascribed to these various reasons by all age-groups with the single exception of 'medicinal reasons' which appears much lower in the average set of reasons given by young people than it does for either the middle-aged or the elderly. With this solitary exception, therefore, the relative importance attached to these reasons by individuals of different ages seems more or less the same.

Quite striking differences do, however, appear between the groups in the absolute weight they attach to various of the different items in this list. Thus, young people attach much greater absolute importance to easier social contact as a reason for drinking, as they also (along with the middle-aged) do for the view that it is easier to relax when drinking. Young people were also more likely to endorse 'other reasons'; although unfortunately, respondents

Table 3.24

Age and reaction to being served wine at a function

	Young	Middle-aged	Elderly
Drink it*	75.6	62.9	47.4
Allow it to be poured and only sip it*	6.7	11.3	19.0
Request something non-alcoholic	5.0	9.9	17.8
Say want nothing to drink	3.5	7.0	4.0
Don't know — depends on the situation	9.2	8.9	11.7

* a statistically significant difference in the response of the different age-groups to this statement.

Table 3.25

Age and main reasons for drinking

	Young	Middle-aged	Elderly
Easier social contact*	2 (57%)	4 (38%)	2 (42%)
Easier to relax*	1 (63%)	1 (60%)	3 (39%)
In order not to appear self-righteous*	8=(6%)	8 (15%)	7 (15%)
Abstinence is out of date	12 (2%)	11 (5%)	11 (3%)
Atmosphere better with a little alcohol	4 (37%)	3 (40%)	5 (34%)
Increase the value of a good meal	3 (56%)	2 (54%)	1 (48%)
Difficult to be TT in my job	11 (3%)	12 (3%)	12 (2%)
Don't believe I would be damaged	6 (24%)	5 (19%)	6 (27%)
Want to use Christian freedom	8=(6%)	10 (5%)	10 (10%)
Don't want to be different from friends	7 (7%)	9 (10%)	9 (11%)
Medicinal*	10 (6%)	6 (18%)	4 (35%)
Other reasons*	5 (27%)	7 (16%)	8 (13%)

* a statistically significant difference in the response of the different age-groups to this statement.

were asked to provide no further information where their answers were placed in this particular box. In contrast, elderly people are much more likely to claim to drink for medicinal purposes and also (along with the middle-aged) in order not to appear self-righteous.

Thus, young people appear to have a more instrumental attitude towards drink, seeing it as a catalyst in social relationships. Older people, on the other hand, seem to require to justify their alcohol consumption to themselves, their endorsement of the need not to appear self-righteous possibly being particularly revealing in this respect, containing as it does a rather negative form of rationlisation, rather than seeing alcohol as having some potential beneficial effects in individual and social affairs.

The question asking drinkers why they did not drink more produced generally similar rank-orderings between the age-groups. Table 3.26 does, however, show some variation between elderly people and the two younger groups in the desire to avoid a hangover (on which they are lower) and solidarity with friends (on which they are higher). Similarly, younger people place a rather higher priority on the dangers to the foetus during pregnancy and rather less importance than their elders upon the risk of becoming dependent and the need to set an example for others. All of these five items render a significant difference in the absolute priority attached to the reason in question by the three groups; and in addition, elderly people attach more importance to the danger drinking might create in traffic and to a dislike of the taste of alcohol.

Twenty eight young people (6.8% of their total number), 45 middle-aged (14.9% of their total) and 46 elderly (18.4% of this group as a whole) did not drink at all. Although certain perceptible differences appear in the importance attributed by the three age-groups to various reasons for not drinking, the relatively small numbers involved and the rather long list of statements from which their selections had to be made, reduce the confidence one can place in any differences emerging on this particular question. However, for what the findings are worth, middle-aged people gave a somewhat higher ranking to the desire to avoid a hangover and the risks caused to the foetus by drinking during pregnancy. Young abstainers, on the other hand, gave greater weight to having drunk too much in earlier life and (along with elderly people) a desire to set an example for others; whilst elderly non-drinkers cited resisting social pressure, fear of becoming dependent, and danger to traffic, relatively more frequently than the other age-groups. Moving from relative to absolute differences between the groups, we find that elderly people place significantly higher importance upon the fear of damaging their health and on Christian conviction as reasons for abstaining.

Although the great majority in all three age-groups rejected the notion that a Christian should be a total abstainer, older people proved significantly less opposed than their younger brethren to this statement. Indeed, Table 3.27 indicates that elderly people are far more divided in their views on this matter, with a significantly larger proportion agreeing that Christians should

Table 3.26

Age and reasons for not drinking more

	Young	Middle-aged	Elderly
Damaging to my health	1 (46%)	1 (50%)	1 (47%)
Avoid a hangover the following day*	6 (22%)	8=(17%)	16 (3%)
Resisting social pressure	17 (3%)	16 (3%)	17 (2%)
Drinking in pregnancy damages the foetus	15=(4%)	18=(1%)	19 (0%)
Don't want to risk dependency*	9 (17%)	6 (22%)	3 (26%)
Drank too much in earlier life	14 (5%)	15 (4%)	18 (0.7%)
For sake of those damaged by alcohol	19 (1%)	17 (1%)	15 (4%)
Drinking and driving is dangerous and against the law	3 (33%)	2 (37%)	4 (26%)
Don't want to be a danger in traffic*	13 (5%)	12=(7%)	11 (11%)
Don't like the taste*	11 (8%)	10 (10%)	9 (16%)
Don't want to lose control	8 (18%)	8−(17%)	7 (18%)
Don't want to gain weight	12 (7%)	12=(7%)	12 (7%)
Example for my children	7 (20%)	7 (18%)	8 (17%)
Example for others*	15=(4%)	11 (10%)	10 (12%)
Can't afford it	4 (27%)	5 (23%)	6 (20%)
Have seen what alcohol has done to others	5 (28%)	4 (30%)	5 (22%)
Solidarity with friends*	18 (2%)	18=(1%)	13=(5%)
Don't want to get drunk	2 (38%)	3 (34%)	2 (28%)
Other reasons	10 (10%)	14 (7%)	13=(5%)

* a statistically significant difference in the response of the different age-groups to this statement.

be total abstainers and a large additional proportion unable to express an opinion on the matter. Very probably related to these figures is the fact that about 50% of elderly people felt that Communion wine should be non-alcoholic, with much smaller proportions in the other two age groups selecting this option. The association with age on both of these variables is significant at well beyond the 0.1% level.

No association existed between age and smoking, with a majority in all three age groups declaring they do not smoke. And on the very last question

Table 3.27

Age and attitude towards notion that Christians should be total abstainers

	Young	Middle-aged	Elderly
Yes	3.7	6.5	15.1
No	87.5	82.5	68.6
Don't know	8.8	11.0	16.3

Table 3.28

Age and attitude towards legalisation of cannabis

	Young	Middle-aged	Elderly
Yes	14.0	1.3	0.8
No	72.2	89.9	91.5
Don't know	13.8	8.7	7.7

in the schedule, a majority of all age groups were resistant to the idea that people should be allowed to use cannabis freely. Nonetheless, a very significantly higher proportion of young people expressed their support for such a policy; and indeed, cannabis may well be replacing alcohol in the demonology of the young, since significantly more in this age-group also chose the don't know response. Again, these differences were significant at well beyond the 0.1% level of confidence. Responses to this question on the free use of cannabis are summarised in Table 3.28.

Conclusions

One may summarise the above findings relatively briefly. It has become apparent that the elderly have had a religious upbringing which has been strict in comparison with that which the younger generations have received. The effects of this are still manifest in their much higher level of involvement in formal Churchgoing and prayer and their general degree of commitment to the Church. Age and religiosity are thus tied strongly to each other and this probably means that many of the differences in religious activities that were noted in Chapter 2 may be ascribed to the effects of age, rather than Church of Scotland membership *per se*. Because the factors of age and religion do interact in this way, however, it seems necessary to disentangle them further by comparing the behaviour of old and young Church of Scotland communicants with their age-peers in other denominational groups, and this will form the focus of our analysis in a later Chapter.

The relationship of age to the more subtle content of religious belief is, however, both weaker and less systematic. It accordingly seems less important as an explanatory factor for these aspects of the questionnaire. Again, however, an analysis which controls simultaneously for age and religious affiliation may elicit some interesting trends.

Age has a very powerful relationship with lifestyle and indeed seems more influential than does religion in this respect. In particular, age proves to be closely linked to people's level of contentment with life which seems more or less unaffected by people's religious affiliations. (Whether or not it is affected by the content of religious belief remains an interesting question, which we may be able to explore further.) The apparent stoicism of elderly people is almost certainly a generational phenomenon and religion may have played some role in producing the attitudes on which older people diverge so markedly from the generations who are succeeding them. Whether or not religion influences elderly people's predilection for more active involvement in politics and social organisations should also be illuminated by an analysis that holds both age and religion constant.

Elderly people have significantly more negative attitudes towards alcohol. This is very likely due to their stronger religious loyalties and consciousness; but this notion can be relatively easily tested in a future Chapter.

REFERENCES

Morrison, D E (1971) Some notes toward theory in relative deprivation, social change, *American Behavioural Scientist*, 14, pp.675–90.

Robertson, A (1980) The welfare state and 'post-industrial' values in N Timms (ed) *Social Welfare : Why and How?* London : Routledge and Kegan Paul.

CHAPTER FOUR

LIFESTYLE AND BELIEF:
DIFFERENCES BETWEEN THE SEXES

Having tried to disentangle the effects of age, we must now undertake a similar exercise in respect of sex-differences. This Chapter will follow the same basic structure as Chapters 2 and 3.

Of the 997 returned schedules, 571 had been completed by women and 426 by men. This gives a ratio within the sample of 57.5% women to 42.5% men.

(i) General background factors

The analysis discussed in Chapter 3 has of course already pointed out that no association exists within the sample between sex and age and we may thus infer with reasonable confidence that any differences in responses between the sexes will not be contaminated by the effects of age. The age-distribution as between males and females is presented in Table 4.1, which shows broadly similar ratios of men to women within the three main age-groups discussed in Chapter 3. Obviously, the preponderance of women over men within the sample is not attributable to the effects of age.

Sex also proved unrelated to the length of time people had been living at their present address. Nor did it show any significant association with either income or the likelihood that a person had attended college or university.

Table 4.1

Age-distribution within the sample

	Young	Middle-aged	Elderly
Female	43.2	29.7	27.1
Male	41.7	33.5	24.8

There is no significant relationship between age and sex in the sample.

There is, however, a significant relationship between sex and civil status. Table 4.2 shows that many fewer women were married and many more widowed than was the case for men, with relatively minor differences appearing in the other groupings in this Table. This suggested that there were perhaps proportionately more very elderly women than men within the 'elderly' portion of the study-sample. However, more detailed scrutiny of the age-distribution as between elderly members of the two sexes showed this not to be the case. But whether or not because of the higher proportion of widowed members, women tended to live in rather smaller households, with 50% of their number living in households of one or two (17% living on their own), as opposed to 40% for men (of whom 11% had no other persons in the household). Significantly fewer women than men were in paid employment.

Table 4.2

Marital status

	Male	Female
Married	73.3	65.2
Separated	0.5	1.6
Divorced	1.9	1.1
Widow/widower	4.9	12.9
Single	18.7	17.9
Co-habiting	0.7	1.3

Men were no more or less likely than women to hold public office. Nor did any significant difference emerge between them in respect of their political affiliations.

The only significant factor differentiating the two sexes in these basic background characteristics was thus the larger number of men still living with a spouse and the correspondingly higher proportion of women who were widowed. And almost certainly related to this, proportionately more women were living on their own, or with only one other person.

(ii) Religion and the Church

In contrast to the rather similar pattern presented by the domestic circumstances and social contexts of men and women, a considerable number of differences were highlighted in their commitments and activities within the church. Thus, Table 4.3 shows women reporting a substantially higher degree of commitment to the church, with fully 55% of their number claiming to be 'highly' or 'fairly' committed, as opposed to 43% of men. And consistent with this (and with casual observation) women proved to be much more assiduous church-goers, with 43% of them reporting they attended church several times or once a week, as opposed to 33% of men. Fully one-quarter of the male sample claimed to attend church 'only for baptisms, weddings and funerals', whilst only 13% of women characterised their pattern of attendance in these terms.

Table 4.3

Degree of commitment to the Church

	Male	Female
Highly committed	13.9	16.4
Fairly committed	29.6	38.6
Not very committed	29.8	30.4
No commitment	26.7	14.6

Table 4.4 shows a remarkably similar pattern between men and women as to their frequency of church attendance in the past, as compared to now, and indeed these figures yield no statistically-significant association between sex and current frequency of church attendance. And there was substantial similarity between men and women in their predictions as to their likely pattern of church attendance in five years time.

Table 4.4

Reported frequency of Church attendance in
earlier adult life, as compared with the present

	Male	Female
More frequently	44.0	49.3
About the same	39.7	38.5
Less frequently	16.3	12.2

There is no significant difference between men and women on this issue.

Twenty five per cent of women and only 16.5% of men regularly listened to or viewed religious programmes on radio or television. Differences in responses to this question yielded an association with sex that was significant at the 1% level, with women clearly tuning in more frequently to religious broadcasts. Women also proved much more regular readers of the Bible; although Table 4.5 also shows that only a minority of both sexes read the Bible at least once a week. Thirty per cent of women (as opposed to 20% of men) read the Bible once a week or more, whereas 47% of men replied that they never or hardly ever read the Bible, with 33% of women falling into this category.

Table 4.5

Frequency of reading the Bible

	Male	Female
Every day	5.6	7.9
2–3 times per week	3.9	6.5
Once a week	10.5	15.6
Seldom	33.1	37.1
Never or hardly ever	47.0	33.0

Table 4.6 reveals that women also pray much more frequently than men, with over half of them praying at least two to three times a week. At the other end of the scale, almost a third of men report that they never pray. As in the case of those for Bible-reading, these data yield a difference between the sexes that is significant at far beyond the 0.1% level of confidence. However,

women proved no more likely than men to pray together with their family, with only some 10% of either sex reporting that their family prayed together once a week or more. Sixty two per cent of men and 58% of women reported that their families never pray together.

Table 4.6

Frequency of prayer

	Male	Female
Every day	24.1	40.1
2–3 times per week	7.1	13.7
Once per week	9.8	9.0
Seldom	27.3	21.0
Never or hardly ever	31.7	16.2

Table 4.7

Extent to which a devotional life was the rule in childhood

	Male	Female
Yes	32.4	40.7
No	60.2	51.5
Doubtful, don't know	7.4	7.8

In the midst of what appears to be a substantial shift on the part of people in late twentieth-century Scotland towards more secular views and lifestyles, women accordingly appear to have remained more resistant to the influences of whatever forces have caused this clear and fairly rapid transformation of popular values and commitments. They remain significantly more committed to the church than men. They are also much more frequent attenders at services, read the Bible more often and say prayers with greater regularity than men. Inside the home, however, their devotional activities are overwhelmingly limited to individual expressions of piety, as few women as men participating in joint prayer-sessions with other members of the family.

Various potential explanations suggest themselves for these findings. But the primary possibilities perhaps reduce to three.

First, the child-bearing and rearing roles may keep women closer to the demands and rhythms of biological existence and tend to make them less accepting of alternative views and explanations of the human condition. Second, and not unrelated to this, the lives of women may (at least traditionally) on average entail a rather narrower range of social contacts and a more restricted exposure to alternative values, explanations and experiences. Less extensive social lives, more solitary lifestyles and the need to depend on their own mental resources may accordingly make women more sensitive and amenable to religious views and perspectives upon life. Finally, parents may be more punctilious in communicating moral standards to daughters than to sons and this may make women more resistant to alternative, and possibly opposing, attitudes.

Table 4.7 is at least consistent with this last view, in that it shows significantly more women than men reporting that a devotional life was the rule in their childhood. Since there is no significant difference in the age-structures of the male and female samples, this difference (which is significant only at the 5% level of confidence) cannot be attributed to the more strongly religious upbringing that seems to have been typical of the elderly. That said it should, however, be noted that, in both sexes, only a minority of people gave affirmative response to this question.

When one considers the sources from which individuals obtain their knowledge about church events, Table 4.8 shows men as attaching greatest importance to newspapers, whilst women see the Minister or Priest as the most important agent in this respect. Apart from the (relatively small) differences in the position accorded these, however, the average ranks ascribed by the two sexes emerge as very similar. Nonetheless, the greater importance women apparently attach to religion and church affairs is demonstrated in the significantly higher proportion of them who obtain information from the Minister or Priest, from *Life and Work* and from other church literature. On the other hand, significantly more men (though still a relatively tiny minority of the total) describe themselves as 'not interested in church events'.

Table 4.8

Importance ascribed to sources of knowledge of Church events

	Male	Female
Newspapers	1 (58.3)	3 (53.3)
Radio	5 (30.6)	6 (28.1)
Television	2 (57.5)	2 (57.1)
*Life and Work**	6 (24.2)	5 (32.7)
Other Church literature*	4 (31.0)	4 (40.4)
Minister or Priest*	3 (44.4)	1 (59.0)
Not interested in Church events*	7 (12.7)	7 (8.4)

* Indicates a significant difference in the proportions of men and women attaching importance to an item.

Significantly more men than women read a 'quality' daily newspaper, although no perceptible difference exists between the two sexes in their readership of other types of newspaper. There was no significant difference between men and women in the kinds either of Sunday or religious newspapers that they read. As might possibly be expected, there were substantial differences between the sexes in the types of weekly magazines they read, this being mainly attributable to the 32.3% of women reading women's magazines (as opposed to 2% of men); although 20% of men (as opposed to 4.7% of women) read professional or leisure magazines; and 75% of men but only 61% of women read political weeklies.

Insofar as differences were discovered between denominational groups in their readership of newspapers and magazines, the numerical preponderance of women within the Church of Scotland could obviously account for the Church of Scotland's greater readership of women's magazines. None of the other differences, however, can be attributed to the influence of sex. Other explanations must accordingly be sought.

The answers given by men and women to the question as to why they are members of the church show a virtually identical pattern. Thus, the rank-ordering of the first eight items is exactly the same for either sex. And

Table 4.9

Reasons for Church membership

	Male	Female
Wish to support the Church and Christian values	1 (75.3)	1 (75.7)
Opportunity for baptism, marriage and funerals	4 (27.3)	4 (27.5)
Participate in services/Communion	2 (58.7)	2 (64.1)
Fellowship and contact with others	3 (46.7)	3 (53.4)
Support missionary work	12 (3.2)	10= (3.9)
Support everyday Christian life	5 (22.1)	5 (26.2)
Want to strive for justice and Christian solidarity*	9 (8.4)	10= (3.9)
Natural for me to be a member of the Church	6 (18.6)	6 (23.2)
Family expectations	8 (9.1)	8 (6.2)
Don't want to upset a relative/ friend by leaving	13 (2.1)	13 (0.9)
Other reasons	11 (4.6)	9 (4.1)
Never thought of leaving	7 (9.5)	7 (6.6)
Nothing special	10 (6.3)	12 (3.4)

Table 4.10

Perception of self as a Christian

	Male	Female
Yes	75.9	82.3
No	10.5	5.4
Doubtful/don't know	13.7	12.3

the only item which shows a significant difference between men and women is the higher importance attached by (though still only a very small minority of) men to a desire to strive for justice and Christian solidarity. Both place 'missionary work' near the bottom of their hierarchy of importance. The higher preponderance of women within its ranks may thus at least partly explain the lower priority — in comparison to the Catholic Church — attached by Church of Scotland members to the former item. These trends are displayed in Table 4.9. (It should perhaps be stressed that, since this question applied specifically to church members, only 69% of the male sample responded to it. The replies of women comprised 79.7% of their total number.)

In looking at those organisations of the Church of Scotland of which people in the sample claimed membership, a minuscule proportion (2% of men and 0.4% of women) claimed membership of the Bible Class. These differences were, however, sufficient to yield an association with sex that was significant at the 5% level. As opposed to this, 28.3% of women were members of some form of women's organisation; whereas only 6.1% of men belonged to equivalent organisations for the male sex. This very substantial difference was significant at far beyond the 0.1% level.

Men proved much more likely to be members of the Kirk Session (17.3%, as opposed to 2.7% of women) and the Congregational Board (12.2 and 2.7%, respectively). Conversely, 54.2% of women and 41.7% of men affirmed that they had no position of responsibility in the Church — a difference which is significant at the 1% level.

Despite their substantial numerical superiority within the Church, women are much less likely to attain to a position of responsibility in its organization. This stands in marked contrast to their much higher ratio of membership of those Church organisations that were included in the questionnaire. Whether this disparity is attributable to a historic tendency for women to be omitted from its decision-making bodies that will rectify itself in time as members of a generation more used to the notion of feminine responsibility filter through in greater numbers to senior posts within the Church; or whether the data reflect a tendency — for whatever reason   for women to prefer to retain a purely social involvement in the Church, or whether it reflects the widely held theological view that the roles of men and women differ within the organisation of the church is a question that can be better answered from the Church's own experience than from the present data. The lower significance attached by women in general to a search for 'justice and Christian solidarity' may, however, suggest that part of the answer lies within the attitudes of female Church members themselves. Whether women outside the Church think differently is of course another interesting question that we may be able to explore in a later Chapter.

In the light of what has unfolded earlier in this Chapter, it is hardly surprising that significantly (at the 1% level) more women than men regarded themselves as Christian. These trends are portrayed in Table 4.10. There was, however, no difference between the sexes in the proportions who had been baptised, in either the Church of Scotland or another Church.

Proportionately slightly more men than women (7.3, compared with 4.5% of those who actually answered this question) had never attended Sunday School at any time. And of those who had attended, slightly more women (7%) than men (3.7%) had tended to leave at the age of 16, rather than 15. But these facts notwithstanding, no significant difference appeared between the sexes on this factor. It should, however, be noted that 20% of men and 12.4% of women did not reply to this question.

There was no significant difference between men and women in their perceptions of the regularity with which either their mothers or fathers attended Church. Nor was there any association between sex and attendance at the services of other denominations or membership of ecumenical groups.

Women proved significantly more likely to affirm a belief in God and a belief that He controls our lives here and now. Thus, Table 4.11 shows 8% more women than men professing to believe in God; whereas some 21% of men and 12% of women are agnostic. Both this and Table 4.12 yield an association that is significant at the 0.1% level.

Table 4.11

Belief in God

	Male	Female
Believe	72.5	84.6
Don't believe	6.8	3.2
Don't know	20.7	12.2

Table 4.12 shows an even greater disparity between men and women in the extent to which they believe that God controls our lives here and now. Whilst 22% of male members of the sample refute this assertion some 55% accept such a belief. This stands in some contrast, however, to the 71% of women who subscribed to this view and the 11% who reject it.

Table 4.12

Belief that God controls our lives here and now

	Male	Female
Believe	54.5	70.5
Don't believe	22.4	11.4
Don't know	23.1	18.2

The question concerning people's conception of God also yielded very substantial differences between the sexes. Table 4.13 shows that women were more likely to see God as all-powerful, as loving and controlling our lives, and as a father concerned to save and help; whilst men either expressed no opinion, or saw God as 'a sort of distant, impersonal power or force'. Thus, although a majority of men adhered to concepts of God that are firmly rooted in the Judaeo-Christian tradition, fully 43% either felt unable to express an opinion or subscribed to a somewhat 'secularised' vision of the Deity. Just under three-quarters of the female sample, however, professed to more traditional views of God.

Table 4.13

Concept of God

	Male	Female
All-powerful judge who sees and judges our sins and virtues	10.6	13.6
Loving, He hears our prayers and controls our lives	28.7	40.2
A father whose concern is to serve and to help	17.2	20.4
A sort of distant, impersonal power or force	17.2	12.4
No opinion	26.3	13.5

Women also proved more likely to believe that Jesus died for our sins, 75% of their number supporting this statement as compared with 56% of men. 28% of men didn't know what to believe, this proportion being exactly 10% greater than the number of women who endorsed this response. These answers are outlined in Table 4.14. And asked whether they believed that Christ is risen from the dead, both women and men gave responses that were virtually identical in proportional terms to those contained in Table 4.14.

Table 4.14

Belief that Jesus died for our sins

	Male	Female
Believe	55.7	74.6
Don't believe	16.5	7.6
Don't know	27.7	17.8

Answers to the question as to whether respondents believed in eternal life again show women possessing more religiously-influenced views than men. Table 4.15 shows exactly similar proportions of the two sexes replying that they don't know what to believe. Less than fifty per cent of the men, however, and 59% of the women do respond in the affirmative; with twice as many men as women denying this possibility. Answers to the question concerning belief in the individual's life after death yielded a very similar set of trends, with the answers to both these questions again giving a difference between the sexes that is significant at the 0.1% level.

Table 4.15
Belief in eternal life

	Male	Female
Believe	47.1	59.2
Don't believe	24.3	13.1
Don't know	28.6	27.7

Related to the question just considered, a substantial association also exists between sex and people's beliefs about what happens after death, but not with their opinions about heaven and hell. Table 4.16, dealing with the former question, shows almost three times as many men as women asserting that death is the end of everything, whilst rather fewer men than women accept views that imply the continued existence of the soul. The other possibilities attract extremely similar proportions from either sex. It is thus men's greater acceptance of the idea that human beings cease to exist after death that accounts for the highly-significant statistical association between sex and these replies.

Table 4.16
Belief as to what happens after death

	Male	Female
After death, man stands before God and his judgement	28.3	31.0
Man's soul lives forever without judgement	2.5	5.4
Man's soul goes to another existence	9.8	12.8
Death is the end – man ceases to exist	17.7	6.7
We don't know what happens after death	39.6	40,8
No opinion	2.2	3.2

Although Table 4.17 shows some slight variations between men and women in their conceptions of heaven and hell, these render no statistically-significant difference between the sexes.

Table 4.17

Opinions of heaven and hell

	Male	Female
Heaven and hell are places with eternal bliss or suffering where man must live after God's judgement	24.1	28.5
The expressions 'heaven' and 'hell' mean that after death man may live near or far from God, but otherwise there are no possibilities	17.6	22.1
As such, heaven and hell do not exist – everything is related to man's life here and now	29.5	24.7
No heaven or hell now or in the future	7.6	5.5
No opinion	21.1	19.2

No significant difference between the sexes on these opinions.

Responses to Question 43 of the schedule, concerned with individuals' opinions of the Bible, also yielded a significant association with sex. Scrutiny of Table 4.18, which presents these trends, shows that one-third fewer men than women conceive of the Bible as 'God's word — true in every detail'. On the other hand, twice as many men (though still a tiny proportion of their total number) conceive of the Bible as 'a normal book'. It would thus again seem that men take a more sceptical and secular view of a religiously-significant item.

Table 4.18

View of the Bible

	Male	Female
God's word – true in every detail	14.3	21.8
Written by men who were inspired by God and therefore must be interpreted	56.7	57.3
Contains much vision but God has not affected it specially	10.6	7.3
A normal book	5.7	2.9
No opinion	12.8	10.7

There was no significant difference between men and women in the extent to which they view mankind as basically good, basically bad or a mixture of good and bad. Nor did any difference emerge between them on the frequency with which they claimed to think about the above issues. About 50% of both sexes professed to think 'often' about such questions (although it should be noted that 12% of male and 8.5% of female respondents did not answer this question). This would suggest that (a) differences noted on this variable in earlier Chapters cannot be attributed to sex-differences and (b) men's apparently more sceptical attitude towards religion and religious explanations is based upon no lower level of thought about the matter than is given it by women.

Table 4.20 summarises the degree of importance attached by men and women to various possible developments within the church. As in the earlier analyses of responses to this question, the rankings ascribed by the two groups concerned are extremely similar. When, however, we consider the *absolute* importance attached by men and women to each item in this series, we find — consistent with their apparently higher degree of religiosity on earlier questions — that women attach significantly more importance to items 1, 2, 3, 4 and 8. Whether there is any significance in the fact that no statistically-significant association exists between sex and items 5–7 is a question which can only be raised for speculation at this point. It is, however, interesting to note that men and women agree in ascribing highest ranking to improved co-operation between the Church of Scotland and other Protestant churches, to joint effort in relation, for example, to under-developed

Table 4.19

Importance attached to possible developments within the Church

	Male	Female
1. Joint services for Church of Scotland and other denominations*	6 (65.2)	4 (75.1)
2. Improved co-operation between the Church of Scotland and other Protestant Churches*	1 (82.3)	1 (89.3)
3. Joint Communion for Church of Scotland and other denominations*	8 (49.7)	8 (60.6)
4. Local Bible Study and prayer groups including Church of Scotland members and members of other Churches*	7 (58.1)	7 (65.8)
5. Joint effort, e.g. information campaigns re under-developed countries	2 (79.4)	3 (83.0)
6. Church of Scotland and other Churches should have a common view on Bible translation	5 (67.4)	5 (72.3)
7. Improved co-operation with the Roman Catholic Church	4 (72.4)	6 (66.4)
8. Improved co-operation on inter-Church marriage*	3 (75.3)	2 (83.3)

* = significant difference between the sexes in degree of importance attached to an item.

countries, and to improved co-operation on inter-church marriage; whilst those to which both sexes attach least priority are joint Communion and local Bible study and prayer-groups involving different churches.

Table 4.20

Importance ascribed to various activities for the future of the Church

	Male	Female
Political awareness*	11 (2.48)	11 (2.69)
Evangelisation	9 (2.20)	9 (2.18)
Social work	3 (1.78)	4 (1.79)
Help to developing countries	6 (1.91)	5 (1.83)
Work with pensioners and the sick	1 (1.62)	2 (1.63)
Personal renewal*	8 (2.00)	7 (1.92)
Increased awareness of economic and social justice	7 (1.98)	8 (2.10)
The position of women in the Church	10 (2.41)	10 (2.35)
Efficient organisation and good financial management	5 (1.89)	6 (1.90)
More spiritual leadership	4 (1.87)	3 (1.76)
Christian education*	2 (1.65)	1 (1.51)

* = significant difference between the sexes in absolute importance attached to this item by the two sexes.
(Numbers in parentheses specify the average scores obtained by each group on the item in question on a scale from 1 to 3.)

The same high degree of agreement between the sexes is apparent in their responses to that question which asked people to rank a number of areas of potential social involvement in the order of importance these were seen to have for the churches' future. Thus, Table 4.20 reveals only the most trifling differences between men and women in the relative importance they ascribe to these issues. Men do, however, attach greater absolute importance to political awareness (although this appears at the very bottom of the listings of both sexes), whereas women vote significantly more often than men for both Christian education and personal renewal (although the latter of these is significant only at the 5% level). Perhaps surprisingly, both sexes attach similar (low) priority to the position of women in the church.

Viewing this section as a whole, we may accordingly conclude that women are both more active within and more personally committed to the church, than are men. The pattern presented by Church of Scotland members in Chapter 2 was of course of lower religious involvement than was the case for other denominations. In so far as women constitute a larger group within the membership of the Church of Scotland, the lower degree of religious commitment shown by its members clearly cannot be attributed to sex differences. Some other factor must be operating here. The same conclusions must be drawn in respect of the various items of religious interpretation and Christian belief, in which women's more clearly orthodox religious views are inconsistent with the heterogeneity shown by Church of Scotland members. Finally, although certain interesting differences appear between men and women in the priority they ascribe to the various items in the two lists contained in Tables 4.19 and 4.20, none of these differences takes us any further in explaining such divergencies as exist on these factors between Church of Scotland members and those affiliated to other churches.

(iii) Social and moral issues

There was a significant difference in the extent to which women differed from men in thinking that nuclear weapons provided an effective deterrent. Significantly too, more women than men gave no opinion about the effectiveness of such weapons.

Table 4.21

Attitudes to nuclear weapons

	Male	Female
An effective deterrent against war	54.1	42.2
Morally unacceptable	37.6	42.1
No opinion	8.3	15.7

As might perhaps have been predicted, women were substantially more supportive of the idea that greater control should be introduced over the amount of sex and violence shown on television. Table 4.22 shows proportionately more than twice as many men as women opposed to the notion of televison censorship; although it should be stressed that a majority of both sexes endorse this proposal overall.

Table 4.22

Support for control over TV sex and violence

	Male	Female
Support control	65.0	80.2
Don't support control	28.6	13.7
Don't know	6.4	6.1

90

But while there was a significant difference between the sexes in their degree of support for a policy of classifying home videos, Table 4.23 shows that this is due to differences in the proportions of men and women endorsing the 'no' and 'don't know' responses, with a virtually identical (and very large) percentage in both sexes supportive of video classifications. Both of these sets of results are similar to those for Church of Scotland members, as reported in Chapter 2.

Table 4.23

Support for classification of home videos

	Male	Female
Support	77.8	78.6
Don't support	14.5	8.9
Don't know	7.6	12.5

With regard to the importance ascribed to the six occupations listed in Question 52, women accorded significantly higher priority to Ministers, while men placed school teachers very significantly higher than women. No other differences were apparent.

We may thus be some way towards understanding the divergence between Church of Scotland members and other groups in their answers to this question. Women and elderly people (both groups showing a higher degree of religiosity than their comparators; and both also over-represented within the Church of Scotland) rank the Minister significantly higher and the teacher significantly lower. We are still, however, unable to explain the higher esteem accorded to policemen by Church of Scotland members.

Women were significantly less likely to endorse the idea of strike action. No difference, however, existed between the sexes in their views of the present level of unemployment.

A majority of men (54%) saw nuclear weapons as an effective deterrent against war, this ratio being significantly higher (at the 0.1% level) than the 42.2% of women who subscribed to the same view. Clearly, therefore, Church of Scotland members' support for nuclear weapons cannot be attributed to their numerical bias towards the female sex. We have of course already seen that age has an important influence over peoples' answers on this item; although it may work in combination with some other factor to produce the results reported in Chapter 2. This possibility will be tested at a later point.

Although a minority of both sexes saw membership of the Orange Order as consistent with Christianity, a significantly higher proportion of men than women (11.3 as opposed to 6.3%) answered in this vein. Twenty five per cent of men (contrasting with 13.8% of women) also saw Freemasonry as consistent with Christianity, this difference being significant at the 0.1% level. There was, however, no difference between men and women in their attitude towards the Knights of St Columba.

There was no association between sex and attitudes towards abortion. Women were, however, very significantly less supportive of premarital sexual intercourse. Table 4.24 shows vastly more men than women endorsing the affirmative response, whereas 10% more women than men would not countenance it under any circumstances.

Table 4.24

Opinion over rightness of sexual intercourse before marriage

	Male	*Female*
Yes	39.8	26.0
Yes, but only if couple intend to marry	24.4	25.1
Not under any circumstances	25.7	35.4
Don't know	10.1	13.5

The responses of women to questions concerning sexual morality have so far been consistent with the more conservative stance adopted by Church of Scotland members, in common with those of other churches. Table 4.25, however, reveals a pattern which diverges significantly from the general uniformity of this trend. This shows a very substantial majority (59%) of men construing homosexuality as 'an unnatural act', with only 47.6% of women responding in these terms. These differences are significant at the 0.1% level.

Table 4.25

Attitude towards homosexuality

	Male	*Female*
An unnatural act	59.2	47.6
Sexual love between members of the same sex is acceptable	4.0	2.6
A personal matter – up to the individual	33.8	40.1
Don't know	3.0	9.7

By contrast with religious affiliation and (especially) age, sexual status yielded a small and rather uninteresting crop of associations with the various lifestyle questions. The ten items from this section of the questionnaire that show a significant association with sex are listed in Table 4.26. This shows women as significantly less enamoured of exciting or unconventional experiences, but less in agreement with the notion that one should live in an area where all the neighbours have a similar standard. Relating as they appear to do to conventional attitudes towards life and social relationships, these two items yield contradictory trends. On a second cluster, throwing up items which we have also seen before in relation to the elderly, women show a significantly stronger preference for paying for purchases by cash; and a significantly greater proportion of them would also like to change society so that material things matter less. Women proved significantly less likely than men to feel that private motoring has more disadvantages than advantages, (an anti-materialist view) and ironically were significantly more likely to agree that they are fashion conscious (a materialistic view).

Consistent with their repudiation of premarital sex, women were significantly less likely to approve of a teenage son's going on holiday with his girlfriend. And to complete a rather mixed bag, women (very surprisingly, to this observer at any rate) were significantly less accepting of showing one's feelings at work. Less surprisingly, 15% more women than men reported that religion was important in their life, whilst 13% more men asserted that they liked to discuss politics and community questions.

It would seem possible to account for only a few of the associations that were noted between lifestyle and religious affiliation in Chapter 2, in terms of the statistical bias towards women within the ranks of the Church of Scotland. The preference for paying in cash, the greater dislike for unconventional experiences, the opposition to a teenage son's going on holiday with a girlfriend and the affirmation that religion is important in their lives all resonate with certain of the inter-church differences in lifestyle which were noted in that Chapter. Moreover, all of these factors also differentiated elderly from younger people. The Church of Scotland's greater preparedness to endorse these responses may accordingly be attributed to a preponderance of women and elderly people in the Church of Scotland. In so far as a preference for living in areas where all the neighbours have a similar standard was more strongly stated by members of the Church of Scotland, men's endorsement of this item did, however, contradict the general pattern. Overall, the most sensible conclusion would seem to be that sex has a fairly limited influence upon such aspects of lifestyle as were included in the questionnaire and that those aspects on which differences do emerge between the sexes help to explain only a small part of variations between the members of different churches.

Moving on to Questions 61–4, men and women were no different from each other in the ways in which they prefer to spend their spare time. Men did, however, express a rather stronger preference (significant at the 5% level) for being with people whose ideas and values diverge from their own. And although sex proved unrelated to people's perception of themselves as happy or unhappy, Table 4.27 shows that significantly greater numbers of women admitted to feeling lonely, with 48% of the female sample reporting that they experienced such sentiments sometimes or often.

In comparing these data with those presented in Chapter 2, one is again

Table 4.26

Lifestyle

			Male	Female
(i)	I like new exciting experiences even if they are a bit frightening or unconventional	Agree	53.5	38.7
		Disagree	46.7	61.3
(ii)	It is best to live in an area where all the neighbours have a similar standard	Agree	58.4	51.6
		Disagree	41.6	48.4
(iii)	I prefer to pay cash even if I have to wait for larger purchases	Agree	72.0	80.0
		Disagree	28.0	20.0
(iv)	I would like to change society so that material things matter less	Agree	57.5	68.3
		Disagree	42.5	31.7
(v)	I think that private motoring has more disadvantages than advantages	Agree	23.4	19.4
		Disagree	76.6	80.6
(vi)	I am not specially fashion conscious	Agree	79.1	65.8
		Disagree	20.9	34.2
(vii)	If I had a teenage son I would let him go on holiday with his girlfriend	Agree	58.8	46.3
		Disagree	41.2	53.7
(viii)	One shouldn't show one's feelings at work	Agree	48.4	56.2
		Disagree	51.6	43.8
(ix)	I like to discuss politics and community questions	Agree	52.0	39.2
		Disagree	48.0	60.8
(x)	Religion is important in my life	Agree	56.7	71.1
		Disagree	43.3	28.9

Table 4.27

Frequency of feeling lonely

	Male	Female
Often	6.1	9.0
Sometimes	27.1	39.0
Seldom	44.4	32.9
Never	22.4	19.1

struck by the relative absence of overlap between the two sets of findings. Although women are similar to members of the Church of Scotland in their general lack of enthusiasm for being with people of different views, they are no more likely than men to prefer to spend their spare time with their family and experience significantly more frequent feelings of loneliness — a factor which failed to differentiate between the denominational groups. It thus seems safe to conclude that the responses of Church of Scotland members have been relatively little influenced by the higher proportion of their female members. Indeed, given that elderly people are significantly more prone to report feeling lonely, one would expect the combination of age and sex to produce a similar tendency within the Church of Scotland. Church membership is thus perhaps an important factor in giving immunity from sentiments of isolation.

(v) Alcohol

Table 4.28 provides the statistical summary of people's reports on their consumption of alcohol. Women are manifestly less regular drinkers of alcohol than men. And with regard to what is actually consumed, men report more frequent intake of beer, wine and spirits; but there is no difference between the sexes in their consumption of fortified wine.

Table 4.28

Consumption of alcohol

	Male	Female
Never drink alcohol	9.5	21.2
Very occasionally drink alcohol	28.5	37.7
Occasionally	40.0	32.5
Regularly	22.0	8.5

People's reports on how they would react if they were served wine at a function were consistent with these trends. Thus, Table 4.29 shows that significantly more men than women would drink it, whilst significantly more women would either request something non-alcoholic or express a preference for not drinking at all.

Table 4.29

Reaction to being served wine at a function

	Male	Female
Drink it*	71.1	58.3
Allow it to be poured and only sip it	9.8	12.4
Say that you want something non-alcoholic*	6.6	12.2
Say you don't want anything to drink*	1.0	6.8
Don't know – depends on the situation	11.3	10.4

* = significant difference between the proportion from either sex endorsing this item.

As experience of previous comparisons on these data has by now led one to expect, there is no difference between men and women in the relative importance they attach to various reasons for drinking. Substantial and interesting differences do, however, emerge between the sexes in the absolute importance they attach to certain of these reasons. Table 4.30 shows that men ascribe greater significance to alcohol's role in making for easier relaxation and social contact and in improving the 'atmosphere'. In addition, a tiny proportion (5%) of men claim to drink because it is 'difficult to be TT in my job', but this is significantly greater than the even tinier proportion (1%) of women who offer the same reason. Women, by contrast, are significantly more likely to refer to the benefits of alcohol in increasing the value of a good meal and are also significantly more likely to deny that they would be damaged by alcohol. These differences clearly indicate that men see drinking taking place within an essentially social context and use alcohol in an instrumental way to enhance their enjoyment of that setting. Where women do ascribe significance to the role of alcohol in social settings, it is in the context of eating, whilst the two other responses which they are significantly more likely to give than men perhaps suggest a greater need for self-justification.

Table 4.30

Reasons for drinking

	Male	*Female*
Easier social contact*	2 (53%)	3 (42%)
Easier to relax*	1 (61%)	2 (54%)
In order not to appear self-righteous*	9 (7%)	8 (14%)
Abstinence is out of date	12 (3%)	11 (3%)
Atmosphere is better with a little alcohol*	3 (45%)	4 (31%)
Increase the value of a good meal*	4 (43%)	1 (62%)
Difficult to be TT in my job*	11 (5%)	12 (1%)
Don't believe I would be damaged*	5 (19%)	5 (27%)
Want to use Christian freedom	10 (5%)	10 (8%)
Don't want to be different from friends	8 (10%)	9 (8%)
Medicinal	7 (14%)	7 (17%)
Other reasons	6 (18%)	6 (23%)

* = significant difference between the proportion from either sex endorsing this item.

Asked why they do not drink more, male and female drinkers again provide very similar rank-orderings, with the notable exceptions of 'drank too much in earlier life' (placed twelfth by men and nineteenth by women) and 'don't like the taste' (which women placed ninth, as opposed to men's fifteenth). The difference between men and women in the absolute importance they accord to these two items is in fact statistically highly significant. Men are also significantly less likely than women to refer to the need to resist social pressure and are also more likely to be deterred by the fact that drinking and driving is dangerous and against the law; whilst women accord significantly greater weight to the dangers created for the foetus by drinking during pregnancy.

Table 4.31

Reasons for not drinking more

	Male	Female
Damaging to health	1 (47%)	1 (48%)
Avoid a hangover next day	7 (19%)	10 (14%)
Resisting social pressure*	17= (1%)	15 (4%)
Drinking in pregnancy damages the foetus*	19 (0.6%)	16 (3.7%)
Don't want to get drunk	3 (37%)	2 (33%)
Don't want to risk becoming dependent	6 (20%)	7 (20%)
Drank too much in earlier life*	12 (7%)	19 (1.7%)
For the sake of those damaged by alcohol	17= (1%)	18 (2%)
Drinking and driving is dangerous and against the law*	2 (42%)	5 (25%)
Don't want to be a danger in traffic	10 (9%)	14 (5%)
Don't like the taste*	15 (4%)	9 (16%)
Don't want to lose control	8 (17%)	8 (19%)
Don't want to gain weight	14 (5%)	11 (9%)
Example for my children	9 (16%)	6 (22%)
Example for others	13 (7%)	12 (26%)
Can't afford it	4 (27%)	4 (26%)
Have seen what alcohol has done to others	5 (25%)	3 (31%)
Solidarity with friends	16 (2%)	17 (2%)
Other reasons	11 (9.1%)	13 (7%)

These differences are generally perhaps in tune with the expectations of commonsense. However, it does seem interesting that proportionately more women feel the need to resist social pressure in drinking, whereas a small but significant minority of men are influenced by what they see to have been their own over-indulgence earlier in life.

Thirty-nine men and one hundred and seventeen women indicated that they never drink alcohol. And once again, the relatively small numbers involved, together with the fact that their preferences had to be distributed over a list of 20 items, meant that no very useful analysis could be undertaken of the congruence between the rank-orderings they ascribed to these items. It is interesting, however, that 19% of the non-drinking men ascribed their teetotalism to having drunk too much in their earlier life (as opposed to only 2% of women); while a significantly higher proportion (31%) of women than men asserted that they do not drink because they do not like the taste of alcohol. The item accorded highest importance by both sexes was the need to avoid damage to their health.

Only a small minority of both men and women felt it necessary that Christians should be total abstainers and no significant difference exists between the two sexes in this regard. Significantly more women than men, however, felt that Communion wine should be non-alcoholic, the responses to this question being outlined in Table 4.32.

Table 4.32

Whether communion wine should be alcoholic

	Male	Female
Alcoholic	7.4	3.5
Non-alcoholic	26.4	40.4
Doesn't matter	59.4	48.4
Don't know	6.9	7.7

Whilst a minority of either sex reported that they smoked, the 30% of men who did so was significantly higher than the 23.7% of women who gave an affirmative reply to this question. Finally, a significant difference also emerged between the sexes in their support for a policy of free use of cannabis. Thus, although the overwhelming majority of either sex were opposed to such a development, the 11% of men who did support this proposal were, in proportionate terms, significantly greater (at the 0.1% level) than the 3% of women who would also give their blessing to such a development.

Conclusions

Considering these findings as a whole, it seems reasonable to conclude that the inter-denominational differences identified in Chapter 2 are only marginally attributable to the numerical predominance of women within the Church of Scotland. Whilst significant differences emerge between men and women in their responses to a considerable number of the areas covered by the questionnaire, relatively few of these are consistent with the general direction of the responses endorsed by Church of Scotland members in the aggregate. Indeed, on a number of these — but perhaps especially on those items pertaining to church attendance and devotional activities — the differences established between men and women are directly antithetical to those between other churches and the Church of Scotland.

What may we then say about the effects of sexual status upon the behaviour and religious, social, moral and political attitudes of the individual? In general, women are manifestly more committed to the church and assiduous in church attendance and the performance of such devotional activities as praying and reading of the Bible. They are also firmer than men in their belief in God, in life after death and Christ's role as a saviour. But the fact that, even with its predominance of female members, the Church of Scotland is unable to make a superior showing to the Roman Catholic Church on these elements suggests that a religious factor must be operating here.

Sex appears to be related to individuals' beliefs as to what happens after death, and to their views of God and the Bible. It has no significant association, however, with respondents' opinions of heaven and hell. Scrutiny of how similar women's responses are to those for the Church of Scotland sample suggests that Church of Scotland members' views of what happens after death may be influenced by a 'feminine factor', but that conceptions of God and the Bible are more strongly shaped by other influences. It also seems worth noting that, despite their lower degree of religiosity, men think no less frequently than women about the issues covered in this section of the questionnaire.

Sex has no discernible effect upon people's perceptions of the importance of various possible developments within and future activities by the Church. Women adopt a much more moral stance than men on control over TV sex and violence, classification of home videos, and sexual intercourse before marriage. All of these may be reflected in the generally more conservative stance of members of the Church of Scotland upon these issues. Again, the effects of sex may interact with those of age to produce the harder stance of Church of Scotland members on these issues; although the fact that Roman Catholics share the same general position as Church of Scotland members on these matters would indicate — given the more even distribution between the sexes in the Catholic sample — that age is the more influential factor here. The greater hostility of women to nuclear weapons runs counter to the fact that Church of Scotland communicants tend to support them. Church of Scotland members' position on these weapons must therefore be explained in other terms. The same must be said of attitudes towards homosexuality, where the link with sex is again contrary to that for religious affiliation.

In the case of lifestyle, some similarities do exist between the responses of women in particular and those of Church of Scotland members in general. This suggests that the more conventional lifestyle of Church of Scotland communicants is to some degree explained by the preponderance of women among them. But on the whole, sex seems to have a relatively minor role in shaping people's attitudes and behaviour in these areas.

Comparison of women's responses to the questions on alcohol with the inter-group trends identified in Chapter 2 suggests that part of any peculiarly Church of Scotland response may be attributable to the effects of its uneven sex-composition, with both women and those affiliated to the Church of Scotland being significantly less likely to see alcohol as making for relaxation or ease of social contact and more likely to use alcohol to improve a good meal. Both women and Church of Scotland members also point to the dangers of drinking and driving as reasons for not drinking more. The lack of a complete fit between the two sets of data, however, again suggests that other factors are probably operating here.

Whilst it would be premature to conclude that religion is more influential of sex than vice versa, a reasonable case could be constructed on the basis of the present evidence. Women, as has been emphasised above, are much more involved in and committed to the Church, and religion seems to have a very much more potent influence upon their daily lives — an influence which one might expect to extend into their attitudes and opinions on social, moral and political issues. But this possibility awaits an analysis of the interaction between religion and sex and the relative strengths of their separate and combined influences.

CHAPTER FIVE

COMMITMENT TO THE CHURCH*

Chapters 3 and 4 have indicated that certain of the interdenominational differences observed in Chapter 2 may largely be attributable to the influences of age and sex. A substantial part of those differences between the churches do, however, appear to remain independent of those influences. It is now time to examine the extent to which religious belief *per se* has a bearing on the divergencies in question. Our starting point in this analysis will be the part played by commitment to the church, in shaping people's attitudes and behaviour. Our discussion will follow the same essential structure as earlier chapters. 'Commitment to the church' was in this instance gauged by people's responses to the question in the schedule that asked them 'what is your level of commitment to the church?'. Respondents were then asked to insert a tick in whichever one of four boxes came closest to their own view of their level of church commitment. The responses offered were: highly committed, fairly committed, not very committed, and no commitment; and these categories have been used as the basis for the analysis in the present Chapter.

(i) General background factors

It has already been established in Chapters 3 and 4 that a high degree of commitment to the church is significantly more likely to be found among elderly people and among women (see Tables 3.2 and 4.3). Almost certainly related to the former of these findings, people with a high degree of commitment to the church are significantly more likely to be found among those who have been living in the same neighbourhood for 11 years or more, as well as among the widowed and (to a lesser extent) married, whilst people who are separated, divorced or (again, to a lesser extent) co-habiting report lower degrees of church commitment. Similarly, pensioners reported them selves in significantly greater numbers as committed to the church than did those in employment, the unemployed, self-employed, housewives and students. Individuals who had attended university or college also reported a very much lower level of church-commitment than did those who had not enjoyed such opportunities. There was, however, no relationship between commitment and annual income, despite the obvious potential bearing of old-age pensions upon this. Finally, the owner-occupiers of houses and of rented flats were for some reason more likely to report themselves as highly committed to the church than the owner-occupiers of flats and people living in

---

* Non-Church members were excluded from the data for this Chapter.

rented houses. This (from a statistical point of view, highly significant) finding is most probably attributable to the social and other characteristics associated with particular forms of housing tenure, rather than to the effects of age or sex; although the data themselves offer no hints of the factors that might be important.

Finally, level of church-commitment showed no relationship with whether or not people held public office. It was, however, significantly related to party-political loyalties, with Conservatives and (less markedly) Liberals reporting a stronger commitment to the church than supporters of the Labour, Scottish National or Social Democratic parties.

For the most part much of the above is attributable to the effects of age. It does, however, seem likely that the inverse relationship between commitment to the church and higher education and certain forms of housing tenure is independent of the age-factor.

(ii) Religion and the Church

Predictably, those claiming a high or fair degree of commitment to the church reported a far higher level of attendance, with the majority attending at least once a week (over a quarter of the highly committed giving a figure of several times a week), whilst more than half those with no commitment confine their attendances to baptisms, weddings and funerals (Table 5.1).

Table 5.1

*Commitment to Church in relation to frequency
of attendance at Church*

Commitment	Highly %	Fairly %	Not very %	Not at all %
Several times a week	28.8	3.3	0.3	—
Once a week	67.1	57.5	5.9	5.7
Approximately once a month	2.1	25.0	18.1	0.5
Once a quarter	—	9.6	30.2	5.7
Twice a year	—	1.5	15.6	5.7
Once a year	—	0.3	8.0	8.9
Only for baptisms, weddings and funerals	—	2.1	19.8	57.8
Never	2.0	0.6	2.1	15.6

Table 5.2 shows that the frequency of church attendance of 'highly committed' members of the sample was in the majority of cases about the same in their earlier adult life as now, whereas two-thirds of the 'not very committed' attended church more frequently in their earlier adult life than

now. A majority of those affirming no commitment to the church also report having attended more frequently in their earlier adult life than at present, although the proportion (54%) offering this response is appreciably smaller than among the 'not very' committed; and this, in conjuction with the 37% of the uncommitted who claim their present frequency of church attendance to be about the same as 5 years ago, suggests that a high proportion of this group have never had any commitment to the church. Finally, in this respect, Table 5.3 shows that although a majority in all four groups think that their level of church attendance will be about the same in 5 years time as it is now, these proportions are far higher for the two 'committed' groups, whilst the groups reporting low levels of commitment to the church are substantially more likely to find their future frequency of church attendance difficult to predict.

Table 5.2

Frequency of Church attendance in earlier adult life

Commitment	Highly %	Fairly %	Not very %	Not at all %
More frequently than now	19.0	37.4	67.2	54.2
About the same	58.5	44.6	24.5	36.5
Less frequently than now	22.4	18.0	8.3	9.3

Table 5.3

Expected frequency of Church attendance in 5 years time

Commitment	Highly %	Fairly %	Not very %	Not at all %
More frequent than now	2.7	8.4	17.6	3.1
About the same	82.9	70.4	52.8	53.6
Less frequent	2.1	4.2	5.2	3.6
Difficult to know	12.3	17.1	24.5	39.6

Responses to the question concerning frequency of reading the Bible again yielded a predictably significant association with church commitment. As opposed to 29.1% of the highly committed, only 1.6% of those professing no commitment claimed to read the Bible every day; whereas 5% of the highly committed and 79% of the uncommitted 'never' or 'hardly ever' read the Bible. Similarly, there was a highly-significant association between level of church commitment and reported frequency of prayer, with 77% of the highly committed claiming to pray every day, whilst 59.7% of the uncommitted never or 'hardly ever' pray. This association also extended into the frequency of praying together as a family.

In this connection, Table 5.4 shows another extremely significant association between church commitment and the extent to which respondents saw a devotional life as having been the rule during their childhood. The frequency of positive answers declines with a reduction in the level of church commitment, whilst negative answers diminish proportionately as church commitment increases. Of some interest here is the very high proportion of the 'not very committed' and uncommitted groups reporting a devotional life as *not* having been the rule in their childhood. Perhaps negative influences are stronger in this respect than positive ones.

Table 5.4

Extent to which a devotional life was seen as having been the rule in respondents' childhood

Commitment	Highly %	Fairly %	Not very %	Not at all %
Yes	59.3	46.7	28.0	18.0
No	36.6	44.3	65.1	73.5
Doubtful/don't know	4.1	9.0	6.9	8.5

Turning to a consideration of the sources from which people obtain their knowledge about church events, Table 5.5 shows significant differences between the committed and the uncommitted in the regularity of their listening to or viewing religious programmes. Thus, 32.3% of the uncommitted never tune in to such broadcasts, whereas a virtually equivalent proportion of the highly committed do so regularly, this group being proportionately three times greater than their counterparts among the uncommitted. Even so, a majority of all four groups listen to or view religious programmes at least sometimes, with fully 57% of the uncommitted appearing in this catergory,

Table 5.5

Regularity with which respondents listen to or view religious programmes on radio and TV

Commitment	Highly %	Fairly %	Not very %	Not at all %
Regularly	31.1	28.7	15.5	10.4
Sometimes	65.5	66.5	72.5	57.3
Never	3.4	4.8	12.0	32.3

There was substantial variation between the four 'commitment' groups in what they reported to be their most important sources of knowledge about church events. These are outlined in Table 5.6. For the most highly committed group, the Minister or Priest emerges as the single most important point of contact, whereas for the two groups with the lowest levels of commitment, newspapers and television are given the highest rating. Indeed, for the most committed group of all, the three sources most directly connected with the church constitute the most important fonts of information, whereas among the uncommitted, they are accorded least priority. It is thus obvious that if the churches consider it important to communicate information about their activities beyond their own memberships, they must rely heavily on mainly secular vehicles of dissemination.

Table 5.6

Importance ascribed to the following as sources of knowledge about Church events (Percentages ranking sources as among the first three in importance)

Commitment	Highly %	Fairly %	Not very %	Not at all %
Newspapers*	36 (4)	48 (3)	68 (1)	65 (2)
Radio*	16 (6)	23 (6)	32 (5)	47 (3)
TV*	32 (5)	52 (2)	67 (2)	73 (1)
*Life and Work**	61 (2)	35 (5)	20 (6)	4 (7)
Other Church literature*	48 (3)	40 (4)	39 (4)	14 (5)
Minister or Priest*	80 (1)	70 (1)	42 (3)	12 (6)
Not interested in Church events*	0 (7)	2 (7)	10 (7)	37 (4)

* significant association between degree of commitment and importance ascribed to source.

Church commitment showed no association with readership of daily newspapers nor of weekly magazines. Consistent, however, with the findings in Table 5.6, those committed to the church showed a far higher incidence of readership of religious newspapers and magazines. A significant relationship was also found between church commitment and readership of Sunday newspapers, with the highly committed being concentrated among those reading either the 'heavier' popular Sundays like the *Sunday Express*, or those not taking a Sunday paper at all, whereas the uncommitted showed significantly higher proportions reading the 'quality' Sunday papers. Both the 'fairly' and 'not very' committed harboured significantly more readers of the *Sunday Post* within their ranks.

Table 5.7 shows the relationship between commitment to the church and specifications as to the most important reasons for remaining in communion with the church. In interpreting this Table, it should be borne in mind that only 50 of the 192 people professing no commitment to the church gave responses to this question. The Table does, however, in general show fairly substantial similarities between the four groups in the *relative* importance they ascribe to the various reasons given. Thus, support for the church and Christian values and participation in services are both ranked high by all four groups, whilst fellowship and contact with others is ranked high by the three most church-committed sets of respondents. Not unexpectedly, the opportunity for baptism, marriage and funerals comes first in importance for those with no commitment: amongst the most committed, only 6% rate this as an important reason for church membership. Perhaps the most interesting finding in this Table is the tiny proportion of committed members who see missionary work as a powerful incentive to membership, the same being true of the priority ascribed to the search for justice and Christian solidarity. This is of course consistent with the extremely low priorities these two elements received from the various denominational groups.

Table 5.7

*Importance ascribed to the following as reasons for Church membership
(Percentages ranking factors as among first three in importance)*

Commitment	Highly %	Fairly %	Not very %	Not at all %
Wish to support the Church and Christian values*	87 (1)	89 (1)	58 (1)	38 (2=)
Opportunity for baptism, marriage and funerals*	6 (6)	21 (5)	46 (3)	46 (1)
Participate in services/ Communion*	76 (2)	68 (2)	50 (2)	38 (2=)
Fellowship and contact with others	73 (3)	57 (3)	33 (4)	25 (6=)
Support missionary work	6 (6=)	5 (8)	1 (13)	0 (13)
Support everyday Christian life*	25 (4)	27 (4)	25 (6)	6 (10=)
Want to strive for justice and Christian solidarity	6 (6=)	6 (7)	5 (11)	6 (10=)
Natural for me to be a Church member*	13 (5)	18 (6)	27 (5)	35 (4)
Family expectations*	0.7 (11)	1 (11=)	17 (7)	25 (6=)
Don't want to upset someone by leaving	0 (12=)	0.3 (13)	3 (12)	6 (10=)
Other reasons*	1.4 (10)	1 (11=)	9 (9)	13 (9)
Never thought of leaving*	3 (9)	3 (9)	11 (8)	33 (5)
Nothing special*	0 (12=)	2 (10)	7 (10)	25 (6=)

* significant association between commitment and importance ascribed.

Degree of commitment to the church was significantly correlated with membership of Church of Scotland organisations; and the uncommitted were significantly more likely to be married to people who were themselves not members of any church, whereas the spouses of 'highly' and 'fairly' committed individuals were (in almost exactly equal proportions) themselves significantly more likely to be members of a church. The more committed people are, the more likely they also are to regard themselves as Christians and to be baptised and to have attended Sunday School until a fairly late age. To complete this list of rather predictable findings, both their parents were significantly more likely to have been regular church attenders.

Asked whether they attend services in other denominations, the highly committed seem significantly more likely to 'shop around' other forms of worship, although the majority do this on a very occasional basis. Relatively small proportions of the highly committed groups (5.8% and 3.1%, respectively) were members of ecumenical groups, but these were still significantly greater in number than those 'not very committed' and uncommitted individuals who claimed such membership.

Committed individuals significantly more often affirm a belief in God and that God controls our lives here and now. Very significantly higher proportions of them also believe that Jesus died for our sins and that He is risen from the dead. The highly committed also contain a substantially higher proportion (91%) of individuals who believe in eternal life and in the individual's life after death (82%).

Table 5.8

Relationship between commitment to Church and concept of God

Commitment	Highly %	Fairly %	Not very %	Not at all %
All powerful judge who sees and judges our sins and virtues	12.3	15.6	12.5	6.5
Loving, He hears our prayers and controls our lives	52.7	46.8	26.4	14.5
A father whose concern is to save and to help	31.5	20.7	17.7	8.6
A sort of distant, impersonal power or force	2.7	9.0	22.6	21.0
No opinion	0.7	7.8	20.8	49.5

Table 5.8 shows how level of commitment to the church is (highly significantly) associated with individuals' opinion of God. This shows that those with the greatest degree of commitment see God as a loving or helping being, whilst those with lower levels of commitment either see God in rather impersonal terms (a 'sort of distant, impersonal power or force') or profess to no opinion on the subject.

Similarly, Table 5.9 shows significant differences between the four groups in the beliefs they hold about what happens after death. Among the highly committed, fully 60% believe that after death man stands before God and his judgement, with the 3 remaining groups subscribing in regularly declining proportions to this view. Conversely, lack of commitment correlates with professions of uncertainty as to what happens after death, with more than a quarter of the uncommitted also subscribing to the view that 'death is the end'.

Answers to the question concerning opinions about heaven and hell also showed a significant association with commitment to the church. The majority of those professing a high or fair degree of commitment subscribed either to the view that heaven and hell are places with eternal bliss or suffering where man must live after God's judgement, or to the statement that the expressions 'heaven' and 'hell' mean that after death, man may live near or far from God. Conversely, the majority of those professing lesser or no commitment either endorsed the statement that heaven and hell do not exist as such, everything being related to man's life here and now, or professing no opinion on the matter. Similarly, and again according to expectation, church commitment was correlated with people's views of the Bible. The majority of the highly, fairly and not very committed groups saw the Bible as written by men (albeit, inspired by God) and therefore requiring interpretation; whereas as many of the uncommitted endorsed this view as felt unable to express any opinion on the matter. By contrast, some 40% of the highly committed see the Bible as 'God's word — true in every detail'.

Table 5.10 also shows a significant association between church commitment and opinions of humanity. This seems entirely attributable to the rather smaller proportion of the highly committed who see human beings as a

Table 5.9

Opinion as to what happens after death

Commitment	*Highly* %	*Fairly* %	*Not very* %	*Not at all* %
After death man stands before God and His judgement	61.0	39.6	16.6	9.0
Man's soul lives forever without judgement	4.8	6.6	3.5	0.5
Man's sould goes to another existence	9.6	9.9	15.2	10.1
Death is the end – man ceases to exist	0.7	3.6	13.5	29.6
We don't know what happens after death	23.3	37.8	48.8	45.0
No opinion	0.7	2.4	2.4	5.8

mixture of good and bad and the rather higher proportion of this group who subscribe to the doctrine of Original Sin, the 8% of those highly committed who endorse this view being proportionately many more than their counterparts in the three remaining groups. This Table also shows a remarkable degree of similarity between the fairly committed, not very committed and uncommitted groups in the proportions among them subscribing to the different views offered. Finally, and by their own report, the highly committed think significantly more often about these issues than members of the other groups: 87% of their number report thinking in these terms, whilst 63% and 71%, respectively, of the not very committed and uncommitted groups 'seldom' or 'never' give thought to these issues.

Table 5.10

Opinion of humanity

Commitment	*Highly* %	*Fairly* %	*Not very* %	*Not at all* %
There is good and bad in everyone	84.8	92.5	92.5	92.6
Everybody is basically good	6.8	6.9	7.1	6.8
Everybody is basically bad	8.3	0.7	0.4	0.6

Table 5.11 shows the degree of importance attached by the four 'commitment' groups to the various possible developments within the church. The first thing to note about this Table is that there is a significant difference between the four groups on all of the items in this section of the questionnaire, with the sole exception of improved co-operation with the Roman Catholic Church. On all items apart from this, much higher importance is ascribed by the committed than the uncommitted groups. Although the rank ordering ascribed by each of the four groups is roughly similar, highly committed respondents give much higher priority to the development of local Bible study and prayer groups than do those with lesser degrees of commitment, whilst the least committed place improved co-operation with the Roman Catholic Church and inter-church marriage rather higher in their own relative systems of priorities than do highly committed informants. Conversely, the least committed give rather less priority to improved co-operation between the Church of Scotland and other Protestant churches than the three more committed groups.

A number of differences also emerge between groups with varying degrees of commitment to the church in the importance they believe various activities to have for the church's future. That there is a difference in the *absolute* importance they ascribe to each of the activities listed in Table 5.12 is evidenced by the fact that a significant difference emerges between the four

Table 5.11

Importance ascribed to the following:
(Percentages rating items as 'very important' or 'important')

Commitment	Highly %	Fairly %	Not very %	Not at all %
Joint services for Church of Scotland and other denominations*	78 (4=)	81 (4)	67 (6)	54 (5=)
Improved co-operation between the Church of Scotland and other Protestant Churches*	92 (1)	94 (1)	88 (1)	66 (4)
Joint communion for Church of Scotland and other denominations*	67 (8)	63 (8)	50 (8)	44 (7)
Local Bible Study and prayer groups including Church of Scotland members and members of other Churches*	83 (3)	70 (7)	59 (7)	40 (8)
Joint effort, e.g. information campaigns about the under-developed countries*	90 (2)	84 (2)	81 (3)	72 (1=)
Church of Scotland and other Churches should have a common view on Bible translations*	76 (6)	76 (5)	72 (4)	54 (5=)
Improved co-operation with the Roman Catholic Church	69 (7)	72 (6)	71 (5)	67 (3)
Improved co-operation on inter-Church marriage*	78 (4=)	83 (3)	82 (2)	72 (1=)

* a significant association between commitment and importance ascribed to item

groups on all eleven items. It is also noticeable from this Table that the relationship between commitment to the church and the degree of importance ascribed is linear (in the sense that the average score for each group increases or declines in a regular way as one moves from left to right) on all items with only some (slight) variations to this pattern. With regard to the *relative* importance attributed to these by the groups in question, spiritual leadership, Christian education, personal renewal and evangelisation are all given supreme priority by the highly commited. Among those with no commitment to the church, Christian education is ranked relatively high, but the other three factors are given a very much lower priority. Conversely, social work, work with pensioners and the sick and (to a lesser extent) help to developing countries are ranked high by the uncommitted and given a rather lower grading by those with a high commitment. It is thus obvious that those who see themselves on the periphery of church concerns attach somewhat higher importance to its pastoral activities, whereas those whose commitment to the church is strong accord greatest priority to its spiritual and evangelical functions. Interestingly, however, all four groups give minimal priority to the need for 'political awareness' in the church, although the two most committed groups see this as significantly less crucial than those with marginal church commitments. Overall, these findings do not run very much counter to expectation.

Table 5.12

Importance ascribed to following items for the Church's future
(Average scored ascribed each item on a scale from 1–3)

Commitment	Highly %	Fairly %	Not very %	Not at all %
Political awareness*	2.8 (11)	2.8 (11)	2.2 (9)	2.3 (9=)
Evangelisation*	1.7 (3=)	2.2 (8)	2.3 (10)	2.4 (11)
Social work*	2.0 (7)	1.8 (4)	1.8 (4)	1.5 (2)
Help to developing countries*	2.0 (6)	1.9 (6=)	1.7 (3)	1.7 (3)
Work with pensioners and the sick*	1.8 (5)	1.8 (4)	1.5 (1)	1.4 (1)
Personal renewal*	1.7 (3=)	1.9 (6=)	2.0 (7=)	2.2 (8)
Increased awareness of social and economic justice*	2.2 (9)	2.2 (8=)	2.0 (7=)	1.9 (5=)
The position of women in the Church*	2.6 (10)	2.3 (10)	2.5 (11)	2.3 (9=)
Efficient organisation and good financial management*	2.1 (8)	1.8 (4=)	1.9 (5)	1.9 (5=)
More spiritual leadership*	1.4 (1=)	1.7 (2)	2.0 (7=)	2.1 (7)
Christian education*	1.4 (1=)	1.5 (1)	1.6 (2)	1.8 (4)

* significant association between commitment and degree of importance ascribed to item

(iii) Social and moral issues

A majority of the highly, fairly and not very committed groups (90%, 86% and 68% respectively) would welcome greater control over the amount of sex and violence shown on television. Only 48% of the uncommitted subscribed to this view, however, whilst 40% opposed it and 12% opted for the 'don't know' response. This last response represented a much higher proportion of don't knows than for the two most committed groups (2% each), although 9% of the 'not very committed' also chose this answer. In the related question as to whether respondents thought there should be classification of home videos, a majority of all four groups agreed with this statement, but with

111

declining strength as stated commitment to the church decreased. Thus, 87% of the highly committed, but only 63% of the uncommitted, agreed with this proposal. Conversely, fully one-quarter of the uncommitted were hostile to this suggestion, as opposed to the mere 2% of the highly committed who expressed a negative opinion.

Table 5.13

Attitudes to nuclear weapons

Commitment	Highly %	Fairly %	Not very %	Not at all %
Effective deterrent against war	46.9	51.7	49.3	37.7
Morally unacceptable	41.5	37.8	36.8	48.7
No opinion	11.6	10.5	13.9	13.6

Commitment to the church was also significantly related to the importance people ascribed to five of the six occupations which they were asked to rank in order of their significance for society, the only one on which no difference emerged being opinions on school teachers. Thus, the highly committed appear to value doctors significantly less highly, relative to other occupations, than do any of the other three 'commitment' groups, as was also the case on the views held of the importance of policemen. In this latter instance, however, it is also interesting to note that the importance ascribed increases as commitment to the church declines, with 43% of the highly committed, 59% of the fairly committed, 66% of the not very committed and 73% of the uncommitted placing policemen among the first three occupations in their rank ordering. In the case of judgements of social work, the position is somewhat different, in that people with no commitment to the church value social work as a profession significantly more highly than do the three remaining groups, who seem very similar in their opinions in this regard.

Highly committed churchgoers value Ministers significantly more than the remainder, with a regular decline in the importance attached to clerics by individuals with progressively lower degrees of commitment to the church: 72% of the highly committed place the Minister in first or second place in their rank order, whilst only 14% of the uncommitted do so. Finally, support for lawyers increases as one moves down the scale of church commitment; although it should also be said that lawyers seemed generally to be the least popular profession among all of the six between which respondents were asked to judge.

Asked whether, if they were currently in employment, they would ever go on strike, only 21% of the highly committed responded affirmatively, with 23% and 30% of the fairly and not very committed responding in the same vein. Exactly 50% of the uncommitted, however, gave a positive reply. With perhaps some passing comment on the relative smallness of the proportions of those giving an unequivocal 'yes' to this question, we should also note that these differences were statistically highly significant. There was, however, no association between church commitment and people's opinions of the present level of unemployment. Nor did commitment to the church correlate with people's opinions of nuclear weapons. Opinions on whether it was consistent with Christianity to be a member of the Orange Order, Freemasons, or Knights of St Columba all failed to show any relationship with commitment to the church.

Table 5.14

Attitude towards abortion

Commitment	Highly %	Fairly %	Not very %	Not at all %
A matter entirely for the persons concerned	20.5	30.3	38.9	57.4
Justifiable in certain circumstances	56.8	54.8	55.2	33.2
Always wrong	19.2	9.4	4.9	6.3
Don't know	3.4	5.5	1.0	3.2

Table 5.14 shows that there is a highly-significant relationship between degree of church commitment and attitudes towards abortion. But whilst the 19% of highly committed people who view abortion as 'always wrong' is much higher than each of the proportions in the three remaining groups, the most significant feature of this Table is the high proportions of those with some degree of commitment to the church who regard abortion as justifiable in certain circumstances, whereas the majority of those with no commitment see abortion as a matter entirely for the persons concerned. Those committed to the church are clearly in favour of the selective use of abortion.

It seems entirely predictable that individuals with a high degree of commitment to the church would view sexual intercourse before marriage as

Table 5.15

Attitude to sexual intercourse before marriage

Commitment	Highly %	Fairly %	Not very %	Not at all %
Right	5.0	15.1	43.6	63.6
Right, but only if couple intend to marry	19.9	28.6	29.1	15.0
Not under any circumstances	61.7	43.7	16.0	10.2
Don't know	13.5	12.6	11.3	11.2

entirely unacceptable under any circumstances. What is also interesting about Table 5.15 is, however, that, apart from the 64% of uncommitted people who see premarital intercourse as acceptable, the largest single proportion of the fairly committed see premarital sex as unacceptable under any circumstances, whilst an equivalent proportion of the 'not very committed' give their unqualified approval to this statement.

Table 5.16 also yields a (possibly predictable) significant relationship between commitment to the church and views on homosexuality. Thus, the majority of both the 'committed' groups view this as an unnatural act, whilst a (bare) majority of the uncommitted view it as a personal matter and therefore up to the individual to choose. Also of some possible interest in this Table is the apparent ambivalence of the not very committed, with virtually equal proportions within this group seeing homosexuality as either 'an unnatural act' or 'a personal matter'.

Table 5.16

Attitude towards homosexuality

Commitment	Highly %	Fairly %	Not very %	Not at all %
An unnatural act	72.3	58.5	46.1	36.3
Sexual love between partners of the same sex is acceptable	2.1	1.9	3.9	4.9
A personal matter – up to the individual	19.9	30.3	45.0	51.6
Don't know	5.7	9.3	5.0	7.1

The results in this section of the questionnaire accordingly support the view that people who are highly committed to the church tend towards rather conservative views on moral issues, but that their opinions on social and political issues are much less predictable. Thus, whilst their attitudes towards abortion, homosexuality, premarital sex, television sex and violence and home videos are all in an essentially predictable direction, their views on unemployment and nuclear weapons divide along the same lines as their fellow citizens with lesser degrees of church commitment. Nor do their views on the Orange Order, Freemasons and the Knights of St Columba diverge from those of other groups. These facts perhaps make it doubly interesting to consider their responses on the 'lifestyle' section of the questionnaire.

(iv) Lifestyle

Table 5.17 shows the relationship between 'lifestyle' and commitment to the church, concentrating as in previous Chapters only upon those items which show a significant relationship to church commitment. The first seven items in

114

that Table clearly centre on the varying degrees of life-satisfaction reported by the groups in question. And as in the case of Chapter 3, in particular, it seems possible to sub-divide these into three subsidiary clusters. Thus, items (i) to (iv) all appear to centre on the degree of contentment the individual feels in reviewing his/her current life-situation. All four items show those with higher degrees of commitment to the church to report higher levels of satisfaction, although it is interesting that in the case of items (i) and (iv), the 'fairly committed' group emerge as the most satisfied of all. Items (ii) and (iii), however, show a directly linear relationship with church commitment. Possibly related to these (although perhaps also more directly an indicator of mood) is item (v), which again shows that, of the relatively small minorities in all four groups who assert that they 'feel miserable most of the time', this features much less frequently among the groups with some degree of commitment to the church than among those professing no commitment whatsoever.

The next dimension of life-satisfaction is like that range of statements identified in Table 3.19 as concerned with cognitive appraisal of one's past experiences and current life situation. Item (vi) in Table 5.17 again shows those with the highest degree of commitment to be also those with the highest level of satisfaction with their past life; although it is once more interesting to observe that the 'fairly committed' report the highest levels of retrospective satisfaction in the sample. Finally, item (vi) would appear to focus on assessment of more direct and recent experience. This shows the highly committed endorsing this statement in a far greater proportion than those with lower commitment-levels.

It is thus apparent that commitment to the church either gives the individual immunity from dissatisfaction with various aspects of his/her life, or so affects people's lives and activities that they experience genuinely higher levels of satisfaction in whatever they undertake. The former possibility would suggest that religious commitment creates a perceptual 'filter' through which people interpret their experiences which makes them view them in a positive way; whilst the latter would indicate that such commitment transforms their way of engaging with tasks and responsibilities in the world, so that their activities become more fulfilling in themselves. Which of these two is correct — or whether indeed there are other possible ways of interpreting these results — might be an interesting topic for another analysis.

Items (viii) and (ix) show the church-committed expressing the degree of disapproval of sexual permissiveness that one would expect from their answers to earlier questions. Items (x) to (xiv) suggest the stoical attitude to life that was again identified in Table 3.19, in relation to the elderly. These all show people with higher degrees of commitment to the church to like simple things, to agree that the only way to get something valuable is to save for it, to prefer to pay cash even if they have to wait for bigger purchases, and to desire to change society so that material things matter less. Whether these differences are specifically influenced by age, or whether the more forbearing attitudes of the elderly have been shaped by their own previous upbringing

Table 5.17

Commitment to the Church by 'lifestyle'

	Commitment %	%	Highly %	Fairly %	Not very	Not at all
(i)	I've got pretty much what I expected out of life	Agree Disagree	80.0 20.0	85.0 15.0	75.8 24.2	67.6 32.4
(ii)	I have to a great extent the things that make life really pleasant and satisfying for people of my age	Agree Disagree	96.4 3.6	93.5 6.5	90.3 9.7	76.6 23.4
(iii)	I am as happy now as when I was younger	Agree Disagree	80.4 19.6	79.3 20.7	78.3 21.7	68.4 31.6
(iv)	My life could be happier than it is now	Agree Disagree	40.6 59.4	31.3 68.7	44.9 55.1	52.7 47.3
(v)	I feel miserable most of the time	Agree Disagree	1.5 98.5	2.8 97.2	2.9 97.1	7.0 93.0
(vi)	I wouldn't want to change my past life, even if I could	Agree Disagree	65.4 34.6	69.2 20.8	60.5 39.5	57.4 42.6
(vii)	During the past few weeks I have felt pleased about having accomplished something	Agree Disagree	85.9 14.1	74.4 25.6	70.5 29.5	72.5 27.5
(viii)	If I had a teenage daughter I would let her go on holiday with her boyfriend	Agree Disagree	34.5 65.5	45.3 54.7	58.0 42.0	64.6 35.4
(ix)	If I had a teenage son I would let him go on holiday with his girlfriend	Agree Disagree	37.4 62.6	48.3 51.7	62.9 37.1	71.4 28.6
(x)	In order to work more efficiently, I cut down on social life and pleasure	Agree Disagree	54.6 45.4	50.5 49.5	47.3 52.7	34.6 65.4
(xi)	I like simple things and a natural way of life	Agree Disagree	98.6 1.4	95.7 4.3	90.6 9.4	85.2 14.8
(xii)	The only way to get something valuable is to save for it	Agree Disagree	85.1 14.9	88.4 11.6	82.5 17.5	71.1 18.9
(xiii)	I prefer to pay cash even if I have to wait for larger purchases	Agree Disagree	82.5 17.5	82.7 17.3	72.3 27.7	67.4 32.6
(xiv)	I would like to change society so that material things matter less	Agree Disagree	79.3 20.7	67.1 32.9	58.9 41.1	54.1 45.9
(xv)	Solidarity with the weak is important to me	Agree Disagree	70.6 29.4	64.6 35.4	48.5 51.5	45.9 54.1
(xvi)	I want to change society	Agree Disagree	41.9 58.1	28.4 71.6	28.4 71.6	38.5 61.5

(xvii) I restrict my circle	Agree	41.3	44.4	51.2	53.3
of friends to a few	Disagree	58.7	55.6	48.8	46.7
(xviii) I like new experiences even					
if they are a bit frighten-	Agree	37.6	38.3	51.2	52.4
ing or unconventional	Disagree	62.4	61.7	48.8	47.6
(xix) In an election I would always					
vote for a party with a	Agree	48.1	53.2	41.5	35.5
strong defence policy	Disagree	51.9	46.8	58.5	64.5
(xx) When I join a club or					
society I engage myself	Agree	81.1	62.6	42.4	40.2
fully in its work	Disagree	18.9	37.4	57.6	59.8
(xxi) Religion is important	Agree	97.2	93.1	47.5	16.8
in my life	Disagree	2.8	6.9	52.5	83.2
(xxii) I like to discuss politics	Agree	53.6	47.7	36.7	45.4
and community questions	Disagree	46.4	52.3	63.3	54.6
(xxiii) Regular exercise is	Agree	78.2	79.4	76.1	67.4
important for me	Disagree	21.8	20.6	23.9	32.6
(xxiv) Our family do many	Agree	80.2	83.8	75.1	59.7
things together	Disagree	19.8	16.2	24.9	40.3

and higher degree of commitment to the church is of course a question that we have raised before and which clearly cannot be answered from these data.

Items (xv) and (xvi) in Table 5.17 perhaps reflect a concern with social justice. Commitment to the church shows a very strong association with the affirmation that solidarity with the weak is important to the informant. Only a minority of the two least committed groups give it their support. A more complex relationship emerges, however, in respect of the desire to change society. The highly committed prove most supportive of this opinion, but they are closely followed in this opinion by those individuals with no commitment whatsoever to the church. The two remaining groups report uniform, and much lower, support for this view.

Items (xvii) and (xviii) suggest that those who are committed to the church prefer to be more selective in their friendships and also that they are wary of unconventional experiences. Again, it is interesting to speculate whether these results reflect the influence of age, although again it is impossible to answer this within the current analysis.

The six remaining items present a rather mixed bag. The fact that the most committed would always vote for a party with a strong defence policy (though this view is more strongly held by the 'fairly' committed) seems at some slight variance with the fact that no difference emerged in their views on nuclear war. That those who are highly committed to the church should be very significantly more likely to engage themselves fully in the work of clubs or societies of which they are members is, however, entirely congruent with the trends evinced in Chapters 2 and 3 and suggests that church membership and activity 'spill over' into other areas of the individual's existence. Whether or not this suggests there is a positive basis for their higher satisfaction with life (as noted above) is again an interesting question. This particular finding perhaps also relates to that for item (xxii) which shows a positive relationship between church commitment and a liking for discussing politics and community questions. Again, this is consistent with the results of analyses reported in earlier Chapters.

It is not in any way surprising that those expressing high degrees of commitment to the church also affirm that religion is important in their lives. The positive relationship between church commitment and items (xxiii) and (xxiv) again make sense in terms of earlier findings. The importance claimed for regular exercise by the most committed groups perhaps gives further credence to the view that the church-committed are more active in various spheres and that this eventually manifests itself in higher levels of satisfaction with life. The fact that the most committed also claim that their family do many things together may of course simply reflect the higher incidence of married people in the most highly committed groups. These trends do, however, also resonate with two earlier findings in this section. First, the 'doing' may again emphasise the apparently active nature of the lives of people who are committed to the church. Secondly, the fact that these are undertaken in the family may be a practical manifestation of the fact that people with a high degree of commitment to the church tend to restrict their circle of friends.

Perhaps the overwhelming impression given by Table 5.17 is the generally 'positive' lifestyles of those with a high degree of commitment to the church. Not only do they express much higher levels of life-satisfaction, but they also show a more forbearing attitude towards material goods and generally appear to live more active and participatory lives than their counterparts with less religious commitment. At the same time, they prefer their experiences to remain within more or less predictable boundaries (not liking frightening or unconventional new experiences) and to be undertaken within a relatively predictable circle of friends and acquaintants.

Moving on to the last four questions in this section of the schedule, Table 5.18 further strengthens the impression that those with a commitment to the church on the whole spend more of their time with the family than do those with no such commitment. Although the largest single group of the uncommitted also profess to prefer to spend their spare time with members of the family, a very substantial number of their members also prefer to be with friends. It should, however, again be stressed that these differences may simply reflect the lower proportion of married people within the 'uncommitted' sample.

Perhaps somewhat contrary to certain of the inferences drawn from part of the results in Table 5.17, the highly committed showed no less liking for being with people whose ideas and values differ from their own. Nor was there any difference between the four groups concerned in the extent to which they reported feeling lonely. Table 5.19 finally, shows proportionately many more of the highly committed to describe themselves as 'very happy' than any of the

118

Table 5.18

Preferred ways of spending spare time

Commitment	*Highly*	*Fairly*	*Not very*	*Not at all*
Alone	9.7	9.1	9.4	11.6
With the family	68.1	67.0	61.0	49.2
With friends	22.2	22.7	27.5	37.6
In a crowd	—	1.2	2.1	1.6

Table 5.19

Description of oneself

Commitment	*Highly*	*Fairly*	*Not very*	*Not at all*
Very happy	39.7	27.5	27.3	26.2
Quite happy	56.8	69.2	67.8	64.4
Not particularly happy	3.4	2.7	4.2	9.4
Not at all happy	—	0.6	0.7	—

three remaining groups. Although the commonest response for all four is to see themselves as 'quite happy', a higher proportion of those with no commitment to the church describe themselves as 'not particularly happy'. These findings of course lend further support to the analysis of life-satisfaction in Table 5.17.

(v) Attitudes and behaviour in respect of alcohol

Table 5.20 reveals a very significant association between commitment to the church and the consumption of alcohol with, as might be predicted, more frequent consumption being reported by those with the lowest levels of commitment. This lower level of consumption was manifested in the significantly lower levels of beer, wine and spirits consumed by those with a high or fair degree of commitment to the church. As a matter of interest however — and again resonating with the findings of earlier Chapters — their consumption of fortified wine was rather (and significantly) greater than that of people who were not very committed or possessed no commitment at all to the Church.

Table 5.20

Frequency of consumption of alcohol

Commitment	*Highly*	*Fairly*	*Not very*	*Not at all*
Never drink alcohol	28.1	16.8	12.5	11.5
Very occasionally	43.2	39.9	30.9	20.9
Occasionally	20.5	35.7	39.6	40.8
Regularly	8.2	7.5	17.0	26.7

Asked how they would react if wine were served at a function, people in the four 'commitment' groups responded in the patterns presented in Table 5.21. This shows that, although the commonest response was to 'drink it', this was selected significantly less frequently by the highly committed than by any of the three remaining groups. Conversely, very many more of the highly committed would request something non-alcoholic (with the 'fairly committed' also being relatively numerous on this response). Other responses are presented in the Table, which yields a highly-significant difference between the groups in their reaction to this (hypothetical) situation.

Table 5.21
Reaction to being served with wine at a function
(Percentage choosing each response)

Commitment	*Highly*	*Fairly*	*Not very*	*Not at all*
Drink it*	50.0	61.6	70.4	67.4
Allow it to be poured and only sip it*	13.7	13.8	9.1	8.4
Say you want something non-alcoholic	17.9	10.4	7.7	5.8
Say you don't want anything to drink	6.2	3.9	4.9	4.7
Don't know – it depends on the situation	12.4	10.3	8.0	13.7

* significant association between commitment to Church and proportion choosing this item

The reasons proffered by individuals for drinking are contained in Table 5.22. Although seven of the twelve responses in this Table show a significant difference between groups with varying degrees of commitment to the church, the general order of importance of these twelve items remains very similar between all four groups. As against this, it should however be noted that the two least committed groups are significantly more likely to report using alcohol to relax, to facilitate social contact and create a better atmosphere; whereas those with a strong commitment to the church significantly more frequently report using alcohol to increase the value of a good meal, for 'medicinal purposes', in order not to appear self-righteous, and because they want to use their Christian freedom. It is obvious that, in the case of the least committed, the use of alcohol is woven into a fabric of social contact and relationships; whereas the fact that those with a high level of commitment to the church appear to feel the need to justify their use of alcohol to others or themselves again resonates with the findings of earlier Chapters.

Table 5.22 summarises the reasons for which those people who do drink do not drink more. It is apparent that there is rather more variation in the rank

Table 5.22

Reasons for drinking
(Percentage placing items in their first three choices, in order of importance)

Commitment	Highly %	Fairly %	Not very %	Not at all %
Easier social contact*	47 (2)	38 (3)	55 (2)	58 (2)
Easier to relax*	38 (3)	51 (2)	66 (1)	68 (1)
In order not to appear self-righteous*	21 (7=)	11 (8)	9 (9)	7 (7=)
Abstinence is out of date	6 (9)	4 (11)	2 (12)	2 (11)
Atmosphere is better with a little alcohol	24 (4)	32 (4)	42 (4)	49 (3)
Increase the value of a good meal*	70 (1)	56 (1)	47 (3)	48 (4)
Difficult to be TT in my job	1 (11)	3 (12)	3 (11)	3 (10)
Don't believe I would be damaged	23 (5)	26 (5)	22 (5)	21 (6)
Want to use Christian freedom⁺	17 (8)	8 (10)	6 (10)	0.6 (12)
Don't want to be different from friends	5 (10)	10 (9)	10 (8)	6 (9)
Medicinal*	22 (6)	23 (6)	11 (7)	7 (7=)
Other reasons	21 (7=)	21 (7)	21 (6)	22 (5)

* significant association between commitment to Church and degree of choice for this item

orderings of these items between the four groups, although on only eight of the nineteen items in this Table do significant differences appear. Thus, the less committed restrict their drinking in order to avoid a hangover, because they cannot afford it, and because a proportion of them feel they drank too much in earlier life. As against this, those more committed to the church limit their intake of alcohol because they do not want to risk dependency (although the trend is not entirely consistent across the four groups on this variable), as an example for their children and as an example for others (with highly-committed members of the sample being very different from all other three groups in this last respect) and because they have seen what alcohol has done to others. Finally, the most highly committed were less likely to point to 'other reasons' as their primary motives for restricting alcohol intake. Overall, one may infer that the reasons that the least committed avoid drinking more alcohol refer essentially to their own current life-situation or past experience, whilst the more committed are motivated either by moral considerations (such as setting an example) or fear of the effects alcohol might have upon themselves (avoiding the risk of dependency and the impression created by having seen what alcohol has done to others).

Table 5.23

Reasons for not drinking more
(Percentage placing item among first three choices in order of importance)

Comment	Highly %	Fairly %	Not very %	Not at all %
Damaging to health	40 (1)	46 (1)	53 (1)	46 (1)
To avoid a hangover the next day*	10 (11)	10 (10)	19 (7)	26 (5)
Resisting social pressure	6 (13=)	2 (17)	1 (18)	3 (15=)
Drinking in pregnancy damages foetus	2 (19)	3 (15)	2 (16=)	2 (18=)
Don't want to get drunk	33 (3)	29 (4)	39 (2)	39 (2)
Don't want to risk becoming dependent*	25 (5=)	18 (7)	25 (6)	14 (8)
Drank too much in earlier life*	4 (16=)	2 (18=)	4 (14=)	8 (12)
For the sake of those damaged by alcohol	4 (16=)	2 (16)	0.8 (19)	2 (18=)
Drinking and driving is dangerous and against law	21 (7)	35 (2)	34 (3)	35 (3)
Don't want to be a danger in traffic	6 (13=)	8 (12=)	6 (13)	7 (13=)
Don't like the taste	13 (10)	13 (9)	8 (11)	7 (13=)
Don't want to lose control	17 (8)	16 (8)	19 (8)	22 (6)
Don't want to gain weight	7 (12)	7 (14)	7 (12)	9 (10=)
Example for my children*	26 (4)	26 (5)	16 (9)	9 (10=)
Example for others*	25 (5=)	8 (12=)	4 (14=)	2 (18=)
Can't afford it*	16 (9)	26 (6)	28 (4)	34 (4)
Seen what alcohol has done to others*	37 (2)	34 (3)	24 (5)	21 (7)
Solidarity with friends	2 (18)	2 (18=)	2 (16=)	3 (15=)
Other reasons	5 (15)	8 (11)	8 (10)	10 (9)

* significant association with commitment to the Church

Non-drinkers in the sample were also asked why they do not drink, being offered the same range of responses as contained in Table 5.23. The numbers involved were too small to merit their being presented in a similar Table. It is, however, of note that teetotallers with a high degree of commitment to the church cited 'Christian conviction' significantly more often as a reason for total abstention. The less committed (and particularly the 'not very committed') on the other hand, more frequently pointed to the effects of having seen 'what alcohol has done to others' as a reason for their non-indulgence and they again proved more likely to refer to 'other reasons'.

Finally, highly-committed churchgoers proved more likely to believe that Christians should be total abstainers, to believe that Communion wine should be non-alcoholic, not to smoke and to be opposed to the freer availability of cannabis. All of these seem entirely consistent with expectation.

Conclusions

In the whole of the preceding analysis 'commitment to the church' has of course been entirely subjectively defined, the divisions around which our discussion was organised stemming from people's responses to a single question in the schedule. Within the present study, the concept of church commitment is thus perforce a rather ambiguous one and it is possible to identify at least three different meanings that might be attached to this term and which may accordingly be reflected in the findings we have reported.

In the first place, the term 'commitment' may have an essentially theological significance, referring to the strength of the individual's religious beliefs. From this perspective, the analysis in this Chapter would be assessing the effects of profound faith or conviction upon lifestyle, perceptions and behaviour. Secondly, the main referents of individuals when using the term 'commitment to the church' might be *organisational*, implying a loyalty to the institutional form(s) of Christianity, or to the more particular characteristics of their own religious denomination or place of worship. Finally, the factor(s) people have in mind could be of a more direct and social nature, referring to the (formal) activities and groupings that exist in their own local place of worship. This last would obviously connote involvement in a network of social relationships and emphasise that aspect of 'fellowship and contact with others' which featured as one of the answers given by several people as among their most important reasons for church membership.

Whilst all three of the above are likely to be inter-related, it also seems probable that each will weigh rather differently in the motives and perceptions of particular people. Whilst it is impossible to disentangle the influence of these factors from each other within the present data, it may be useful to bear these possibilities in mind in attempting to interpret particular sets of findings. However it is defined, commitment to the church clearly holds influence over a broad swathe of the issues and activities covered by the questionnaire. How, then, may we interpret its significance; and how might its influence relate to those of denomination, age and sex that have been shown in earlier Chapters to be important?

Commitment to the church has already been shown to be greater among women and the elderly. It seems highly probable that the higher degree of church commitment among pensioners, the widowed and those living in the same neighbourhood for eleven years or more may be explained in terms of the greater proportion of elderly people within the ranks of the committed. In the case of the widowed, we are probably also seeing the effects of the bias towards women among those committed to the church. The preponderance of political Conservatives among people committed to the church almost certainly bears witness to the influence of age; although it is harder to explain their slightly greater support of Liberalism in these same terms. Since all of these factors — with the sole exception of 'commitment to the church' — were also characteristic of Church of Scotland members, we may thus infer either that elderly members of the Church of Scotland will be less committed than the elderly members of other churches, or (as seems more plausible) that younger members of the Church of Scotland are less committed than their elderly co-denominationists and the younger members of other churches. If it is the latter, we cannot of course (at present) decide in what way they are less 'committed'. Why the owner-occupiers of houses or tenants in rented flats should emerge as more committed to the church than people who are renting houses or who are the owner-occupiers of flats is rather difficult to determine. In relation to the above one could, however, suggest that people who are renting houses or who are the owner-occupiers of flats will contain proportionately more individuals who are 'moving up' the housing market. This finding may therefore simply underline the apparently rather settled nature of the lives of most people who are highly committed to the church.

Not unexpectedly, the highly committed emerge as leading much more devotional lives than their counterparts with lower degrees of commitment, attending church, reading the Bible and praying more frequently, reporting a devotional life as having been the rule in their childhood, and having in most cases attended church with the same frequency throughout their adult lives. In all of these respects, trends among the highly committed are the direct antithesis of those reported by members of the Church of Scotland, who also predicted that their future level of church attendance would remain the same as at present. Since the concentration of elderly people within the Church of Scotland would lead one to expect no differences in these respects, one must conclude that a religious factor is operating here. This interpretation is further strengthened by the fact that women (who of course form the greater numbers in both the Church of Scotland and among church-committed individuals) also report higher levels of devotional activity, standing again in marked contrast to the apparent tendency within the overall membership of the Church of Scotland.

One area, however, where Church of Scotland members share a common pattern with women, the elderly and the church-committed is in the frequency of their tuning in to religious broadcasts and in the greater importance they (along with Roman Catholics) ascribe to the Minister or Priest as a source of information about church events. Reasons for people's membership of the Church seem only weakly related to any of the factors so far considered.

Those reporting a high degree of commitment to the church in general possess a more coherent system of beliefs in God, eternal life and life after death, see God as loving and helping, believe that Jesus died for our sins and is risen from the dead, that we stand before God after death, that heaven and hell are places of eternal bliss or suffering and that the Bible is a 'special' book, either in the sense of being 'true' in every detail or written by men who were inspired by God. On these and most of the other more subtle questions relating to the content of religious belief, age and sex play very little part. It seems very likely that here, we are talking of commitment in the sense of strength of faith and given the fact that Church of Scotland members are, as a group significantly less committed to their church than the members of other denominations (see Table 2.7, p.16) it is hardly surprising that Church of Scotland members reveal much less certain or uniform views upon these topics. This probably relates to the fact that, whilst the great majority of people in the sample saw human beings as a mixture of good and bad, the minority whose views on this matter appear to be shaped by the notion of Original Sin belong to the 'other' church group and that this view is also significantly over-represented among the highly committed. In further contrast to their highly-committed brethren, members of the Church of Scotland think less often about these issues.

People with a high degree of church commitment attach greater priority to the development of local Bible study and prayer groups and to improved co-operation between the Church of Scotland and other Protestant churches, on both of which factors their views correspond more closely to those of elderly people and of women. With women they are also at one in seeing Christian education as an area of priority for the church's future, whilst they share with elderly people an emphasis upon the need for spiritual leadership. Church of Scotland members also ascribe priority to Christian education, but disagree with people committed to the church in stressing the importance of social work and work with pensioners and the sick, both of which (along with help to developing countries) are seen as important by those with a lesser degree of commitment to the church. In the case of these questions, it seems likely that people are in the first instance adopting an 'organisational' concept of the church, although their views as to the priority that deserves to be attached to particular activities will then be tempered by more theological aspects of commitment. In this latter respect, Church of Scotland members clearly adopt a more pastoral (and perhaps more secular) perspective, which possibly reflects the rather less systematic pattern of their beliefs about God, Jesus, the Bible and the after-life.

The views of women, the elderly, the church-committed and the generality of the membership of the Church of Scotland converge over matters of personal and sexual morality, reflected in such issues as TV sex and violence, the classification of home videos, premarital sex and homosexuality. Church of Scotland members, however, are more inclined to see abortion as justifiable in certain circumstances, whereas the church-committed are significantly more likely to regard it as always wrong. Views on social issues are rather more diffuse. Church of Scotland members probably reflect the age and sex bias of their membership in their disinclination to go on strike (an attitude which they shared with the more committed), but commitment to the church diverges from the other three factors in showing no relationship to attitudes towards nuclear weapons. A complex interaction is clearly occurring here and it is impossible to tell whether age and sex are more influential than denomination or church-commitment in forming sexual mores but not social attitudes; or vice versa.

People with a high commitment to the church are remarkable for their significantly and consistently higher levels of satisfaction with life and for their apparently higher level of engagement in social activities. On many of these aspects, their responses are very similar to those of members of the Church of Scotland. One is initially tempted to explain this correlation in terms of their common core of elderly people. Elderly people, however, show generally lower levels of life-satisfaction than the young and it therefore seems that on this aspect, at any rate, a 'religious factor' does operate — an interpretation which gains extra credence from the fact that Roman Catholics share the same overall pattern. Stoical attitudes towards life and a tendency to do many things together with the family do, however, seem more likely to reflect the age-bias within the two sub-samples. Whether the higher degree of engagement in the life of clubs and societies and a liking for discussing politics and community questions are determined by a religious factor or by age is a question we may be able to disentangle in a subsequent analysis.

Religion has an undoubted influence on people's attitudes towards consuming alcohol and it seems highly probable that age-differences may be explained in these terms. The committed and members of churches in general consume less alcohol, although the committed and Church of Scotland members consume more fortified wine. The reasons given for drinking or controlling one's intake of alcohol seem extremely similar between the church-committed and the Church of Scotland, indicating that Christians have a more moral and self-conscious attitude towards imbibing alcohol; whereas those with less strong or no religious beliefs view alcohol as an aspect of one's social context, emphasising its functions as a social lubricant and personal relaxant. Again, we may be able to take these matters further in a later analysis.

CHAPTER SIX

DISENTANGLING THE PRIMARY INFLUENCES

Our analysis has thus far considered the possible separate effects of religious affiliation, age, sex differences and commitment to the Church upon attitudes, lifestyle and moral, social and political beliefs. Throughout our discussion we have, however, been made constantly aware of the possibility that these factors are related to each other in ways that may have an important bearing on our results. In particular, and to repeat a question that has been raised at several points already, how far can the differences that have been noted to exist between individuals affiliated to the Church of Scotland and the members of other groups within our sample, be attributed to aspects of their religious understanding and beliefs, or to the preponderance of women and elderly people within their ranks? The data-analysis in Chapters 3 to 5 has already thrown some light on this and other questions, but a more specific analysis of these interconnections and their effects may add a greater degree of confidence to our interpretation of those effects and/or introduce other possibilities into the conclusions we may draw.

The present Chapter will accordingly trace the relative strengths of the influences exerted by these factors, either individually or in combination, upon certain of those aspects of behaviour and belief that relate more closely to the essential objectives of the survey. With that end in view, the analysis reported in this chapter had recourse to a set of (suitably modified) procedures based on a statistical technique known as analysis of variance. In essence, this provides a test of the *homogeneity* of a set of data by testing how much of the total amount of variation within a sample is due to particular factors. To take an example from agriculture, if several varieties of potatoes are sown in different types of soil and treated with different types of fertiliser, the variation in the various yields of tubers may be affected by variety of seed, by variety of soil or by variety of fertiliser. An analysis of variance of the yields obtained from particular types of seed in varying conditions would enable us to disentangle the relative effects which these difference factors had upon the final results. Moveover, we could also assess the effects of interactions between these factors. Does, for example, a particular variety of potato do especially well in particular soil conditions? Applying the same logic to our present interests, we may be able to discern how far variations in those aspects such as lifestyle in which we are interested are attributable to denominational affiliation, sex or age. For present purposes, and because of the limitations imposed in the number of sub-divisions that can be made within the data by the relatively small numbers particularly of Catholics and those professing allegiance to 'other' churches, our attention will be confined to the effects of age, sex and church membership.

In this chapter the term church membership should usually be taken to mean denominational affiliation.

(i) General background factors

Our analysis in Chapter 2 pointed to a Church of Scotland membership who were rather more settled in their social position, this being reflected in the significantly higher proportion within their number, of people who had been resident at the same address for 11 or more years; and the high proportion, particularly in the non-church and other church groups, who were separated, single or divorced. The greater proportion of Conservative voters among Church of Scotland communicants might also suggest a greater acceptance of the social and political status quo than was the case for other groups within the sample. These associations were, however, complicated by the various patterns of interconnection that were also noted to exist with sex and age.

The analysis of these interactions and their effects suggests age to be the dominant factor in the apparently more settled and conservative position of Church of Scotland members. Thus, individuals' length of residence at their present address is entirely attributable to age, with religion having no significant effect. Similarly, when the effects of age, sex and religion are weighed against each other, age appears as the only factor that correlates significantly with political support. One may thus conclude that the apparently greater support for the Conservative party among Church of Scotland communicants is due to their greater average age, rather than aspects stemming from their religious beliefs. Age also proved (perhaps not unexpectedly) to be the primary factor relating to people's income before tax, with sex also emerging as a secondary influence in this respect. However, the results also show that age, sex and religion exercise a significant combined effect upon income, suggesting that elderly female members of the Church of Scotland and Roman Catholic Church have lower incomes than their counterparts in other church (or non-church) groups.

When the effects of other factors are taken into account, age (again, not unexpectedly) remains significantly associated with marital status. The interesting finding here is, however, that church membership shows a stronger relationship with marital status than does age *per se*. In other words, married or widowed people appear more likely to be members of the Church of Scotland and the Roman Catholic Church; and church membership is a better predictor of an individual's marital status than is age. Single, divorced and separated people thus seem less attracted to church membership than do those whose marital background has been more conventional or settled. Finally, and as suggested in earlier chapters, the single most important factor determining whether or not an individual had attended College or University was age. College or University education does, however, also show a significant (though secondary) relationship with religious affiliation. The most important determinant of failure to acquire further or higher education would thus seem to be the restricted opportunities that were available to earlier generations. However, people whose education has terminated with school appear more likely to be members of the Church of Scotland or the Roman Catholic Church, and the fact that age and church membership show no significant combined effect in this respect indicates that the tendency for the members of these two churches to have spent shorter periods of their lives in full-time education is related to some factors specific to the churches themselves, rather than to the older average age of their members. By contrast, members of other churches and individuals with no religious affiliation are significantly more likely to have gone through tertiary education.

To summarise briefly the apparent meaning of these findings, the position of Church of Scotland members established on the above matters in Chapter 2 seems largely attributable to their higher average age. The findings with regard to the relationship between church membership and marriage in particular, but also with attendance at College or University, do, however, leave some residual questions unanswered about the bearing which religious belief might have upon these factors. Our later analysis may provide some insights into these connections.

(ii) Religion and the Church

(It may be worth noting that non-church members were excluded from most of the other analyses in this particular section.)

Our analyses in Chapters 2 and 3 showed Church of Scotland members to be less committed to the church than communicants within other denominations; and that elderly people showed a higher degree of commitment than members of the younger generation. Given the high proportion of elderly people within the Church of Scotland (which should of course tend to make for a greater average Church of Scotland commitment to the church), these results, in combination, point to a generally lower level of church commitment to church affairs and activities within all or parts of the Church of Scotland sample. This interpretation would tend to be confirmed by the significantly higher degree of commitment, as reported in Chapter 4, by women whose numerical preponderance within the Church of Scotland should again make for a higher average level of commitment within that denomination.

When these factors were weighed against each other in the present analysis, age emerged as the single most important correlate of commitment to the church, with sex ranking second in statistical significance and church membership showing only a marginally-significant association with this variable. There was no significant interaction between age and church membership, and the suggestion that younger Church of Scotland members had for some reason become significantly less committed to the church than their age-counterparts in other churches and the older members of their own church is therefore not supported. The single most important correlate of church commitment was accordingly confirmed as age. The influence of church affiliation in this respect appears rather weaker than expected, but apparently still vigorous enough to account for the trends noted above.

Age and denominational affiliation were also highly (and more or less equally) significantly associated with frequency of attendance at church services, with the effects of sex being rather less important. These variables, however, showed no significant combined effect upon frequency of church attendance.

The pattern for the answers to the question as to how often respondents read the Bible shows all three factors to be significantly correlated, with age being the single most important determinant of this behaviour, followed by church membership, with sex in third place. Sex emerges as the factor correlating most highly with the frequency with which people pray; although in this case age also appears as a secondary factor almost equivalent in importance to sex, exercising an apparently much stronger influence than the denomination to which the individual belongs. In the case of Bible-reading, age and sex also showed a signficant combined effect, the direction of this association suggesting that elderly women are more assiduous or habitual readers than any other group, of this ultimate reference point for Christian belief.

These various results point fairly clearly to age as the most important determinant of strength of church commitment and devotional behaviour, with sex and denominational affiliation playing a more subsidiary role in shaping these areas of behaviour. Exactly the same pattern appears in respect of people's reports of the regularity with which they listen to or view religious broadcasts on radio or television. Again, age shows by far the major influence, with religious denomination and sex (in that order) showing secondary (though still statistically-significant), associations with this form of behaviour. Age and church membership also prove to have an extremely powerful effect in combination with each other, with elderly members of the Church of Scotland apparently tuning into religious radio and television programmes significantly more often than younger Church of Scotland members or communicants (whatever their age) within the two remaining denominational groups. Analysis of the relative significance of the relationship between age, sex and denominational affiliation and the various responses offered as reasons for retaining membership of a church again show age to be by far the most important of the three factors concerned. Thus, Table 6.1 (p.132) shows age to correlate significantly with a propensity to specify support for the church and Christian values; opportunity for Baptism, marriage and funerals; participation in services and communion; fellowship and contact with others; a wish to support everyday Christian life; and family expectations, as important reasons for continuing in communion with the church. In all of these cases, the values concerned are endorsed more heavily by the older members of the sample, and since these elements correspond very closely to those endorsed by Church of Scotland members in Table 2.13, it would appear that the generally more social and instrumental considerations proffered by Church of Scotland communicants as reasons for their church membership are largely attributable to their older average age.

By contrast, the fact that an emphasis on missionary work correlates significantly with denominational affiliation is consistent with the greater importance ascribed to this factor by Roman Catholic and other church members; but the data in the interactions column also demonstrate the combined effect of age and the denomination to which one belongs to be a more important determinant of attitudes in this respect than denominational affiliation alone. It would therefore seem that there is something about the value and belief systems of younger Roman Catholic and other church members which makes them attach greater importance to this sphere of church activity than their counterparts in the Church of Scotland. The only other factor of potential importance in this Table is the apparent significance of the combined effects of sex and denominational affiliation in shaping people's propensity to perceive support for the church and Christian values as an important reason for church membership. The interaction between these two factors is in fact rather less important in this regard than age *per se*; but it does appear that the female members of 'other' churches attach less importance to this variable than do women of the Church of Scotland or Roman Catholic Church. Overall, one may therefore conclude that the less radical views of Church of Scotland members concerning their position in the church are primarily attributable to the preponderance of older people among them, with sex and specific denominational beliefs being considerably less important.

Turning to individuals' reports of whether or not their parents had been regular church attenders, and including within this analysis those who are not members of any church, we find religious affiliation to be significantly associated with the reported frequency of church attendance of both father and mother; indicating (not unexpectedly) that current church membership is heavily influenced by the regularity with which both father and mother themselves attend(ed) church. In the case of fathers' church attendance, however, there is an additional (though less strong) association with age, which supports the interpretation attached to the trends in Table 3.7, that there has been a decline over the generations covered by this study in the frequency of church attendance by men (or at any rate, fathers) which has not been matched by a decline in church attendance among women.

Moving to that part of the questionnaire which dealt with individuals' beliefs in and about God and certain aspects of the Christian faith, by far the most important correlate of individuals' professed belief in God was denominational affiliation; although this effect disappeared when non-church members were removed from the analysis. Sex, however, showed a significant association with professed belief in God both when non-church members were *included* and when they were *excluded* from the data-analysis. Indeed, the influence of sex differences was increased when non-church members were included, giving strong support to our earlier finding concerning the relationship between sex and belief in the existence of the Deity, and suggesting that a high proportion of women who do not attend church do in fact believe in God. There are obvious implications here for a significant and potentially receptive group within the population whom the church's message is failing to reach; although perhaps more important is the apparently

Table 6.1

What are the most important reasons for being a church member?
*What are the effects of denomination, age and sex?**

	Denomination	Age	Sex	Interactions
Wish to support the church and Christian values	—	1	—	Sex and religion (2)
Opportunity of baptism, marriage, funerals	—	1	—	—
Participate in services/ Communion	—	1	—	—
Fellowship and contact with others	—	1	—	—
Support missionary work	2	—	—	Age and denomination (1)
Support everyday Christian life	—	1	—	—
Want to strive for justice and Christian solidarity	—	—	1	—
Natural to be a member of the Church	—	—	—	—
Family expectations	—	1	3	Sex and denomination (2)
Don't want to upset a relative/friend by leaving	—	—	2	Age and sex (1)
Other reasons	—	1	—	—
Never thought of leaving	—	—	—	—

* The figures in the columns of this and other Tables in this chapter indicate the relative strengths of the influence of particular variables (church membership) on the statement in question. Thus, a '1' indicates the variable to have been first in importance, a '2' second in importance, and so on.

increasing disinclination of males to believe in God or involve themselves in religious matters and activities.

Again omitting non-church members from the analysis, we find that denominational affiliation still correlates significantly with the belief that God controls our lives here and now, this trend being accounted for by the firmer endorsement by Catholics of this assertion. Again, however, church affiliation appears as secondary in importance in its association with this particular belief, with women expressing agreement with this opinion in far greater numbers than do men. The same essential pattern holds for people's beliefs in whether Jesus died for our sins and is risen from the dead. When those who are not members of any church are included in the analysis, denominational affiliation emerges as the most significant correlate of the individual's belief, with sex appearing as a secondary, though still important, factor. When, however, the non-church group are excluded from consideration, we find that sex is the most important single variable, with the effects of denominational affiliation being substantially reduced, though still remaining statistically significant. It would thus appear that women are much more likely than men to accept these basic tenets of the Christian credo. Even among churchgoers, sex exercises a much greater influence than denominational affiliation. Nonetheless, Roman Catholics show a significantly firmer endorsement of these beliefs than their counterparts in the two remaining religious groups. Belief in eternal life and in life after death show a somewhat different pattern, in that sex yields no significant association with these assertions when church-members only are considered: it is only church membership that shows any association with these factors, with the strength of belief of Roman Catholics again distinguishing them from their religious counterparts. But when the analysis is extended to include non-church members, we find sexual status emerging as an important secondary (after denominational affiliation) factor, giving further credence to the view that a large proportion of women who have no formal attachment to any church still subscribe to most or all of the basic precepts of the Christian credo. In none of the above is there any evidence of any of the factors of age, sex and church membership working in combination with each other to influence the pattern of people's responses.

Turning to the more detailed content of certain aspects of belief, we find people's views of God to be equally (and very heavily) susceptible to the influence of both sex (in particular) and denomination. Thus, women and both Church of Scotland and Roman Catholic communicants are more likely to view God as a loving figure who hears our prayers and controls our lives, whereas men and the members of other churches (non-church members having been excluded from this analysis) express 'intellectual' images of God. The pattern for denominational affiliation is, however, made more complex by the rather high proportion of Church of Scotland members who profess to 'no opinion' about God, or construe Him as a sort of distant, impersonal force; whereas significantly more Catholics see Him as an all powerful judge. Age also exercises an influence over these views, though this is much less marked than that for sex and denomination.

In contrast, however, to the above, opinions about what happens after death and about heaven and hell are not in any way correlated with sex. Rather, in both cases, the most important determinant of respondents' views is denominational affiliation (whether non-church members are included or excluded), with age adopting a position of secondary importance. We again find church membership appearing as the single most important correlate of the frequency with which people reported that they thought about these matters. Age also emerges as significant, though once again, its influence is secondary to that of denominational affiliation. As before, there are no interactions between the three primary variables of age, sex and denomination, in producing these effects.

There seems to be a broadly discernible pattern in the above findings. Age has undoubtedly had an important bearing on some of the more formal aspects of church membership and attendance; and this seems to reflect a generational difference in the strength of the religious environment within which people have been raised. The findings point quite clearly to a reduction over time in frequency of church attendance and a variety of related activities such as personal prayer, reading of the Bible and taking an interest in religious broadcasts. This trend towards a more secular pattern of life is, however, much more marked among men than women, with respondents having observed an apparently consistent trend towards men (fathers) attending church less frequently than women. Further and perhaps more important indications are, however, contained in the significantly smaller proportions of men who profess to accept a range of fairly fundamental aspects of the Christian creed, such as a belief in Eternal Life or that Jesus is risen from the dead. A number of these trends are overlain by differences between the denominations, with Catholics in particular appearing to subscribe to a much clearer and stronger set of religious beliefs. The fact, however, that no statistically-significant interaction emerges between denomination and either sex or age would suggest that not even Catholics are immune to the trend towards a more secular 'world view'; although one would require to have a similar exercise undertaken with a larger number of people from denominations outside the Church of Scotland before one could feel completely confident about such an assertion.

When we turn to consider the relative influence of the variables of age, sex and denominational affiliation upon the importance people attach to a number of possible initiatives within the church, we find the pattern presented in Table 6.2. This suggests fairly clearly that, of our three factors, denomination exercises the most important influence over the opinions and attitudes in question. Thus, not only is denominational affiliation significantly correlated with all eight of the initiatives specified: in the case of all but one (joint communion for Church of Scotland and other denominations) of these suggested initiatives, denomination shows a stronger association with the proposal in question than either of the two remaining variables. Sex also shows a significant association with six of the eight proposals listed and also combines with denomination to influence people's responses on two of the initiatives suggested. One may thus infer with confidence that the differences noted in Table 2.21 are primarily attributable to variations in the beliefs and attitudes of the different denominational groupings.

The same essential pattern is evident in Table 6.3, which shows that denominational membership is by far the most important determinant of the way in which respondents rank the relative importance for the church's future, of a range of possible activities and emphases. The main difference from Table 6.2 resides in the fact that age supplants sex as the factor that in general stands second in importance to denomination in its influence upon the choices made among these various alternatives. With respect to the questions raised in Chapter 2 about the apparently lower degree of social concern

Table 6.2

The effects of church denomination, age and sex on people's perceptions of the relative importance of the following factors

	Denomination	Age	Sex	Interactions
Joint services for the Church of Scotland and other denominations	1	—	—	—
Improved co-operation between the Church of Scotland and other Protestant churches	1	—	2=	Age and denomination (2=) Age, sex and denomination (4)
Joint Communion for Church of Scotland and other denominations	2	—	1	—
Local Bible Study and prayer groups including Church of Scotland and other churches' members	1	—	2	—
Joint effort about the under-developed countries	1	—	—	—
Church of Scotland and other churches should have a common view on Bible translation	1	—	—	—
Improved co-operation with the Roman Catholic Church	1	—	2	—
Improved co-operation in inter-church marriage	1	—	2	—

among Church of Scotland members over such issues as help to developing countries and increased awareness of economic and social injustice, it may, however, be worth noting that age and denominational affiliation are virtually equal in strength in the influence they exert over individuals' endorsement of help to developing countries as a desirable future priority for the church; whereas variations in the judgements of the importance of developing an awareness of economic and social injustice are in very large part attributable to the influence of denomination. Again the effects of any interactions between these variables is almost negligible.

(iii) Social and moral issues

An analysis of the differential significance of age, sex and denomination in shaping people's attitudes towards a strengthening of control over the amount of sex and violence screened on television, shows age to have by far the most important bearing on opinions on this matter; with sex exercising a strong secondary influence in this area, and denominational affiliation (including

Table 6.3

*Effects of denomination, age and sex on opinions
concerning developments for church's future*

	Denomination	Age	Sex	Interactions
Political awareness	1=	—	1=	—
Evangelisation	1	—	—	—
Social work	1	—	—	—
Help to developing countries	1=	1=	—	—
Work with pensioners and the sick	1	—	—	—
Personal renewal	1	—	—	—
Increased awareness of economic and social justice	1	—	—	—
The position of women in the church	2	1	—	—
Efficient organisation and good financial management	1	—	—	—
More spiritual leadership	1	3	—	Sex and denomination (2)
Christian education	1	2	3	—

Table 6.4

Attitudes on social, political and moral issues

	Denomination	Age	Sex	Interactions
Control over TV sex and violence	3	1	2	Age and sex (4)
Classification of home videos	1	2	—	Age and sex (3)
Would you ever go on strike?	—	—	1	
How acceptable is present level of unemployment?	1=	3	—	Age and sex (1=)
Opinion of nuclear weapons	3	2	1	
Acceptance of premarital sex	2=	1	2=	
Opinion of homosexuality	3	1=	1=	
Attitude to abortion	1	2	3	

non-church members) showing the weakest (though still statistically-significant) effects. Moreover, when one analyses the effects of the interactions between age, sex and denomination in this regard, one finds that age and sex combined exert a statistically-significant influence over people's views on televised violence and sex. Overall, these findings confirm the fact that older people, women and church members (and particularly, members of the Roman Catholic Church) are more supportive of the idea of stronger censorship. In addition, however, older women endorse the idea of official controls much more frequently than other groups, whilst younger men are significantly more likely to reject this proposition than any other group. These latter trends appear to operate independently of individuals' religious beliefs.

Church membership and age (in that order of importance) also correlate significantly with the view that there should be a system of classification for home videos; although contrary to the pattern for television censorship, sex seems to have no significant direct bearing on attitudes towards this topic. Again, however, age and sex do exercise a significant combined influence upon opinions of the need for classifying home videos, with the data again indicating that elderly women express the strongest support for such a policy. The same combination of sex and age also proves to be the most significant correlate of people's opinion of the present level of unemployment, with elderly women again appearing to have more conservative views in this regard, and young men tending to the opposite pole. Denomination *per se* also shows a singificant link with attitudes over this matter, with age also exerting a statistically-signficant influence. However, sex is the sole correlate of people's reported willingness to go on strike, whilst sex (appearing as the most important correlate), age (second) and denomination (in third place) all show a significant association with people's opinion of nuclear weapons.

Sex is thus confirmed as the most potent correlate of attitudes towards the possession of nuclear arms, with women being significantly more rejecting of the deterrent role of such weapons. Denominational affiliation, whilst still significant, is shown to make the smallest contribution to shaping people's attitudes over this matter. Perhaps more interesting for present purposes, however, is the fact that the prediction raised in Chapter 3, that age and church membership would interact to produce a significant effect upon opinions concerning nuclear weapons, is not supported by these findings. One can therefore only conclude that age, sex and church membership exercise independent influences on attitudes in this area, and that the greater willingness of Church of Scotland members to endorse the possession of nuclear weapons is related to factors specific to Church of Scotland beliefs themselves, these exercising a separate though subsidiary influence to those of sex and age.

In the case of opinions about television censorship, home video classification and the present level of unemployment, broadly similar (though not identical) patterns appear to hold. Thus, religion emerges as a strong correlate of people's opinions on these matters, with age also playing a correlate of people's opinions on these matters, with age also playing a significant role. The significant interactive effects on opinions concerning all between age and sex, with the trends pointing to elderly women as having more 'tough-minded' attitudes in these respects. The more conservative opinions of Church of Scotland members in particular towards the present level of unemployment, and of all three church groups towards video classification and television censorship would thus appear to be due to a substantial degree to some specifically religious factor, although age and sex (either separately or in combination) also appear to account for a significant proportion of the variation between groups in the sample. In other words, being elderly and female seems in particular to have an important bearing on one's attitude concerning such issues. Denomination, however, exercises a separate and highly significant influence on such attitudes, so that the religious differences noted in Chapter 2 with particular regard to members of the Church of Scotland cannot simply be attributed to the age and/or sex structure of the different church groups.

These and the other trends discussed above are all outlined in Table 6.4.

Also portrayed in Table 6.4 are the trends relating to abortion, homosexuality and premarital chastity. Age, sex and denomination are all significantly correlated with these three sets of opinions, although the overall pattern of the influence of these factors is rather different between the three areas. Thus, attitudes towards abortion are primarily linked with church membership (mainly reflecting the difference between Roman Catholics and the other groups); whilst views concerning the acceptability of premarital intercourse are most closely linked to age, with sex and denominational affiliation showing an equal degree of subsidiary influence. Attitudes towards homosexuality are most strongly correlated with sex and age, with men and older people being significantly more rejecting of such behaviour.

(iv) Lifestyle

Table 6.5 (pp.139–41) presents the results of an analysis of the relative contributions made by denomination, age and sex to variations in the responses on the 'lifestyle' section of the questionnaire. In order to facilitate interpretation and discussion, the statements have, as in previous Chapters, been organised into groupings that *prima facie* appear to be related to each other. The results are further organised into columns, with the first three columns outlining the effects exercised by the three primary variables considered independently of each other, and the remaining four portraying the influence exerted by each of the possible sets of interactions between them. As in previous Tables in this Chapter, the figures appearing in each column represent the degree of influence exerted by each variable relative to the others. Thus, a '1' means that the effect of the variable or interaction in question is greater than any other for that particular statement. Similarly, a '2' or a '3' point to influences that are of secondary or tertiary importance. It

Table 6.5

Differential strength of the links between lifestyle, denomination, age and sex

	Single effects			Interactions			
	Denomination	Age	Sex	Denomination and age	Denomination and sex	Age and sex	Denomination, age and sex
(i) In order to work more efficiently I cut down on social life and pleasure	—	1	—	—	—	—	—
(ii) One shouldn't show one's feelings at work	—	1	3	—	—	—	2
(iii) I like simple things and a natural way of life	1=	1=	—	4	3	—	—
(iv) The only way to get something valuable is to save for it	—	1	—	—	—	—	—
(v) I prefer to pay cash even if I have to wait for larger purchases	3=	1	2	—	3=	—	—
(vi) I think that private motoring has more disadvantages than advantages	—	2	1	—	—	—	—
(vii) I would like to change society so that material things matter less	2	—	1	—	—	—	—
(viii) Regular exercise is important for me	—	—	—	—	—	—	—
(ix) It would be useful for me to reduce my material standards	—	—	—	—	—	—	—
(x) Compared with other people of my age I've made a lot of foolish decisions in my life	—	1	—	2	—	3	—

(continued overleaf)

	Single effects			Interactions			
	Denomination	Age	Sex	Denomination and age	Denomination and sex	Age and sex	Denomination, age and sex
(xi) When I think back over my life I didn't get most of the important things I wanted	—	1	—	—	—	—	—
(xii) I've got pretty much what I expected out of life	2=	2=	—	1	—	—	—
(xiii) I wouldn't change my past life even if I could	—	—	—	—	—	—	—
(xiv) I have to a great extent the things that make life really pleasant and satisfying for people of my age	1	—	—	—	—	—	—
(xv) My life could be happier than it is now	1	—	—	—	—	—	—
(xvi) I am just as happy now as when I was younger	—	—	—	—	—	—	—
(xvii) These are the best years of my life	—	1	—	—	—	—	—
(xviii) I never felt better in my life	—	1	—	—	—	—	—
(xix) Compared with other people I get down in the dumps too often	—	—	—	—	—	—	—
(xx) I feel just miserable most of the time	—	—	—	—	—	—	—
(xxi) During the past few weeks I have felt particularly excited or interested in something	—	1	—	—	—	—	—
(xxii) During the past few weeks I have felt pleased about having accomplished something	—	1=	1=	—	—	—	—
(xxiii) During the past few weeks I have felt proud because someone complimented me on something I had done	—	2	—	1	—	—	—

(xxiv)	During the past few weeks I have felt on top of the world	—	1	—	—	—	—	—
(xxv)	When I join a club or society I engage myself fully in its work	1	—	—	—	—	—	—
(xxvi)	I like to discuss politics and community questions	—	2	1	—	—	—	—
(xxvii)	Solidarity with the weak is important to me	2=	1	—	—	2=	—	—
(xxviii)	I want to change society	1	—	—	—	—	—	—
(xxix)	In an election I would always vote for a party with a strong defence policy	—	1	—	—	—	—	—
(xxx)	Religion is important in my life	1	3	2	—	—	—	—
(xxxi)	If I had a teenage daughter I would let her go on holiday with her boyfriend	—	1	—	—	—	—	—
(xxxii)	If I had a teenage son I would let him go on holiday with his girlfriend	—	1	—	—	—	—	—
(xxxiii)	I like new exciting experiences even if they are a bit frightening or unconventional	—	2	1	3	—	—	—
(xxxiv)	It is best to live in an area where all the neighbours have a similar standard	—	1	—	—	—	—	—
(xxxv)	I restrict my circle of friends to a few	—	1	—	—	—	—	—
(xxxvi)	Our family do many things together	1=	—	—	—	—	1=	—
(xxxvii)	I am attracted by new religious groups outside the Christian Church	—	1	—	—	—	—	2
(xxxviii)	I am not specially fashion conscious	—	—	1	—	2	—	—

141

should also be noted that, for the sake of clarity, only significant effects are noted in the Table. A blank space in any column therefore means that the variable in question shows no influence of any note over the particular statement being considered.

The first nine statements in this Table relate to what in previous Chapters we have suggested may be interpreted as a stoical attitude to existence. Consistent with the findings and discussion in Chapter 3, we find that age is by far the most potent factor in shaping people's responses to these items. The greater preparedness of older people to endorse such notions as cutting down on social life and pleasure in order to work more efficiently, saving in order to acquire something valuable, and refraining from showing one's feelings at work give credence to the interpretation presented in Chapter 3, that social values have undergone a change over recent decades, so that younger people do not share the forbearing attitudes held by their elders. Perhaps also worthy of note is the fact that denomination appears to have a relatively minor bearing on the trends in this first section of the Table: and indeed, the contents of the particular cluster of items (iii), (v) and (viii) in which religious affiliation is identified as having a significant effect seem to have more to do with attitudes towards material possessions, rather than with what might more strictly be interpreted as stoicism or forbearance. In other words, older people's attitudes seem relatively independent of a 'religious factor' here.

Finally, the effects of sex are relatively modest in responses to this section of the questionnaire, with women wanting to change society so that material things matter less, whilst also rejecting the idea that private motoring has more disadvantages than advantages. The interaction effects in the last four columns yield four significant findings for this set of items, but these all emerge as relatively subsidiary. It is, however, interesting that religious affiliation, which shares first place with age as a determinant of people's liking of simple things and a natural way of life, should also yield significant interactions with age and sex in replies to this particular statement. The former is attributable to the propensity for elderly members of the Church of Scotland to endorse this item; but it is difficult to interpret the significance of the combined influence exercised by religious affiliation and sex in this respect.

The second cluster of items is organised around items that pertain to different aspects of life-satisfaction. Items (x)–(xii) seem to reflect appraisals undertaken by the individual of his or her past experience in life, and the degree of satisfaction this overview gives. Because they obviously have more experience upon which to reflect, elderly people not unexpectedly emerge as more dissatisfied with their previous lives than their younger brethren, and this is displayed in the primary significance attributable to age in the case of items (x) and (xi). In the case of item (x), age also combines with religious denomination (or more strictly, church membership) and with sex in ways that have a significant bearing on people's judgements of their own past foolishness. The interaction of age with sex reflects a greater tendency for young women to deny in greater proportion than either young men or older

142

women, that they have made foolish decisions. With regard to item (xii), elderly and (particularly) middle-aged Roman Catholics and members of the Church of Scotland seem more likely to report that they have got 'pretty much what (they) expected out of life', and this is displayed in the primary significance of the interaction between age and denomination/church membership as an influence upon responses to this statement. The additional independent (though secondary) influences of denomination and age upon responses to the same item confirm what was established in Chapters 2 and 3, reinforcing the impression of higher degrees of contentment (or is it self-satisfaction?) among the middle-aged, Roman Catholics and Church of Scotland members. Item (xiii), which seems to impinge on the same kinds of appraisal as the statements immediately before it, yields no significant findings. With items (xiv) and (xv), the focus of the respondent's reflections would seem to shift more directly towards an evaluation of his or her present life-circumstances; and this shows church membership as the only factor among those under consideration that has a significant bearing on such perceptions. Again, this endorses the finding of an earlier Chapter, which suggested that church members (though particularly, members of the Church of Scotland) are significantly more likely to express contentment with their current life-circumstances. But to repeat an affirmation made in Chapter 2, while remembering also that most people in the sample expressed satisfaction with their life, it would probably be more accurate to conclude that a majority of people succeed in achieving a reasonably satisfying niche or lifestyle, but that church membership gives some degree of immunity from sentiments of dissatisfaction. Alternatively, of course, satisfied people might be rather more likely to become church members.

The statements 'these are the best years of my life' and 'I never felt better in my life' possibly form part of the same nexus of items as were considered immediately above; or might alternatively be seen as relating to individuals' judgement of their physical capacities, rather than circumstances, as seems to be implied in the other statements. Whatever the correct interpretation might be, answers to both statements are significantly influenced by age, with young people more likely to agree with these assertions. Again, this repeats already-established findings. What is perhaps significant to note is that no other factors have any apparent bearing on these responses. Interestingly, the two items (xix) and (xx) relating to fairly constant or frequent feelings of depression show no association with any of the factors under scrutiny.

Items (xxi)–(xxiv) centre on evaluations of more recent experiences, pertaining as they do to such things as having felt particularly excited, pleased or proud about something during the past few weeks. Age is significantly linked to all four factors and as was established in Chapter 2, this is because young people are more likely to have become excited or interested in something, or received a compliment, whereas middle-aged people are more likely to have experienced a feeling of pleasure in accomplishment. In addition, young people are significantly more likely to feel 'on top of the world'. The interaction between age and church membership in their link with feelings of pride at having received a compliment is more difficult to interpret. It does, however, seem that young individuals who are members of a church are more likely to report such an experience.

On the whole, few surprises have been produced by the above analysis, and that continues to be the case for the remainder of these items. Thus, membership of the Church of Scotland is confirmed in item (xxv) as an important determinant of an individual's degree of commitment and activity on joining a society. Similarly, men and elderly people profess a greater liking for discussing politics. Age is also confirmed as a significant determinant of the importance individuals attach to solidarity with the weak; although in this connection, the interaction between age and sex is interesting in showing elderly women to be significantly less likely than their male counterparts to express this view, whilst younger and middle-aged women share more or less identical opinions with their male contemporaries.

The connection between church membership and a desire to change society is perhaps connected to the earlier-stated preference of church members to 'change society so that material things matter less'. Its referents, in other words, may be evangelical, rather than political in the more everyday sense of that word. Without more information, it is difficult to interpret this finding. Item (xxix) confirms age as the sole determinant of the preference for voting for a party with a strong defence policy and it would therefore seem that Church of Scotland members' greater support for this statement is due to their age-structure, rather than to factors related to the beliefs they hold. While it is fairly obvious why church affiliation should be the most significant determinant of people's agreeing with the statement that 'religion is important in my life', its endorsement by a significantly higher proportion of women and elderly men underlines the comments made earlier in this Chapter about the apparent decline of interest in religious affiliation among men and in the younger generation.

The statements concerning permission to teenage sons and daughters to go on holiday with a partner of the opposite sex show age to be the only factor exercising a significant influence over such attitudes: it does perhaps give some cause for surprise that church denomination plays no significant role in this regard. In only 3 of the remaining items (xxxiii), (xxxvi) and (xxxviii) does church denomination, either on its own or in interaction with other factors, show any significant effect upon the pattern of responses given. Thus, membership of the Church of Scotland is confirmed as a significant determinant of an individual's propensity to report that 'our family do many things together'. In addition to, and independent of, this specifically religious effect, elderly women are also significantly more likely to report regular involvement in family activities. Elderly Roman Catholic and Church of Scotland members also emerge (in the interaction effect reported for item (xxxiii)) as significantly more averse to new or unconventional experiences; although in this case, being female or elderly are in themselves apparently more important determinants of timidity or diffidence about confronting the unusual. Finally, there is a significant interaction effect between sex and

144

church membership which has a bearing on individuals' predilection to be interested in fashion; but one finds this hard to explain. In most of this section of the questionnaire, age is in fact confirmed as the most important single determining factor.

Perhaps the single most important conclusion to be drawn from the above analysis is that, whilst religious affiliation/church denomination is confirmed as exercising an influence over a variety of the 'lifestyle' areas considered in the present questionnaire, its overall effects are subordinate to those in particular of age; and that the two aspects of lifestyle in which it seems to exercise its most specific and coherent influence pertain to people's acceptance of their lot and tendency to report their life as satisfying, and to the clear propensity of Church of Scotland communicants to play an active role in societies of which they are members. These two phenomena are quite possibly related, in that the contentment reported by Church of Scotland members stems from their wholehearted commitment to groups and activities in which they are involved. It is perhaps in these areas that one sees the greatest redemption of and compensation for the rather 'static' picture that has emerged of Church of Scotland members from earlier parts of our analysis. One feels bound to reiterate the view that the current dependence of the Church of Scotland for its membership upon women and elderly people cannot be healthy for the Church (nor, one hastens to add, would it be satisfactory if its membership were mainly male and young); and the problems of reversing this trend seem particularly severe in view of the apparent change that has taken place towards more secular views among men and the young. The fact that the statement 'religion is important in my life' is supported by church members, women and the elderly serves only to underline this conclusion. Across the spectrum of lifestyle statements, the above analysis has, however, pointed to the overriding significance of age as a determinant of attitudes and responses.

(v) Attitudes to and consumption of alcohol

Age, sex and church membership all emerge as significantly correlated with the reported frequency of alcohol consumption. Sex seems to be the most important determinant of a person's alcohol consumption, with age second and church membership seen as third in importance. A significant interaction effect between these three elements in fact confirms elderly female church members to be significantly more abstemious with regard to alcohol than other groups.

The same broad pattern emerges in respect of beer-drinking with sex, age and church membership (again in that order) all being significantly related to the reported frequency with which individuals drink this beverage. Here, however, the significant effects of interaction are confined to those between age and sex, with elderly women being confirmed, whatever their religious affiliation, as the group who drink beer least. But sex exercises no independent influence over the likelihood that people will drink wine. Age is by far the most significant determinant of this behaviour, with denominational affiliation having only secondary significance. Elderly women are, however, again identified as least likely to indulge in consumption of this form of alcohol, with a significant interaction effect emerging between these two variables; and the interaction effect between age, sex and membership of the church also proves to be significant. The findings in respect of wine consumption accordingly point once again to elderly female church members as the least frequent users. The fact that age exercises no significant independent effect on this area of alcohol consumption does, however, suggest that younger women (particularly those who are not church members) have taken to wine drinking.

Age emerges as the sole significant determinant of consumption of fortified wine; and it would thus appear that the greater frequency with which Church of Scotland members were noted in Chapter 2 to indulge in the consumption of sherry or port for instance, is entirely attributable to the greater average age of Church of Scotland members. However, reported consumption of spirits shows the by now familiar pattern, with sex, age and membership of the church correlating in that order with individuals' propensity to consume this strongest form of alcohol. Again, age and sex combine to form a highly significant influence, with elderly women proving to be the least inclined to consume spiritous liquor; with the three-way interaction between age, sex and denominational affiliation also yielding a significant association. Elderly female church members, therefore, are the ones who least frequently drink spirits.

Greater age and being a member of the female sex and of an organised church all have a significant effect upon the likely frequency with which a person will imbibe beer, spirits or wine — though, interestingly enough, not fortified wine. The lack of a direct correlation between sexual status *per se* and wine drinking does, as mentioned above, suggest that women are beginning to drink wine more frequently; although the reverse pattern could of course explain this finding, in that men may simply drink less wine than either beer or spirits.

The pattern of responses in Table 6.6 suggests denomination to be a relatively unimportant factor in shaping people's reasons for drinking. Thus, age is the strongest correlate of a propensity to report easier social contact, ease in relaxing, a wish not to appear self-righteous, and 'medicinal' purposes as the main reason one drinks, with younger people proffering the two former, more social and instrumental, reasons for indulgence in alcohol consumption, whilst older people emerge as possibly more inclined to feel the need to justify alcohol consumption, with their more frequent appeal to medicinal benefits and a desire to avoid appearing self-righteous as their main reasons for indulgence. In the case of sex, the tendency for men to cite the improvements rendered in the social atmosphere, the difficulties created by the work environment for anyone who wants to abstain, and a belief that it

Table 6.6

Importance ascribed to reasons for drinking

	Denomination	Age	Sex	Interactions
Easier social contact	3	1	2	—
Easier to relax	2	1	3	—
In order not to appear self-righteous	3	1	2	Sex and denomination (4)
Abstinence is out of date	—	—	—	—
Atmosphere is better with a little alcohol	—	—	1	—
Increase the value of a good meal	—	—	—	—
Difficult to be TT in my job	—	—	1	Sex and denomination (2)
Don't believe I would be damaged	—	—	1	—
Want to use Christian freedom	—	—	—	—
Don't want to be different from friends	—	—	—	—
Medicinal reasons	—	1	—	—

would in any case not be detrimental to individual health or constitution emerge as the most significant influences on drinking behaviour. Denominational affiliation, however, appears subordinate in its effects to those of both age and sex.

Table 6.7 shows church membership to be an apparently more powerful determinant of why those people who do drink do not drink more; although even here, the range of its influence again appears inferior to that of both age and sex. Thus, a specifically denominational influence seems primary in respect of people's desire not to lose control, to set an example for children (supported also by a less marked association with a desire to set an example for others) and to remain within their financial budget, as reasons for restricting their intake of alcohol. Membership of a church also predisposes people to refer to the dangers of drinking and driving (though in this case subordinate to the effect of sex) as a reason for exercising restraint in the use of alcohol; and significant interactions between age and church affiliation suggest that older church members are more likely to restrict their alcohol intake in order to avoid either getting drunk or gaining weight, whilst elderly female church members also refer to the risks of becoming dependent if their intake of alcohol were to be greater. Sex, however, is highlighted as perhaps

Table 6.7

Reasons for not drinking more

	Denomination	Age	Sex	Interactions
Damaging to my health	—	—	—	—
To avoid a hangover the following day	—	1	—	—
I am resisting social pressure	—	—	1	—
Drinking in pregnancy damages the foetus	—	1	2	Age and sex (3)
Don't want to get drunk	—	2	—	Age and denomination (1)
Don't want to risk becoming dependent	—	2	—	Sex and denomination (1)
Drank too much in earlier life	—	—	1	—
For sake of those damaged by alcohol	—	—	—	—
Drink and driving dangerous and illegal	2	—	1	Age and sex (3)
Don't want to be a danger in traffic	—	3	1	Age and sex (2)
Don't like the taste	—	2	1	—
Don't want to lose control	1	—	—	—
Don't want to gain weight	—	—	1	Age and denomination (2)
Example to my children	1	2	—	—
Example to others	2	1	—	—
Can't afford it	1	2	—	—
Seen what alcohol has done to others	—	—	1	—
Solidarity with friends	—	1	—	—

the most important factor in shaping people's responses to this question, with 7 of the 16 first-place responses occurring in relation to this variable.

With regard to the few remaining questions, variations in opinion as to whether Christians should be total abstainers seem almost entirely attributable to variations in the responses of church and non-church members. Church membership also emerges as a significant determinant of the opinion that communion wine should be non-alcoholic; although the influence of age over answers to this question is even more significant, showing the high resistance of older people to the thought that alcoholic wine should be imbibed at a communion service. These two results present a slight paradox, in that the significantly greater support (though still by a minority) of elderly people for a policy of total abstention among Christians seems due to the effects of religious belief, whilst endorsement of the notion that communion wine should be non-alcoholic appears to be rather more influenced by age than by affiliation to a church.

Finally, although denominational affiliation is confirmed as a significant determinant of whether people smoke, its effects emerge as inferior to those of sex. Sex differences are also confirmed as highly significant in shaping people's attitude to the freer use of cannabis; although here, it shares equal influence with the combined effects of age and denomination, with older church members also repudiating more permissive practices in the use of cannabis.

Conclusions

The above analysis has, at times, of necessity, had to simplify certain technical points; though one hopes it has been successful in marrying the requirements of statistical validity with at least broad comprehensibility. What, however, would seem to be the main conclusions to be drawn from the above?

First, and to state a point that is a matter of common observation, but which is also borne out strongly by our findings, age is a primary determinant of religious affiliation and the degree of importance individuals attach to formal church attendance, as well as to more informal aspects of their personal beliefs and devotions. The data suggest a decline in recent decades in people's frequency of church attendance, and this therefore seems to be most effectively interpreted as a generational difference. The trend towards a more secular lifestyle is, however, more marked and established among men than among women, with a whole range of sex-related differences appearing over aspects such as prayer and Bible reading, as well as simple attendance in church. Moreover, this trend does not seem to be confined to the Church of Scotland, although its effects may be more pronounced there than within the boundaries of the Catholic Church.

It is at one level perhaps surprising that age and sex seem more important than denomination in shaping individuals' attitudes towards the variety of social and moral matters summarised in Table 6.4. Whilst religious affiliation/denomination does correlate significantly with attitudes to certain of these matters, its influence is in general very much subsidiary to that of the other two variables. This leads one to suggest that attitudes within the church are on the whole more strongly influenced by the characteristics of the individuals who become church members than they are by the belief or teachings of the church itself. This is, of course, no bad thing, given the fact that all of the topics covered in this section of the questionnaire are open to varying interpretations of 'rightness' or its opposite. There is, however, perhaps room for concern in the fact that churches (and particularly the Church of Scotland) are so heavily dominated by women and older people within their membership. If the membership is becoming more homogeneous in terms of sex and age, then where will the variety of other inputs to discussion and debate within the church come from, to ensure diversity and proper consideration of such issues within the church itself?

Responses on the 'lifestyle' section of the questionnaire give further ammunition to the view that church membership exerts a less strong influence than do age and sex over the various aspects of attitude and behaviour encompassed by these questions. Where, however, church affiliation does produce significant effects, they are towards generating greater contentment expressed by people with their lives, and also towards encouraging people to play a wholehearted part in the activities of groups to which they are attached. Thus, people affiliated to a church are less likely to feel that their life could be happier than it is now, and to report that by and large they see themselves as having the things that make life pleasant and satisfying. In addition, older people who are also church communicants also prove significantly more likely than other groups to estimate that they have got 'pretty much what they expected' out of life, and to be less likely to feel they have made a lot of foolish decisions in the course of their lives. Church members also report themselves in significantly greater proportions as liking simple things and a natural way of life, with denominational affiliation also interacting significantly with both age and sex to affect people's attitudes in this regard. We come back to the question of whether the satisfaction reported by church members (though again, particularly by members of the Church of Scotland) may more accurately be equated with complacency or with a deep sense of contentment generated by fulfilment over a range of life tasks. In other words, does satisfaction reflect achievements over areas that are being judged according to a set of high expectations, or is it more strongly due to fulfilment gauged against a much narrower range of goals and expectations? The rather staid impression given by the general profile that has emerged throughout this analysis of Church of Scotland members perhaps inclines one to the latter view. But this is a question that is probably better answered by reflection and discussion within the Church itself.

Finally, denominational affiliation again seems to have a rather limited impact upon attitudes and behaviour concerning alcohol. It does, however, exert some primary influence over people's reasons for not drinking more than they do, and these seem in the aggregate to relate to feelings of responsibility towards other people, covering as they do such items as not wanting to lose control, setting examples for children and for other people, and an acceptance that drinking and driving are dangerous.

With particular reference to the group which sponsored this research, membership of the Church of Scotland would therefore seem to be related to more staid and conservative behaviour and attitudes among its members. At its worst, this may lead to a complacency with a lifestyle that is pursued within a set of rather narrow limits and expectations. At its best, however, it is correlated with socially-responsible attitudes and values and a commitment to social action that may induce Church of Scotland members to play a leading role in social life. Part of the task ahead of the Church is to translate that message into terms that will accord with the needs and commitments of a wider group than it is currently reaching.

II. COMMENTARIES

CHAPTER SEVEN

A CHURCH COMMENTARY

The Very Rev J G Matheson

I have no doubt that this *Survey* is a work of major importance, and ought to be studied by all who are in any position to influence the Church's strategy of mission in our time. Although I have some sympathy with the criticism of the *Lifestyle Survey* made at the last General Assembly, that the questions asked of respondents omitted some matters involving 'essential work of the Church', I would like to congratulate and thank the Board of Social Responsibility for initiating this study.

Since most of my working life has been spent as a Congregational or Parish Minister, and because I regard Parish Ministry and Mission as the basic, continuous, most urgent and most fascinating work we have to engage in, I shall confine the comments that follow to that field. What help does the *Survey* give us in assessing the task before us in our parishes today? What are the priorities it seems to show? And what prospects?

Given that the finding of any statistical survey on such matters as belief and behaviours can be challenged on various grounds (as the *Survey* itself acknowledges) it seems to me that certain trends in the religious scene in Scotland are confirmed beyond doubt. Some of them make gloomy reading.

We have to take home to ourselves the awareness that the Church, and especially the Church of Scotland, has failed to catch the interest and commitment of the young people of Scotland. The *Survey* shows that for the 16 – 24 age groups, so far as the Church of Scotland is concerned, only a tiny percentage, 6.2%, are in that category. We have to ask ourselves why the energy and enthusiasm of young people so largely bypasses the Church? Perhaps we should also ask whether the invitation to the Church, and the invitation to Christian pilgrimage, in the minds of young people, are one and the same.

Until we have enlisted a far higher proportion of young people into the Church it will remain crippled, lacking in the imagination and courage needed to interpret the Word of God for today's world and to follow its guidance.

Similarly a far smaller proportion of men than women are finding their place in the membership of the Church. We knew that, but to see it set out in the statistics is daunting. We must not brush off the question why the attraction of the Christian way means so little to twentieth-century men.

When we come to statements of their belief by Church members and others the suspicion is confirmed that the specific Christian doctrines are losing their hold. Can it really be true that about a quarter of the members of the Church of Scotland are not sure that Jesus died for their sins, or that He is risen from the dead? (There was no question asked about belief in Jesus as the Son of

God.) Only a little over half declared belief in the individual's life after death.

Equally disheartening are the statistics about members' attitudes to the Church's out-thrust in evangelistic mission, and in concern for the underprivileged in the world. The problems of the unemployed in this country and starvation in the third world do not seem to weigh heavily. Indeed the answers here are so startling that they are hard to believe. If they are true they may be part of the answer as to why young people are not attracted to membership. A Church that appears to be elderly, lukewarm in its convictions and uncommitted to its mission, turned in on itself and not unduly concerned with what is happening in the world at large has no drawing power for healthy young minds.

The conclusion is, I believe, thrust on us that it is time for a searching review of the Church's teaching methods.

During the lifetime of those who have responded to the questions addressed to them in the *Survey*, the Church of Scotland has built its teaching programme on three main pillars. Those are, Religious Education in schools, the Sunday School and pulpit preaching. Taken together they have not been effective it appears, even in building up the faith and Christian practice of those Baptised in our Churches, still less in attracting others to join us. Perhaps there should have been a fourth locus of teaching – the class of preparation for membership. It is not mentioned in the *Survey*, and from one's own observation there is such a lack of consistency and thoroughness in this area that it cannot stand alongside the other three.

From the beginning of its story the Reformed Church of Scotland has laid a lot of stress on Religious Education in schools. It will be generally agreed that in our State schools we can no longer place reliance on it for the Christian nurture of our young people. Though we cannot abandon, and must rather increase our efforts to give it its proper place, it is likely that for the forseeable future it will be a marginal rather than central element in our Church's teaching structure.

We have put resources into Sunday School programmes and methods on a large scale. Eminent Bible scholars and trained teachers have given their expertise to preparing both a suitable syllabus and other teaching aids for the various ages. Sunday School teachers are, taken as a whole, a splendid band. The children, at least in the early years, are eager and happy. Yet they leave Sunday School, or so it appears, remarkably ignorant of the foundations of the Faith and even of the Story of the People of God. Only a small minority go on to eventual membership. Are we on the wrong set of rails?

It would be impertinent of me to suggest that I know the answer. In one respect, however, it has long been clear to me that our whole Sunday School apparatus has been at a great disadvantage. For the convenience of parents, classes meet concurrently with Morning Service. Apart from a brief interlude in Church, which bears only a faint resemblance to the essential spirit of worship, children are excluded from the normal worship of the people. That is a serious mistake. Reverence for God comes not through classes for children, but in the act of worship along with the family and community into which they are born and of which they are a vital part. We must encourage

156

them to share in the worship of the faithful.

If I am right in that judgement then we are faced with the necessity, not only of finding a different time for classes, but also with setting forward a radical transformation of our traditional style of Presbyterian worship. Except in rare cases it is simply not adapted to retain the interest and participation of children. That is to say it is unsuitable for family worship. Why should it be thought impossible to reform our pattern of worship? The Reformation Churches did it. The Roman Catholic 'Risorgimento' did it. There are examples of living worship of the people all over the world.

The third pillar of our normal teaching structure is preaching. D T Niles, one of the great preachers of our century, was preaching in my Church in New Zealand. His sermon was a powerful presentation of the Presence of the Risen Christ. As we walked home to the manse he spoke little. I judged he needed to wind down. At the house door we were met by one of the children, aged about eleven. He said, 'Were you in Church this morning?' She said, 'Yes.' 'Did you listen to the sermon?' 'Oh yes.' 'What was I preaching about?' Immediately the answer came, 'You said Jesus is with us, just as really as the person next to us.' Daniel Niles relaxed completely and said with a lovely smile, 'If I get across to a child of twelve I reckon I have succeeded.' How much of our Scottish preaching is aimed at that target – a child of twelve? It is interesting to note that the *Survey* shows our adult membership has a minority of people who have had higher education.

Even at its magnificent best – James Stewart, Murdo Ewen Macdonald, David Read – preaching, if it is to be a teaching medium, has to be supplemented. It can confirm our faith, inspire us to fresh effort, lead us into the holy place of worship. It will always have a high place, our hopes, in the Church's life. But more is needed if the Christian Faith is to be taught in the context of today's secular society. There is no other context. It is interesting to note from the *Survey* that the Roman Catholic Church, which lays less stress on the sermon than the Protestant Churches do, seems to have better results in teaching the fundamentals of the Faith. So far as its teaching function is concerned, preaching has to be followed up by a more intimate relationship with the people. We do not even know the questions in their minds, far less help to answer them, without that. In some congregations the classes of preparation for membership are thorough enough and continue long enough to give opportunity for such closer contact. It would be good to know what priority is being given to them throughout the Church. Meetings for Bible Study attract only a tiny percentage of members (and others) by their very nature. Valuable as they are for those who take part they are not likely to be a major factor in the teaching process. There is also the danger of them becoming an exclusive group. Difficult as it is, however, to find any widely popular method of adult education in the Church, we cannot give up the search. The monologue sermon cannot deal adequately with the great questions all our people, from school days on, have to face; about God, the authority of the Scriptures, the Divinity of Christ, life after death, and the moral dilemmas of modern society such as abortion, euthanasia and the bomb.

It is time for the Church, led by its education experts, to face up to our present failures in teaching. It is time also to look with fresh eyes at our ways of worship. Individually there are brave spirits who are attempting just that. They need the support of the whole Church.

Some of the findings of the *Survey* are positive and hopeful, especially regarding those who do not write themselves down as Church people. It seems the majority of them believe in God. Does that indicate only a residual 'folk religion'? And is 'folk religion' to be written off as of no account? Significant numbers accept the Christian teaching about Christ's death and resurrection and His promise of eternal life. It confirms the view that has grown stronger throughout a long pastoral ministry, that in spite of the corrosions of secularism there is a steady goodwill towards the Christian faith and the Church. We need not be timid in our evangelism, only sensitive. It has been suggested that we are faced today, not so much with unbelief as with indifference. That is not my experience. In many cases it is not so much indifference as disappointment. The issues that trouble human minds today are big and urgent. The Word, if it is the Word of the living God, will bear on those issues, not in tightly defined doctrines and codes, but in signals of hope.

It remains that the ways of the Spirit are essentially different from the ways of the world. In business and commerce we increasingly find profit in bigness: great mergers, expensive publicity, concentration of power. But we work in a different field – from faith to faith. The real evangelism is in personal meeting. Relationship is the veins and arteries of all religion. It is when we know people, that we love them. It is through human love, which is also divine, that God makes Himself known.

CHAPTER EIGHT

A SOCIAL COMMENTARY

Morag Faulds

The *Lifestyle Survey* has been extensive and methodologically sound, involving the selection of a final random group of 605 from Church of Scotland membership, whose responses have been compared with a matched final random group from the general population, representing 103 members from other Churches, and 247 others who have declared no church affiliation.

The *Survey* succeeds in exploring matters of personal belief and the relationship of those to social behaviour and outlook, thus revealing in the final analysis something of the involvement and influence of Church of Scotland membership in the life of the community. Some disappointment must be expressed that early indices reflected the unrepresentativeness of Church of Scotland membership in age terms, thus undermining the hope that the data gathered would be reasonably representative of the (adult) Scottish population.

In this paper I am responding to an invitation to comment on the survey results from the perspective of my own experience as a social worker, drawing upon the interaction as revealed in the analysis, between social factors and matters of personal belief, attitude and behaviour.

In the context of this task, it is perhaps important that I briefly share with the reader my understanding of the focus and relevance of social work, and attempt to explore that inherent conflicts in practice for the individual social worker, especially the Christian social worker.

Social work is founded on three beliefs; firstly, there is the primary belief in the intrinsic worth of every person by virtue of his being human.

As a social worker who believes that the Christian interpretation of life represents the truth, I have turned many times, both in practice and in teaching, to the following words of Margaret Tilley[1] when my responsiveness and compassion were, at times, in grave danger of flagging in the face of social situations which aroused exasperation, sometimes fear, or even repulsion; when it became difficult to love what is not naturally loveable, as in families with enduring multi-problems often self-perpetrated, or as in gross criminal acts and in very profound handicap.

Margaret Tilley writes: 'Witness to the belief that people matter equally is not the monopoly of Christians. Many humanists also show it, but the Christian has no excuse for ignoring its importance, for it lies at the heart of his faith, and he can turn to God to be re-convinced, when it all seems more than usually absurd and irrational. For, in terms of a materialistic world only, it is indeed irrational to believe that every person really matters; and because it is a quite unworldly belief, one suspects that its source, even when not recognised as such, is always spiritual and that as Simone Weil says, "Whenever the afflicted are loved for themselves alone, it is God who is present.'"

Secondly, social workers believe in man's social nature as well as his uniqueness. This recognises the complementary nature of these two aspects of man's nature, and this also implies deeper issues of social responsibility between man and his social world, often involving social workers in situations of crucial moral choices, as in child versus parent rights, in abortion, or in situations where the protection of society conflicts with freedom of the individual.

Thirdly, there is the belief in the capacity of all man to grow and change throughout their lives. The concept of positive freedom to make rational choices is very central to this notion of change. Holding to such a belief is not to deny the various constraints on an inordinate capacity for change, some derived from his biological endowment, limited intelligence or physique, and some derived from his social environment, such as material, emotional or educational deprivation.

The moral dilemmas facing social workers are thus echoed in all society, and for the Church in particular. They are increased by the growing demand for support from different individuals and groups made upon the scarce resources in society and throughout the world. To this is added the number of recent legislative innovations which are perceived by many to have shifted the legal difinition of morality in a permissive direction, and there has been a steady increase in the rates of divorce, delinquency and violent crime, and much of the latter is linked to addictions such as drugs and alcohol.

In the face of the above, value judgements on the relative importance of the need of one individual or one group over that of others, involves social workers in decisions which are often painful and difficult. We often fail in our endeavours.

I do not wish to infer that social workers who do not acknowledge a sense of divine authority in their approach to their work are in any way less compassionate or effective in their service than others who do. For me and for many colleagues employed in the voluntary and statutory sectors, or directly under the auspices of the Church, one simply attests that one's grasp of this authority, even in its weakest form, has proved to be an irresistible and transcendent dimension to our work. It beckons us beyond rational and intellectual understanding of much of the human despair and social injustice with which social workers are daily concerned.

Situations of immense conflict for social workers and other professional groups are often seen to arise along a professional/Christian doctrinal divide, such as in issues relating to prolongation of life as in abortion and euthanasia. All have to do with one of the great Christian doctrines, the sovereignty of God and the sanctity of human life[2], on the one hand, and responsibilities relating to man's social world, usually his family, on the other.

The knowledge base of social work places new emphasis on psychological theory. The difficulty of assessing human behaviour on the basis of moral standards has been compounded and confused by an assessment which interprets behaviour on the extent to which a person complies with the 'norms' defined by psychological theory, that is, within the mechanics of human behaviour and of personality development.

It has become the 'norm' to talk about the immature rather than the immoral, the inadequate instead of the lazy, the deviant rather than the pervert. This conflict places enormous responsibility on the individual social worker, especially the Christian, to be clear as to the baseline of his values and standards. Students who hold Christian beliefs always experience particular difficulty in handling the moral conflict inherent in behavioural theories.

For social workers and for many other professional carers in our society there exists the temptation to perceive their particular expertise and particular area of knowledge of human relationships as the main answer to the ills of individuals and society in general. Politicians, economists, media representatives and others who shape our lives through legislative, economic and communication means, also believe in the efficacy of their particular efforts to solve the larger social problems.

The disturbing truth is that individual and societal problems now permeate our lives on an ever increasing scale, revealing an increasingly disordered and confused society, with a diminishing faith in the authority of parents, professionals, politicians and others to provide appropriate answers.

It is with a very profound sense of our own powerlessness and our limited effectiveness in the responsibilities undertaken by us, that social workers and other Christian professionals look to the Church for divine authority to guide and influence our interventions in the lives of people. Conversely, of course, the Church needs to harness relevant professional knowledge available within its membership and elsewhere.

The late Dr Martin Lloyd-Jones held the view that 'there is a crisis of authority in society today.'[3] It is one from which the Church cannot stand aside. Indices in the *Survey* in the broad area of religion and the Church, support the view that the source of this crisis lies mainly in the Church itself, in the extent to which it has removed itself from, or, as demonstrated in their responses to questions of fundamental truths of Christian doctrine, some Church members have abandoned the divine authority of Christ, of His Word, and of His Spirit. The gravity of the situation in contemporary society requires a clear and distinctive response from the Church of Scotland and other churches, based upon the authority of the Scriptures. The *Survey* suggests 'that attitudes within the Church of Scotland are, on the whole, more strongly influenced by the characteristics of the individuals who become Church members than by the beliefs or teaching of the Church itself.'

This begs some questions. What body of divine doctrine requires to be accepted by Church members? Have ethics become a growing substitute for Christian doctrine? Or is it possible to detect a growing reluctance now within our society even to think in moral terms? If this is so, is it a reluctance to acknowledge a widespread confusion between what is moral and what is moralistic, compounded by a general decline in religious faith? Perhaps decisions which should command a value judgement are now more often pragmatic, attuned to the economic pressures of an intensely materialistic society, or do they, in large measure, reflect the cynical fatalism of a nuclear age?

Theological issues and Church witness, as reflected in the survey analysis are, and will continue to be, the subject of major concern elsewhere. They have received brief comment in this paper as the power of witness, through preaching and pastoral work on the one hand and the distinctive nature of caring and social responsibility challenging the Church on the other, are inseparable elements of the Church's mission. Caring for others has always been a characteristic of Christianity. Both the Scriptures and tradition indicate the extent to which the Church and all Christian people have a responsible part to play in carrying out such social duties. Like all ideals, that of perfect Christian commitment to the service of mankind, is seldom attainable by human beings.

The Church, across all denominations, attempts to fulfil this mission today through a range of different avenues, of which four can be identified.

Firstly, it is accomplished through a combination of countless, unrecorded acts of individual support given by individual members of a congregation, or through the participation of local churches within a district, in planned and regular forms of social service in collaboration with existing statutory and voluntary social services.

Secondly, a more recent form of service, aimed towards the development of a more caring and healing community, is now being offered through the formal introduction of a Christian counselling service. An example of this work is Network,[4] in Bristol. The aims of Network are (a) to encourage and support the formation of care groups within local churches; (b) to be a referral and resources agency for those involved in Christian counselling; (c) to organise training and (d) to offer Christian counselling to Christians and non-Christians in the Bristol area. Where a Christian is being counselled, Network will wish, with the person's consent, to work where appropriate, with whoever has pastoral responsibility for that person in their own Church. Counsellors will be Christians, chosen for their acknowledged gifts and experience. Network workshops are planned over a twelve month sequence, and the following are examples of current topics: addiction; bereavement; the use of the Bible in counselling; spiritual problems; marriage problems.

The third avenue is through professional social workers, appointed under the auspices of the Church. Most people are agreed that social work, in different forms, is a direct implication of the Christian Gospel, but they may see little place for professional social work on the part of the Church in the modern Welfare State. Others consider that pastoral and social work are indivisible and consider that the Chruch should provide a social services structure of its own, as exemplified by the Church of Scotland. In this way, the Church of Scotland not only supplements but also meets many gaps in the existing statutory services. For example it has led the way forward in the development and provision of resources to meet special areas of need associated with problems of addictions and senile dementia. Its major contribution to residential provision offers the more attractive benefit of choice to persons when making crucial decisions regarding their own future care or that of relatives.

The fourth avenue in the Church's mission of social responsibility lies in the relevance and strength of its distinctive contribution on issues of local and national social policy.

This survey analysis provides some fairly serious clues to some of the social factors which act either as constraints or supports to the attainment of the Church's mission of care and social responsibility in contemporary society.

The analysis of general background factors in the sample as a whole, of Church members and the general public group, reflects two social factors of major significance, a bias towards older age groups and middle class occupations when compared with the Registrar General's census figures for the Scottish population. Closer scrutiny, however, reveals that the age composition of the sample, with many fewer members in the age group 16 – 24 and rather more in the age group 45 and over, compared with the general population, has been clearly weighed in this direction by the age structure of the Church of Scotland members. The age structure of the remaining sample shows no significant difference to that of the country as a whole, when the Church of Scotland group is removed.

A significantly higher proportion of women, either married or widowed, many of pensionable age, are also found in the Church member group, than in the general public group, a factor again possibly related to the difference in the age structure of the two groups.

Another social factor which one would also select as of particular signficance centres on the higher percentage of single persons (31%) in the non-Church member group, compared with 13% in the Church of Scotland. Single people appear less attracted to church membership, as also do divorced and separated people than those whose marital backgrounds have been conventional or settled.

The Church profile, represented by the above analysis, is therefore one which is unrepresentative in terms of age groups, sex, social class and social status. As commented in the report, 'for the Church itself, the problem is the wider and more important one of sustaining a range of opinion and debate within its own ranks, which ensures that its message touches on issues, and is at least tempered by attitudes and approaches, which concern the whole range of society.'

The range of responses to the questionnaire on the attitude of members to social and moral issues, reflect a cluster of core values normally associated with traditional middle class older groups. These include a commitment to the values of hard work, responsibility, delayed gratification, social discipline, reflecting lifestyles associated with fairly staid and conservative behaviour and attitudes, lived within a set of rather narrow limits and expectations, all with a degree of passivity and acceptance. Security and satisfaction seem to lie in 'staying put', with being reasonably content to remain within a fairly circumscribed circle of relationships and attachments.

Data collected under the broad area of religion and the Church would indicate that age and sex were also seen to be the most important determinants of strength of Church commitment. While this is true of women, the survey also indicates a trend towards a falling off in Church attendance and a more secular pattern of life was more marked among men.

By virtue of its particular age structure, the above picture of Church membership is particularly representative of lifestyles in the Church of Scotland, and it raises several important issues which are of relevance within the specific remit of this paper.

It would appear, in the first place, that the Church of Scotland is failing in its mission to many living in the most deprived and vulnerable social areas, of inner urban districts. Cheap accommodation in such areas attracts students, immigrants, young married couples without children who are ineligible for local housing lists, homeless persons and addicts, and now, in addition, an army of young people on the search for employment.

In our highly mobile society many young families experience few opportunities to put down lasting roots in housing estates or in middle class suburbs, into which they move only to be faced with the expectation of a further early move, on to job redundancy, early retirement in the case of older families, or simply to follow in the wake of a highly volatile and rapidly changing industrial structure. Many such families find few social supports in such areas where social relationships are fairly impersonal and can be experienced as uncaring.

There are historical precedents for the Church to reach outside its specific locality to give a direct Christian service across the range of social need described above. Indeed, although this does not emerge in the survey analysis, the Church of Scotland and other denominations have already laid the foundation of such work in a number of inner city areas. While surveys of this kind point up major trends, exceptional and particular areas of divergence may remain unrecorded.

However, the main thrust of the survey's findings clearly challenge the Church of Scotland in particular, to develop more creative ways of being a caring as well as being a strong witnessing community, despite, as clearly depicted in the survey, currently lacking the influence of constant personal mixing with other social classes and interests.

There are many possible answers to this challenge. Certainly the Church of Scotland might more critically examine appropriate ways in which it could use and collaborate with existing social networks and other sectors of society already attempting to find some answers to contemporary social needs. These would include sectors engaged in prompting health education, leisure activities, law enforcement, educational opportunities, social care and many more under the general umbrella of the statutory and voluntary sectors.

The Church could encourage more members to do voluntary work with secular agencies, such as Citizens' Advice Bureaux, Marriage Guidance

Councils, children's panels, and more imaginative and realistic good neighbour activities. Some specialised preparation would be required to undertake some of those tasks, and good neighbour roles would involve some requirement to be kept informed concerning local services.

It might also be possible for the Church to explore different ways of using the existing network of Chaplaincies already attached to schools, prisons, hospitals, hospices, the army and to industry.

The second major issue supported by the age factor revealed in the survey indices, is the belief that the Church of Scotland is failing to attract younger members. This can be regarded as the most worrying and troubling evidence emerging from the *Survey*. It means that the Church is failing to influence young people, amidst a host of other influences competing for this attention and devotion.

For the Church, priorities of concern for young people must surely be primarily directed to action within the Church itself. Many young people, Sunday School teachers and youth leaders do help and support other youngsters within the Church. Important questions concerning the preparation and support which they receive in their teaching need to be asked. What links do they have with parents? Perhaps the most crucial question is, why does the church lose young people at the point in their early teens when they are beginning to think seriously for themselves on many important issues?

Young people appear to be at the receiving end of many confused messages on issues currently in high silhouette in their peer groups, as in the use of alcohol and other drugs, and in the area of sexual relationships. A particular example of this situation arose when the *Clayson Committee (1973)*[5] reviewed the Liquor Licensing Laws of Scotland and made recommendations on what changes might be made in the public interest. In recognising the comparatively much higher incidence of alcohol abuse in Scotland than in England and Wales, the Committee accepted the fiscal controls (Taxation of Liquor) were similar in each country and Licensing Laws were marginally different. The Committee therefore, looked to social controls, controls which derive from the attitudes of a society and its practice in relation to the consumption of alcohol, for an explanation of the major difference in level of alcohol abuse. It found evidence of strong and conflicting attitudes to the use of alcohol. One study, carried out on behalf of the Scottish Home and Health Department's Health Education Unit found that it was youths from homes with the more extreme attitudes and practices to alcohol, abstentionist and heavy drinking, who experienced most difficulty in coping satisfactorily with alcohol in society. American studies further emphasised that strong and conflicting attitudes to alcohol within a society are an obstacle to the reduction of alcohol misuse. The Committee reported, 'We respect the views of those who consider that all consumption of alcohol is harmful and that it should be restricted as far as possible; we do not see why they should be expected to change or suppress their views for what they may regard as a purely expedient purpose. On the other hand, we think it right to say that as a matter of observation, this strong polarity of view is a factor in the situation which conduces to alcohol misuse in Scotland. In particular the message that all consumption is harmful makes it more difficult to establish distinctions between what are socially acceptable and socially unacceptable standards of conduct in the consumption of alcohol.'

These considerations led the Committee to propose that 'whatever changes were later recommended in the licensing Laws of Scotland, in present Scottish circumstances it is in the area of social control that improvement is most required if the serious problem of alcohol misuse is to be ameliorated.'

An analysis of the situation on use of alcohol in the survey reading, age, sex and church membership all emerge as significantly correlated with the reported frequency of alcohol comsumption. Sex seems to be the most important determinant of a person's alcohol comsumption, with age second and church membership seen as third in importance. A significant interaction effect between these three elements in fact confirms elderly female Church members to be significantly more abstemious with regard to alcohol than other groups.

While the overall responses in the *Survey* continue to reflect a range of confusing messages, they also provide an indication of some diminution in polarity of extreme attitudes on the use of alcohol in Scotland. At the same time it demonstrates, in respect of the Church of Scotland, that church membership seems to have a rather limited impact upon attitudes and behaviour concerning alcohol, with overall effects again subordinate to those linked to the lifestyle of elderly female membership.

It would appear therefore, that young people, especially the vast numbers outwith the church, will be even less likely to be aided or influenced by this situation. This must be a major cause for concern, in view of the ever increasing evidence of abuse of alcohol by young people.

One further social factor of considerable significance pointed up in the survey, is the matter of social status and its relationship to current church membership. Overall, with the exception of widowed persons, there is evidence of a relative absence of single, divorced and separated people from membership of the Church. In respect of the Church of Scotland, 13% of this umbrella 'single' group compares with 31% of the non-church member group.

This umbrella group represent a very diverse range of changing family patterns. Nowadays, the one-parent family is more often caused through separation or divorce, than through widowhood and single motherhood.

It is important to acknowledge that many such families with children have happy stable relationships with the same problems which arise in all families as the children grow and develop. Many, however, are very vulnerable to breakdown, due to financial hardship, poor housing, unemployment, lack of support and social isolation, and consequently they are unable to provide children with security and appropriate opportunities for development.

The changing scene is represented in the following statistical picture. At the last census in 1981, there were approximately 98,000 lone parents in Scotland, and of families with children, 1 in 7 are lone parents. A rise of 68% on the

1971 figure is represented in this figure of 98,000. The main contributory factors are the rising divorce rate and the rising proportion of illegitimate births, now 1 in 7 of all births, born both to married and single women.

Every day, on average, 36 marriages are ended. The number of divorces annually is still rising. The 1960 figure was 1,928; in 1983 it was 13,238[6]. It is now acknowledged that 1 child in 5 is likely to experience parental divorce before reaching the age of 16, and 1 in 8 before reaching the age of 10. In the face of these changes, there are one or two trends which have direct relevance to the Church.

Traditional, conventional marriages remain the popular living arrangement but it has now become one of several options, it is more easily broken up, and fewer are marrying. Civil marriages are on the increase and a greater balance between ecclesiastical and civil marriages is developing.

In her early study *Someone to turn to: experience of help before Divorce*[7] Anne K. Mitchell, points out that the many partners in marriages 'at risk' do not have family or friends available to them, and are thus deprived of discrete local help which has many advantages over professional help in that family members are more readily and continuously available, they may share the same personal values, and, unlike professional help they may be given it appropriately when it has not been asked. When professional help is required, medical and legal advice is sought as top priority as such professional services may normally be required.

It is clear from the study however, that the majority are reluctant to seek additional counsel and support, more appropriately available from the Clergy and from social workers. As 50% of all children in care come from one-parent families, their wariness of social worker intervention is perhaps more understandable, though it is as regrettable as in the response to the Clergy.

The situation described above reveals many one-parent families as particularly vulnerable members of society, with a large number of such families as outwith Church fellowship and its caring support. The attitudes expressed by the dominant membership of the Church of Scotland towards premarital behaviour and on unconventional and more liberal family activities, will not be unrelated to the lack of involvement and influence of the Church in the lives of these families. One may also conclude that it is also related, whether consciously expressed or otherwise, to the apparent frequency with which the Laws of the State governing marriage and divorce are not in accord with Scriptural requirements.[8]

As far as children involved are concerned, too many confusing messages again prevail. For many adults concerned, there is a very urgent need for the Church to develop skills in counselling and concileatory work in order to give a contructive contribution to the development of such services in the community.

Finally, the survey analysis clearly confirms the traditional commitment and the continuing priority accorded by members of the Church of Scotland to practical social involvement, in particular through work with the elderly and handicapped. This is achieved through individual members' activities, and by field and residential staff working directly under the auspices of the Church.

This is a priority which will continue to present itself with every increasing insistence in our ageing society. We are now witnessing a perceptible shift in favour of more community care. Families are now expected to undertake more caring of dependent relatives, without any real matching increase in supportive public services.

Frequently the relatives of the very aged, the over 75's are themselves quite aged – perhaps a spouse or a sibling, often a daughter – or they are at least middle-aged, and they have now become the major carers of their elderly relatives.

Perhaps the traditional activities undertaken by the Church of Scotland, in respect of the elderly and the sick and handicapped, could be more usefully directed towards seeking out those 'carer' relatives under strain, in order to provide appropriate and timely respite and support. Such support often prevents an acute crisis from developing into inevitable breakdown. The crucial social factor in this situation is that the main church membership is largely drawn from the elderly female group. They are already much involved in this area of social responsibility and could virtually assume the formal role of an appropriate self-help group in many instances. Alternatively, the Church could act as a catalyst in helping to establish local branches of Associations of Carers, affiliated to the National Association.

Primary health care teams who are engaged in screening of the elderly, pay particular attention to the needs of the recently bereaved, the recently rehoused and those immediately discharged from hospital. It might be in the interests of many elderly people in an area particularly those without a church connection, for the churches to establish links with the local primary health care team in order to offer support and care where acceptable.

In this paper an attempt has been made, through the medium of the survey, to respond to a specific remit by assessing the range and distinctive characteristics of the caring activities of the Church of Scotland, and as a consequence draw some brief conclusions regarding the involvement and the influence of the Church of Scotland membership in the life of the community.

Analysis of responses in the survey clearly indicates how beliefs, social behaviour and outlook relate to social factors of age, sex, social class and social status. In respect of the Church of Scotland membership this combination further determines their perception of the boundaries of their social world and therefore, the range of their social responsibilities. This world is seen to be relatively narrow and circumscribed, creating more disincentives than incentives to the development of the church's mission of caring and its influence in the community.

As already described the church promotes social care through a range of different avenues. Church membership of the Church of Scotland supports and gives priority to traditional forms of social care in respect of the elderly, and sick and handicapped persons. It is argued that these activities, currently undertaken by church members and professional social work staff in the church, must not only be sustained but also be developed in more realistic ways to meet changing patterns of need, resulting from changing policies of care.

Particular emphasis has been expressed regarding the apparent failure of the Church to make a distinctive and influential contribution to the lives of young people in the community in particular to those identified as 'at risk'. In this context, attention has been directed to the experimental, formal counselling services which have been set up with some success under the auspices of the church in other areas. These services are particularly aimed, in some instances, to attract the interest and concern of some people through concentration on social issues of major concern to them.

The rank ordering table in the survey which lists developments for the church's future, rather surprisingly accords low rating by all three church groups to that area of social responsibility which refers generally to issues of local and national social policy. The report reads, 'None of the 3 groups view the Church as a force for justice and social change, but the Church of Scotland in particular is not seen (or desired) as a radically reforming force by its members' and further, 'there is agreement across all four groups on the uniformly low priority they accord to the position of women in the Church and the low importance they attach to "political awareness".' The precedence given to parochial interests, above that of wider societal matters, is exemplified in the preference by church memberships for provincial rather than national newspapers and in the popularity of the *Sunday Post*.

As it is a fairly well established fact that the Church of Scotland intervenes with some rigour and effectiveness on issues relating to local and national social policy, some explanation of this apparent discrepancy with the survey analysis may lie in the low importance attached by women to practical awareness, and the low priority accorded to the position of women in the Church, when set against the fact that elderly women comprise the major membership of the Church of Scotland. A further explanation may rest in the apparent distance between senior church adminstrative activities and those linked to Church membership.

The overall picture represented by the survey analysis reveals serious gaps in the discharge of its caring mission by the Church of Scotland and a corresponding poverty and weakness in the involvement and influence of Church of Scotland membership in the contemporary life of the community. This situation presents the Church of Scotland with an enormous task when considered in conjunction with another important area of the survey analysis, which finds 'that attitudes within the Church of Scotland are, on the whole, more strongly influenced by characteristics of the individuals who become Church members than by the beliefs or teaching of the Church itself.'

The late Dr Martin Lloyd-Jones has left us the following passage in his writing, 'We think that we alone can do it. We are greatly concerned. We hold our conferences and bring out our proposals. But they come to nothing. Then, when we are quite exhausted, after all our great campaigns, conferences and our brilliant organisation and after we have spent all our money and things have still gone from bad to worse, God unexpectedly – in the last place where you would ever have expected Him to do so and through the last person you would ever have thought of – suddenly sheds forth the Spirit. Then the Church rises to a new period of glory, of power and of influence.'

REFERENCES

1. Religion and The Social Worker. *Social Work Quarterly*, April, 1962.
2. As in *Psalm 139*.
3. Authority by Dr D Martin Lloyd-Jones. First banner of Fourth Trust Edition 1984.
4. *Network Newsletter* (**1**) Bristol 1986.
5. *Report of the Departmental Committee on Scottish Licensing Law*, HMSO, 1973.
6. Registrar General *Annual Report (Scotland) 1983*.
7. *Someone to Turn to: Experiences of Help Before Divorce*. Ann K Mitchell, Aberdeen University Press, 1983.
8. As in Matthew 19 vv 3 to 12.
9. Authority by Dr D Martin Lloyd-Jones, *Op.cit,* 1984 p.91.

CHAPTER NINE

A COMMENTARY FROM THE PERSPECTIVE OF THE TREATMENT OF ALCOHOLISM

Dr J Chick

Surveys of drinking habits have been conducted in many developed countries in the past twenty years, including Scotland. Five Scottish surveys, commissioned for various purposes, are listed in Table 9.1. These were based on interviews conducted at the home. Postal questionnaire studies, such as the present study, are not available for comparison. A higher response rate is obtainable using the expensive method of interviewing rather than using a postal method. The present study only obtained an overall response rate of 41%, and the bias towards older people, females and high social class, has occurred. It is probable that the responses in the present study from the general population sampled have a bias towards those with church commitment because of the clear Church of Scotland sponsorship of the general population survey. Furthermore, a church sub-sample has been specially included. Table 5.20 indicates that church commitment is related to less frequent drinking and a higher rate of abstension from alcohol.

Abstension from Alcohol

All surveys of drinking habits in Britain show that being elderly, and being female, are associated with higher levels of abstension from alcohol. The bias in the present study towards older people and women may account for the higher levels at abstension found in the present study (see Table 9.1 above). However, in Clydebank (Saunders and Kershaw 1978) a similar level of abstension was found. Plant and Pirie (1979) also found more abstainers in the South West (Glasgow and Ayr) than in Aberdeen and Inverness (15% as opposed to 8%).

We cannot say from the tables prepared by the study whether the trend towards more abstainers in this study is entirely accounted for by the age and sex bias of the sample. It seems unlikely since if we only look at the 65 year-olds and older, there is still a higher rate of abstension. Dight (1976) found abstainers in this age group amounted to 25% and Ritson et al (1981) found a similar figure.

In the present sample 30.5% of the elderly were abstainers. It seems likely that the whole sample is indeed biased also in favour of church affiliation and that this accounts for the slightly high abstension rates found. The social class bias in the study would not have a bearing, not being a predictor of frequency of drinking.

Table 9.1
General Population Interview Surveys of Adult Drinking Habits in Scotland

Author(s)	Date of Survey	Area Sampled	Response Rate %	Number Responding	Abstension Males %	Abstension Females %
Dight (1976)	1972	All Scotland	80	2453	5	12
Saunders and Kershaw (1978)	1976	Clydebank	82	3608	9	26
Plant and Pirie (1979)	1976	Ayr, Glasgow, Aberdeen, Inverness	70	2056	6	15
Knight and Wilson (1980)	1976	Glasgow, Edinburgh, Dundee, Aberdeen	89	1656	7	11
Ritson et al (1981)	1979	Lothian	71	984	6	15
Crawford et al (1985)	1982	Highlands,	70	797	6	15
		Tayside	70	808	2	7
Present Study (postal)	1984	All Scotland	41	997	10	21

One other possibility is that in postal surveys respondents may dissemble and minimise their drinking more than interview subjects. We know that in interview studies there is under-reporting of alcohol consumed since data on sales or production of alcohol invariably is less than completely covered by surveys. Part of this is due to respondents minimising their consumption, partly because surveys probably miss out some of the heaviest drinkers. This effect is likely to be somewhat greater with postal studies.

It is no surprise to find that there are more abstainers amongst church affiliates than non-church affiliates. However, the rate of abstension, given the bias towards older people and females in this study, is not so high in Church of Scotland members (17.3% versus about 10% for the Scots as a whole) as some might have expected. The Church of Scotland is far from teetotal.

Frequency of Drinking

In the life of Scotland today, frequent drinking is less associated with alcohol problems than is the amount drunk in a session (see, for example, Crawford *et al* 1985). This is also the case in the Scandinavian countries. Since this study did not attempt to quantify consumption, only frequency of consumption, there is no way of saying whether any respondents are putting themselves at risk of social or health problems arising from their drinking.

Reasons for Drinking

The list of reasons for drinking offered to respondents in the present study were not identical with those used in other studies in the United Kingdom. In other work, drinking to celebrate and drinking as part of sociability are the mostly commonly endorsed reasons. Of the options offered in the present study, easier social contact, ease of relaxing and 'increasing the value of a good meal' were the most popular (see Table 2.28). It is curious that 'medicinal' is still offered as a reason for drinking – by 19% of Church of Scotland respondents although only 10% of others. Alcohol's only medicinal usage recognised today is to increase the blood flow to the limbs in certain rather rare types of circulatory diseases. There is a suggestion emerging from the research on the causes of heart disease that small amounts of drinking, that is one or two drinks per day, may reduce the risk of heart disease. This research is still at a preliminary stage. It is most likely that the reason why 'medicinal purposes' was often endorsed by the elderly (by 35%) is that particularly elderly, female Scots were exposed to a belief that drinking alcohol was in some way immoral but could be justified for health reasons.

Church members do not offer as a reason for drinking that the 'don't want to be different from friends' any more frequently than non-church members (Tables 2.29 and Table 5.22). It is amongst the young where such social pressure might be expected to be strongest, although there was no age by

Church membership interaction on this item. Tentatively it can be concluded that Church membership does not place young people in a conflict about being different from others at least with respect to moderate drinking.

Reasons for Not Drinking or
Not Drinking More

Chapter six draws attention to the finding that church membership, even after controlling for the older age and sex bias of church memerbship, is associated with 'not wanting to lose control', 'drinking and driving is dangerous', and setting an example to their children and to others.

Church members also tend to feel that they cannot afford to drink more (Table 6.7). Those church members who drink tend, it seems, to be more socially conscious about their drinking. 'Staying in control of oneself' may be seen either as taking a socially responsible attitude or as a reflection of what we loosely call the 'Calvinist' tradition. Social class may have influenced these findings, however, and has not been controlled for.

Abstinence is slightly more common in church members than in the general population but neither in this survey nor in Dight's 1972 survey, nor Ritson *et al*'s 1979 survey is religious belief the most prominent reason. Amongst women, especially older women, being 'brought up not to drink' is the more important component of their abstinence. But in men, in Dight's survey, the commonest reason offered (and the second commonest in females) was that they had seen the bad effects of alcohol on others particularly in the family. The belief that Christians should be total abstainers is not widely held, even by Christians.

This survey, in common with Dight (1976) and Ritson *et al* (1981) found that people view drinking as a potential health hazard. What we do not know is at what level of drinking the general population believe a risk of hazard to health commences. This is hardly surprising, since the medical profession have yet to decide themselves on what is safe and what is hazardous drinking. A consensus is beginning to emerge between the various medical Royal Colleges that an increased risk can be detected at as little as 12 pints of beer (equivalent to 25 glasses of wine or single measures of spirits) per week (Royal College of Psychiatrists 1986).

Alcohol in Scotland Today

Scotland, like all developed countries, has experienced an economically and socially very costly rise in harm from drinking since 1950. We do not know exactly how much alcohol the population of Scotland drinks, because the most accurate measure of consumption (the Customs and Excise returns) does not distinguish Scotland from the rest of the United Kingdom. Surveys suggest that the amount of alcohol per adult consumed in Scotland is about the same as in England and Wales. However, there are slightly fewer regular drinkers in Scotland than in England or Wales. There is also a tendency for drinking to be compressed into slightly fewer occasions than in England and Wales. Thus, the rate of drinking (for example, the amount of alcohol per hour of a drinking occasion) is slightly higher in Scotland. This may be one reason for the higher rate of alcohol-related accidents and drunk-and-disorderly charges in Scotland, and the higher rate of admitted problems amongst drinkers surveyed in the general population (see, for example, Crawford *et al* 1985).

Increasing the proportion of the population who are abstainers is not thought to be an answer (Scottish Health Education Co-ordinating Committee 1985). Indeed, as stated, Scotland already has a higher proportion of abstainers – although that, in part, might be a reaction to the higher rate of problems here. The present survey shows that abstension is not prominent even amongst churchgoers. Church members of many denominations drink alcohol. This is associated, it would appear, with socially responsible attitudes to drinking. It is these socially responsible attitudes, based on a knowledge of the risks of harm from excessive drinking, that should be fostered. However, we all need to be aware of the mechanisms by which alcohol consumption within a population increases, and the increases in the overall level of drinking in the community are accompanied by greater risk of problems arising from drinking (Royal College of Psychiatrists 1986). Socially responsible drinking in the late 1980s also probably means a diminution by all of us in our overall consumption, particularly on some of those heavier occasions.

REFERENCES

Crawford A., Plant M.A., Kreitman N., Latcham R.W., (1985) Self-reported alcohol consumption and adverse consequences of drinking in five areas of Britian: general population studies. *British Journal of Addiction*, **80**, 421-8.

Dight, S. (1976) *Scottish Drinking Habits*. HMSO: London.

Knight, I., Wilson, P. (1980) *Scottish Licensing Laws*. HMSO: London.

Plant, M.A., Pirie, F. (1979) Self-reported alcohol consumption and alcohol-related problems: study in four Scottish towns. *Social Psychiatry*, **14**, 65-73.

Ritson, E.B., de Roumanie, M., Kendrick, A. (1981) *Community response to alcohol-related problems in Lothian*. Report of a joint SHHD/WHO Project. University of Edinburgh, unpublished.

Royal College of Psychiatrists (1986) *Alcohol – our favourite drug*. London: Tavistock.

Saunders, W.M., Kershaw, P.W. (1978) The prevalence of problem drinking and alcoholism in the West of Scotland. *British Journal of Psychiatry*, **133**, 493-9.

Scottish Health Education Coordinating Committee (1985) *Health education in the prevention of alcohol-related problems*. Scottish Health Education Group, Edinburgh.

Wilson, P. (1980) Drinking habits in the United Kingdom. *Population Trends*, **22**, 14-18.

CHAPTER TEN

A SWEDISH COMPARISON

Gunno Armyr

In Sweden, two lifestyle surveys have been carried out, which are similar to the present one undertaken by the Church of Scotland. These studies have been carried out among members in six associations of free churches in Sweden and among active members in the Lutheran State Church of Sweden. Many of the questions in the present study are identical with those that were used in the Swedish studies.

The Swedish surveys were initiated and sponsored by Ansvar Mutual Insurance Company for Total Abstainers and were carried out in close co-operation with the churches which were included in the surveys. The Ansvar Group of Insurance Companies has its headquarters in Sweden and offers insurance to total abstainers from alcohol in thirteen countries, including the United Kingdom.

The fieldwork of the Swedish survey in the Free Churches was undertaken in 1978 and the results were published in the book *Frikyrkosverige – en livsstilsstudie* (1979) and the data from the Lutheran Church were gathered in 1982 and published in the book, *Aktiva i Svenska kyrkan – en livsstilsstudie* (1983). A parallel study was also undertaken in the secular temperance movement in Sweden in 1978.

The Free Churches' survey is representative for those 3 to 5% of the adult population who are members of these churches. The free churches which participated in the study were; the Methodist Church, the Salvation Army, the Pentecostal Movement, the Baptist Union, the Covenant Missionary Church and the Orebro Missionary Society. In Sweden 95% of the population are members of the Lutheran State Church. In the survey, only those members who are the most active ones were studied. Here, data will be used which is representative for those 7% of the population *who attend church services in the Lutheran State Church at least once a month*. The figures for the Free Churches are based on 2017 interviews and those for the Lutheran Church are based on 396 interviews.

From this description of the groups that were included in the Swedish survey it is evident that there are limitations as far as comparability with Scottish conditions is concerned. However, bearing these limitations in mind, some comparisons will all the same be made between the results of the Swedish study and the results which refer to the members of the Church of Scotland.

Age and sex

The age distribution of the Swedish church members deviates from that of the average adult population of the country in very much the same way as in Scotland. The churches have among their members proportionately fewer in the young age groups and a proportionately higher number in the older age groups, which can be seen in Table 10.1.

Table 10.1

Age Group	Free Churches %	Lutheran State Church %	Swedish population according to census data %
18–29	15	7	21
30–49	25	24	34
50–64	26	28	23
65+	33	40	22

Similar results can also be seen in Sweden and in Scotland in respect of sex distribution. In both cases a higher proportion of females is found within the churches than in the population as a whole (Table 10.2).

Table 10.2

Sex	Free Churches %	Lutheran State Church %	Swedish population according to census data %
Female	56	62	51
Male	41	35	49
Not applicable	3	3	—

Social Class, Education and Income

From answers to questions about education and income it can be seen that regular church attendants of the Lutheran State Church and members of the Free Churches are in a better socio-economic position than the average population. They are relatively well educated and well settled in their social position.

Church Attendance

Since the sampling criterion for the Lutheran Church was church service attendance, a comparison is made here only with the results from the Free Churches. Swedish Free Church members go to church considerably more

178

often than members of the Church of Scotland (Table 10.3).

Table 10.3
How often do you attend church?

Church Attendance	Swedish Free Churches %	Church of Scotland %
Several times a week	40	5
Once a week	34	41
Once or twice a month	10	19
More seldom	8	34
Never	1	2
No answer	8	—

Prayer

Members of the Church of Scotland seem less active in prayer than Swedish church members. A majority of the Swedish church members pray daily, whereas less than half of Church of Scotland members pray daily, as can be seen in Table 10.4.

Table 10.4
About how often do you pray?

Frequency of Prayer	Swedish Free Churches %	Swedish Lutheran State Church %	Church of Scotland %
Every day	86	60	36
2–3 times a week	5	9	13
Once a week	1	3	11
Seldom	3	21	24
Never or hardly ever	1	4	16
No answer	5	4	—

There is a clear difference between Swedish Free Church members and active members of the state church with 21% of active state church members stating that they seldom pray compared to only 3% of free church members.

Regarding Oneself as a Christian

The question whether the respondent regarded him or herself as a Christian was only included in the survey among active state church members. The results were very similar to those in the Church of Scotland, as can be seen from Table 10.5.

Table 10.5
Do you regard yourself as a Christian?

Commitment	Swedish Lutheran State Church %	Church of Scotland %
Yes	86	87
No	4	4
Doubtful, don't know	7	9
No answer	3	—

Theological Questions

In the Swedish survey among active members of the state church a number of theological questions were put, which are identical to those in the Church of Scotland survey.

Asked 'Do you believe that God controls our lives here and now?' very similar answers were given in Sweden and in Scotland (Table 10.6).

Table 10.6
Do you believe that God controls our lives here and now?

	Swedish Lutheran State Church %	Church of Scotland %
Yes	73	72
No	3	10
Don't know what to believe	19	18
No answer	5	—

The responses to a request to indicate which of a range of statements most closely corresponded to the respondents' view of God are shown in Table 10.7.

The view of God is obviously less clear-cut in the Church of Scotland than it is in the Swedish Lutheran Church. In both cases the view of a loving God who hears our prayers and controls our lives is the alternative which attracted the highest percentage of replies. In Sweden, however, the rest of the alternatives were chosen by fairly few of the respondents, whereas in Scotland the answers were more spread among the alternative statements, and for example three times as many in Scotland perceive God as 'a sort of distant, impersonal power or force'.

Asked whether they believed that Jesus died for their sins, 68% of the Swedish respondents answered in the affirmative, compared to 75% of Church of Scotland members.

An identical proportion of the Swedish and Scottish respondents believe that Jesus is risen from the dead (Table 10.8).

Table 10.7
*Which one of the following most closely corresponds
to your own opinion of God?*

	Swedish Lutherian State Church %	Church of Scotland %
All powerful judge who sees and judges our sins and virtues	8	13
Loving. He hears our prayers and controls our lives	64	41
A father whose concern is to save and to help	10	20
A sort of distant, impersonal power or force	5	14
No opinion	7	13
No answer	7	—

Table 10.8
Do you believe Jesus is risen from the dead?

	Swedish Lutheran State Church %	Church of Scotland %
Yes	73	74
No	2	7
Don't know what to believe	20	20
No answer	5	—

A slightly higher percentage give a direct negative response in Scotland, however. In both cases one fifth were undecided.

In both Sweden and Scotland high percentages are recorded as uncertain when it comes to the question of the individual's life after death (Table 10.9).

Table 10.9
Do you believe in the individual's life after death?

	Swedish Lutheran State Church %	Church of Scotland %
Yes	47	53
No	8	14
Don't know what to believe	34	33
No answer	11	—

181

One third say they 'don't know what to believe'. Only about half of the respondents express a firm belief in the individual's life after death.

A number of statements were given concerning opinions of the Bible. Both in Sweden and in Scotland the largest proportion saw the Bible as written by men and therefore requiring interpretation. This alternative reply attracted a higher percentage of responses in Scotland than in Sweden, however (Table 10.10).

Table 10.10
Which one of the following most closely reflects
your opinion of the Bible?

	Swedish Lutherian State Church %	Church of Scotland %
God's word – true in every detail	24	19
Written by men who were inspired by God and therefore must be interpreted	49	63
Contains much vision but God has not affected it specially	9	7
A normal book	—	2
No opinion	9	8
No answer	9	—

About one fifth to one quarter see the Bible as 'God's word – true in every detail'. A very small proportion in the Scottish, and no one in the Swedish sample saw the Bible as 'a normal book'.

Again, very similar responses were given to the question of what happens after death. A higher percentage of the Scottish respondents believe nevertheless, that 'man's soul goes to another existence' (Table 10.11).
In both groups the most commonly-held view is that 'we don't know what happens after death'.

Lifestyle

Respondents were asked to state whether they agreed or disagreed with each of a list of statements regarding behaviours and attitudes relating to social, political and moral questions. Comparisons are made in Table 10.12 for a number of statements which had an identical wording in the Swedish and the Scottish studies.

If we look at the first item in Table 10.12, we see that whereas 81% of the Church of Scotland members agree with the statement that 'our family do many things together', only about half that percentage agree in the Swedish

182

Table 10.11
*Which one of the following is nearest to your
own opinion of what happens after death?*

	Swedish Lutherian State Church %	Church of Scotland %
After death man stands before God and his judgement	28	31
Man's soul lives forever without judgement	10	6
Man's soul goes to another existence	2	12
Death is the end – man ceases to exist	3	8
We don't know what happens after death	46	41
No opinion	11	3

Table 10.12
Indicate your view on each of the following

	Percentage who agree		
	Swedish Free Churches %	Swedish Lutheran State Church %	Church of Scotland %
Our family do many things together	39	45	81
I like simple things and a natural way of life	82	80	96
The only way to get something valuable is to save for it	57	71	85
I prefer to pay cash even it I have to wait for larger purchases	72	81	81
It would be useful for my to reduce my material standards	23	16	16
It is best to live in areas where all the neighbours have a similar standard	—	43	56
If I had a teenage daughter I would let her go on holiday with her boyfriend	15	18	49
If I had a teenage son I would let him go on holiday with his girlfriend	—	21	52
Religion is important in my life	80	62	76
When I join a club or society I engage myself fully in its work	27	25	58

surveys. Obviously the Scottish church members are more family-oriented than the Swedish ones.

On the second item a surprisingly high percentage of Church of Scotland members agree with the assertion that 'I like simple things and a natural way of life'. Also in Sweden the percentages are high, but still significantly lower than the Scottish figure on this aspect of life-satisfaction.

The following statements, covering aspects of people's attitudes towards material objects, show in the first place that the Scottish members are more inclined to believe that the only way to obtain things of value is to save for them. Similar to the Swedish respondents, they also express a preference for paying cash for purchases. Finally, one out of six Church of Scotland members, as well as of active members of the Swedish Lutheran Church, agree with the statement that it would be useful for them to reduce their material standards, whereas one out of four in the Swedish Free Churches agree to the same statement.

About half the Church of Scotland members and active members of the Swedish Lutheran Church think 'it is best to live in areas where all the neighbours have a similar standard'. This statement was not included in the Free Churches questionnaire.

The responses to the two statements concerning approval of a teenage son or daughter going on holiday with a partner of the opposite sex show consistency within each sample, but large differences between Sweden and Scotland. Scottish attitudes are much more liberal than the Swedish ones in this respect.

A slightly lower percentage in the Swedish Lutheran Church agree that 'religion is important in my life' compared to the other two groups, where four out of five affirm that religion in important in their lives.

A surprisingly high proportion of the Church of Scotland sample say that they engage themselves fully in the work of clubs or societies of which they are members. The corresponding Swedish percentages are less than half of the Scottish one.

Alcohol

Quite substantial differences emerge between the groups we compare when it comes to alcohol habits. Table 10.13 shows that the proportion who never drink alcohol is twice as high in the Swedish Lutheran survey compared to the Church of Scotland. On the other hand, since the proportion of abstainers in the general population is about twice as high in Sweden, the proportion who abstain could, from this viewpoint, be said to be comparable in the two churches. In the Swedish Free Churches the proportion of abstainers was 80%. As a matter of fact, against the background of the temperance tradition in the Swedish Free Churches, it caused much distress among Free Church leaders in Sweden when it was realised that the figure was not closer to 100%.

Table 10.13
How would you describe your present consumption of alcohol?

	Swedish Free Churches %	Swedish Lutheran State Church %	Church of Scotland %
Never drink alcohol	80	36	17
Very occasionally drink alcohol	13	48	37
Occasionally drink alcohol	2	11	35
Regularly drink alcohol	1	1	10
No answer	4	4	1

The main reason for drinking given by those who do not abstain is shown in Table 10.14. (The respondents had the opportunity to give more than one answer.)

Table 10.14
If you drink at all, what are your main reasons for drinking?

	Swedish Free Churches %	Swedish Lutheran State Church %	Church of Scotland %
Easier social contact	13	7	42
Easier to relax	8	4	54
In order not to appear self-righteous	5	2	12
Abstinence is out of date	5	3	5
Atmosphere better with a little alcohol	17	10	35
Increase value of a good meal	55	31	57
Difficult to be TT in my job	2	1	3
Don't believe I'd be damaged	11	6	25
Want to use Christian freedom	3	5	7
Don't want to be different from friends	6	3	10
Medicinal	3	8	19
Other reasons	12	7	20
No answer	12	44	—

The most common motive for drinking in all three groups is that alcohol increases the value of a good meal. Other important reason are that it eases social contact, makes it easier to relax and that the atmosphere becomes better with a little alcohol. In the Swedish surveys the motive that alcohol 'increases the value of a good meal' is outstanding in comparison with the other motives.

It is very clear that in all three groups the reason that it is difficult to be a teetotaller in the job is a very unimportant one. Theological reasons, such as 'to use Christian freedom' or 'in order not to appear self-righteous' are also of virtually no importance.

A question asking the respondents why they did not drink more than they do had somewhat different reply alternatives so direct comparisons cannot be made. It can be observed, however, that whereas the arguments 'damaging to my health', 'don't want to get drunk', and 'drinking and driving is against the law', are the most common answers in the Scottish sample, the answer, 'I have no need for alcohol' is the most common one in the Lutheran survey and, 'my Christian conviction makes me abstain from alcohol' is the most common answer in the Free Churches sample. In second place comes 'damaging to my health'. Being an example for one's children is as important a motive in Sweden as it is in Scotland.

Conclusions

Given the limitations in comparability indicated above between the groups which are studied in Sweden and in the Church of Scotland respectively, it can still be observed that many striking similarities exist between church members in Scotland and in Sweden.

The age and sex distribution of the church members are very much the same in Scotland and in Sweden. As in Scotland, Swedish church members are relatively well educated and well settled in their social position.

The question whether one regards oneself as a Christian gave almost identical results. Also most of the theological questions gave very much the same answers. The same proportion affirm a belief that God controls our lives here and now, about the same proportion believe that Jesus died for their sins, and an identical proportion believe that Jesus has risen from the dead. Similar results were given to the question on belief in the individual's life after death and on the way the respondent views that Bible as well as to the question of what happens after death.

Some differences can also be observed, however. Church attendance is lower among members of the Church of Scotland and the frequency of prayer is likewise lower than in the Swedish sample. Some lifestyle differences can also be noted. Scottish respondents are, for example, more inclined to do many things together with the family, to like simple things and a natural way of life, as well as to hold the opinion that the only way to get something valuable is to save for it.

Differences in habits concerning the consumption of alcohol can also be observed, although the differences in the consumption of the average populations in the two countries should be borne in mind when comparisons are made. This being said, it can be noted that 17% of the Church of Scotland members never drink alcohol compared to 36% among active members of the Swedish Lutheran State Church and 80% of the Swedish Free Church members. The most common motive for drinking given by those who do not abstain is in both countries, that alcohol increases the value of a good meal. Whereas 'Christian conviction' and 'no need for alcohol' are the most frequent motives in Sweden for not drinking more alcohol, in Scotland the health motive is the dominant reason.

CHAPTER ELEVEN

WHAT FUTURE FOR THE CHURCH?
SOME SPECULATIONS ON THE RESULTS

Dr A Robertson

What sense can we begin to make of the trends described in Chapters One to Six?

Perhaps the most important findings from the church's point of view are those pointing to its dependence on a largely middle-class membership, and the long-term decline that has apparently taken place in churchgoing and in the frequency with which people indulge in such devotional activities as Bible-reading and prayer. Equally significant, and in many ways more interesting (though it will not form part of our main discussion here), is the fact that women appear to have been less influenced than men by this tendency towards a more secular way of life. This is, moreover, reflected not only in acts of formal religious observance, but also in the more hidden aspects of their personal beliefs, with women as a sex proving much more likely to believe in God and in Eternal Life; and to subscribe to the beliefs that Jesus died for our sins and is risen from the dead, and that God exercises a daily and caring surveillance over our lives. Such beliefs seem also for the most part to be shared by women who are not themselves members of an organised church, as well as those with a formal religious affiliation.

Popular Values and Social Change

With regard to the declension of church attendance and religious behaviour, the data do strongly suggest that a genuine change has been taking place over time in the extent and depth of people's acceptance of religious values. Any attempt to explain this trend will clearly require to take account of factors that are as complex as they are diffuse. The progressive rise over the course of the present century in both the power and the prestige of scientific approaches to the study and explanation of phenomena has almost certainly played a part in this. A set of vaguely 'scientific' notions now probably form the main basis of most people's understanding of the world they live in, more religiously-based interpretations having tended to be set on the defensive. In particular, popular views concerning human nature now seem likely to be shaped by the empiricism and reductionism of social-science models that account for our behaviour in terms of biology, social environment, or specific types of experience, rather than by concepts such as human spirituality, Divine Grace and personal salvation. The essentially pastoral imagery which surrounds Christian teaching may perhaps also have come to be seen as diminishing its relevance for a modern urban industrial society – to the extent that its core message of the dignity of the individual and the brotherhood of man has been incorporated into doctrines that locate these values within a purely secular and materialistic frame of reference, and which promise to attain them in the present world through human effort.

A further element which is perhaps linked to the above is the transition brought about by Keynesian economic policies. From a system based on low average wages and fluctuating high levels of unemployment, Keynesian doctrines transformed the British economy into one in which (until relatively recently) employment was maintained at a fairly high and constant level and earnings were substantially increased. The key to employment policy in the latter half of the twentieth century has been (again, until fairly recently) the regulation of effective demand for goods by such devices as giving consumers extra spending power, or loosening restrictions on credit for purchases. For our present purposes, perhaps the most important consequences of such policies were a rise in the standard of living, and a major increase in the production (and purchase) of consumer goods, with a related growth in advertising.

As a result of this growth of consumer industries, personal consumption has become a dominant factor in the lives of individuals in the West, where Keynesian policies were of course almost universally applied during the period from 1945 to the mid-1970s. This in turn fostered the development of a set of attitudes and assumptions which are appropriate to the notion of consumption as a dominant goal or theme in life. This whole pattern was further reinforced by an increase in both the size and the sophistication of the advertising industry. By contrast, a pre-Keynesian economy encouraged the development of values and attitudinal systems which enabled individuals to adapt more readily to the facts of scarcity and insecurity in their lives (Inglehart 1977).

Work undertaken elsewhere by the present author (Robertson and Cochrane 1976A, 1976B) suggests that these changes led to the development of a system of values based on the premises that:

(i) All human beings are endowed with a set of innate 'potentials', which it is the purpose of life to express, develop or fulfil.

(ii) The extent to which the individual is able to fulfil these potentials is dependent on the social and physical environment within which he or she finds him or herself.

(iii) The responsibility for providing the means for satisfying individual potentials lies in society, rather than the individual. Among other things, this has given rise to pressures for the reform or elimination of social arrangements which are seen as inhibiting, as well as the creation of new agencies to maximise individual fulfilment.

Evidence from this work also suggests that such ideas are held much more strongly by the generation, born after the last World War, which spent its formative years in the era when Keynesian economic policies were being most actively pursued. Ralph Turner (1969) has argued in similar vein that: 'The novel idea ... that a lack of a sense of personal worth is not private misfortune, but public injustice, is carried by youth, who are the main constituency for the new movements in the same manner that a rising industrial class and later a rising working class were constituencies in the earlier era.'

The transfer of allegiance from the church that has apparently taken place among the young may therefore at least partly be explained by a change in values caused by economic policies that gave pre-eminence to individual consumption. Yet Keynesian approaches to managing the economy have clearly had to be revised in the light of the very high inflation that followed the substantial increases in the price of oil and other raw materials which occurred in the mid-1970's. In particular, we are now seeing levels of unemployment which would have been regarded as unthinkable ten years ago; and personal consumption has obviously had to be substantially reduced for a considerable proportion of the population. One might therefore hazard the prediction that popular values will begin to change again over the relatively near future, following the changes which are currently taking place in our economy and the material basis of our society. An opportunity possibly exists here for the church to take on an important role in shaping emerging attitudes and values. This may also be fruitfully linked to the growing debate about the future of the welfare state.

Christianity and the Future of the Welfare State

Part of that debate is about the institutional structure of the Welfare State and its relationship to the needs of an industrial economy. In consequence of the economic trends referred to in the previous paragraph, low or zero growth seems likely to remain a fact of (Western) economic life over the foreseeable future. Among other things, this is causing increasingly obvious strains upon the Welfare State, which was until recently, based on the assumption that higher levels of collective provision could be financed from the surplus accruing from annual 'growth' within an industrial economy. Western Governments are now having to review their welfare systems and to consider ways in which continued investment in social policies may be reconciled with the demands of economic efficiency and attempts at growth.

The response of the present Government, for example, is founded on a belief in the disciplines of the market-place; and upon a reliance on market forces and retrenchment of social expenditure to rectify the economy. Its policies have favoured the advantaged classes, and have conversely imposed considerable costs upon the poor and the generally more under-privileged strata in our society. For instance, the cuts that have occurred in social spending have consistently taken place in services for needy minorities in such areas as housing and unemployment benefit, local authority residential accommodation and the home-help service. The Left's answer has been rather more uncertain, founded as it is upon a desire to protect welfare

191

structures and return to something approaching full employment, together with an apparent unwillingness to consider the prices and incomes policy that would seem necessary to make these targets feasible and which, according to Mishra (1984, especially Chapter 4), has enabled 'Integrated Welfare States such as Austria and Sweden to maintain both full employment and high levels of social spending, whilst also managing a satisfactory level of economic growth.

Indeed, Mishra's valuable analysis points clearly to what seems like a very effective solution to the dilemma we are addressing. Rather than pursuing economic and social objectives largely independently of each other, countries such as Austria and Sweden have set up arrangements which permit representatives of identified interests within society to seek solutions that harmonise economic and welfare objectives.

Whilst undoubtedly important, Mishra's prescriptions do, however, relate only to the decision-making *structures* of the Welfare State and say nothing about the *content* of the system which those decisions are intended to perpetuate. It is perhaps in this area that the greatest potential exists for Christian thought and leadership to exercise some sway over the future progress of events.

Christian Values and the Welfare State

In aggregate, the findings of the present survey suggest the lifestyle, attitudes and goals of members of the Church of Scotland – with their emphasis on sexual morality, their tendency to restrict their social circle and the contentment they appear to feel in surveying their own life histories – to be more governed by the desire to avoid doing what is bad, than by a concern to pursue more positively what is good. This perhaps points to a failing in the teaching of the Church itself. Clearly, personal probity and piety are important aspects of the Christian life. But on their own, they form an inadequate representation of the Christian ideal. As was noted above, the core of Christian teaching rests in its message of the dignity of the person and the brotherhood of man, together with the promise of personal salvation through the gift of Divine Grace. These principles introduce a number of distinctive elements to our understanding of social policy and provide a basis for inserting a set of specifically Christian perspectives into the debate about the future of the Welfare State. Indeed, this is a debate from which Christians cannot responsibly remain aloof.

A founding principle of the Welfare State was, for instance, the promotion of equality through the provision of services that are comprehensive in scope, universal in coverage and free at the point of access. Analyses undertaken by such authors as Legrand (1983) and in the *Black Report* on inequalities in health (Townsend and Davidson 1982) have highlighted not only the failure of the Welfare State to reduce the substantial inequalities that exist in areas such as health, income and educational attainment, but also the extremely ambiguous nature of the concept of equality itself and the uncertainty of its meaning in talk about the Welfare State.

One of the most influential attempts to justify equality as a goal of social programmes has probably been that of Crosland (1956), who equates it mainly with equality of opportunity. Such a view, however, presents a very unsatisfactory vision of equality since although; 'all careers may be equally open to all, ... in the absence of measures which prevent the exploitation of groups in a weak economic position by those in a strong, and make the external conditions of health and civilisation a common possession, the phrase equality of opportunity is obviously a jest' (Tawney 1964, p.110).

Moreover, the notion of equality of opportunity ultimately rests on an individualistic view that all should have an 'equal opportunity to become unequal'. It 'obscures some of the more glaring and obnoxious symptoms of the "disease of inequality" at the expense of making the infection even worse' (Forrester 1985, p.30).

Christians tenets would suggest that welfare transcends individuals and requires to be considered also from a structural point of view – in terms of the relationships of power, advantage and privilege that exist between the constituent members of society. The ends of welfare would therefore seem to require that equality be construed in terms that go beyond the simple notion of equality of opportunity. Rather, it should be concerned with the removal of unjustifiable inequalities that present advantages to certain individuals over others. The debate over what inequalities might be 'justifiable' or otherwise, what procedures might be adopted for removing inequalities and where the limits of legitimate state intervention can be drawn, is of continuing importance for social policy, and is surely one to which the Christian Church can and should make a distinctive contribution. A starting point would be the removal of inequalities that are destructive of human fellowship and mutual respect. The data from the present study do however, suggest that these issues are not seen as primary by members of the Church of Scotland, who place a relatively low priority on increased awareness of economic and social injustice as an area of concern for the Church.

Much has been made of the dangers which such a pursuit of equality would entail for the freedom of the individual within society. Indeed, Friedman has gone so far as to claim that material equality and freedom are antithetical; 'One cannot be both an egalitarian and a liberal' (Freidman 1962, p.195). Under this view, individuals are seen as essentially rational beings, making choices which are designed to obtain the maximum satisfaction to be derived from the various options open to them, given the constraints imposed by the resources they have at their disposal. Government intervention in the interests of promoting welfare is considered unwarranted, except for a very limited range of functions such as defence and a judicial system. The belief underlying this approach is that Government decision-making will, (a) impose collective duties or requirements upon people which, as freely functioning individuals, they might be unwilling to accept and, (b) in any case, prove ultimately less effective in securing welfare and the general good.

At one level, this emphasis on individual liberty is of course consistent with Christian notions concerning the transcendence of God and Protestant teachings about the achievement of Grace through individual action. Weber's famous thesis on *The Protestant Ethic and the Spirit of Capitalism* locates the genesis of capitalism in motivations created by the Calvinistic search for self-denial and other signs of Grace in one's personal life and circumstances (Weber 1930). In the present case, one could perhaps ascribe the apparent emphasis on personal probity among Church of Scotland members at least partly to these individualistic emphases within their religion. Freedom, however, is certainly a more complex notion than is implied in the often crude appeals to the concept of individual responsibility presented by certain protagonists of the 'New Right'.

Against the view that individuals should be allowed to pursue whichever goals they hold personally important, one can, for instance, ask the question as to whether certain standards are not intrinsically better than others; and Christianity must surely have a relevant contribution to make to attempts to answer this question. However, more important for present purposes is the argument that, to view the 'freedom' to make judgements or decisions in isolation from the social and economic conditions in which people live, is to ignore the fact that the power to exercise such freedom is constrained by one's access to economic and other resources which are distributed unequally in society. Within such a system, in other words, economic inequalities will tend to undermine the equalities which people enjoy before the law, and in consquence render individual liberty a formal rather than a substantive entity. There is in fact a good deal of evidence that inequalities in such areas as education, housing conditions and security of income constrain individual freedom and choice in very significant ways (see, for example, George and Wilding 1976, Chapter 6).

It would, therefore, seem legitimate to argue that we cannot regard the liberty of the individual without regard to his or her social circumstances. Within Western society, on the other hand, the problem of economic and social inequality is due only in part to wealth and its associated possibilities for the transmission of advantage through inheritance. Though there is certainly a tendency, in certain quarters, to exaggerate the importance of effort and/or merit as factors in producing inequality, it is perhaps prudent to conclude that, to be persuasive, any argument based on principles of justice will require to stress that the correction of inequalities is legitimate only insofar as factors other than effort or merit are the cause of inequality. Again, Christian values and perspectives deserve to be inserted into this debate. Among other things, however, the findings of the present survey indicate that a major task lies in convincing church members of the importance of trying to do so.

Personal Caring and the Welfare State

Nestled inside the bureaucratic structures and arrangements of the Welfare

State there lies an assumption that the ends of welfare will be secured within a publicly-provided system of services and benefits, staffed by trained professionals. Recent experiences have, however, created a degree of disenchantment with the social services and caused people to call such notions into question. It has, for example, been argued by various authors that the Welfare State's reliance on large bureaucratic structures for the delivery of its services has made it remote from, and insensitive to, the needs and priorities of the public it purports to serve (see, for example, Ignatieff 1984; Williams 1985). Taylor-Gooby has made an extensive investigation of British attitudes towards the Welfare State which highlights the degree of impatience people feel with the regulations and restrictions of the 'nanny state'. He has also underlined the importance they attach to what they see as an 'adequate' level of Welfare-State-Provision (and their resulting opposition to real cuts in a system which they value) (Taylor-Gooby 1985, 1986).

Moreover, the strains and pressures produced within the social services by reductions in financial investment have led professionals to take industrial action as a means of improving their position. Whilst there has been a good deal of sympathy for the difficulties currently faced by personnel inside those services as a result of resource shortages, their use of strike action has undoubtedly also fostered public cynicism towards their claim concerning disinterested service for the public benefit. It has proved, for instance, a chastening experience to hear social workers in Newcastle-upon-Tyne cite as evidence of the need for their services, the fact that in the course of their strike in the early 1980s, the number of deaths among elderly people in their areas had increased by a certain factor above normal expectation; to see teachers in the public sector admit that as a consequence of their progressively-extended industrial action, the educational chances of a generation of children unlucky enough to have been born into these troubled times would be significantly impaired; and to learn of the suffering and discomfort caused to bedridden and handicapped patients in the National Health Service by the withdrawal of necessary laundry and domestic services in support of a pay claim by hospital workers.

Welfare State and Welfare Society

Can state welfare systems be reorganised in a way that reduces or avoids such problems? The most coherent traditional defence of the Welfare State in this respect is probably contained in Richard Titmuss's analysis of *The Gift Relationship* (Titmuss 1970), which starts from the premise that the central issue in social policy is the tension between human tendencies towards egotism and altruism, with social policy seen as representing the triumph of altruistic impulses in human life. For Titmuss, social policy is concerned with the 'social' element in human relations, with the 'social' being largely defined in terms of its distinctiveness from the economic element. The distinguishing feature of the 'social' is held to be 'The grant, or the gift or unilateral transfer

– whether it takes the form of cash, time, energy, satisfaction ... just as exchange or bilateral transfer is a mark of the economic.'

Unilateral transfers can take either of two forms: those that occur within the context of 'personal' and face-to-face relationships ('gifts'), and those taking place between strangers ('grants'). Each of these is justified by a different kind of appeal, the basis of the gift being personal ties and liking, and the knowledge others have of the individual as an individual, whereas the grant is rooted in 'stranger' relationships and based on an appeal to abstract 'social' or 'citizenship' rights. Social policy is essentially concerned with 'stranger' relationships – its prescriptions are built on a foundation of social rights and impersonal fellow feeling, justified by an appeal to the stranger's moral status as a fellow citizen or human being.

Titmuss's argument is an extension of T. H. Marhall's (1963) classic *Citizenship and Social Class*, in which the rights of citizenship are construed as an instrument for guaranteeing social responsibility for, and individual entitlements to, provision for a range of needs pertaining to individual welfare. In a complex industrial society, the abstract rights of citizenship accordingly take the place of the entitlements that arise in simple societies from the more immediate ties of custom and the obligations created by the sentiments woven into a network of intimate relationships.

Unilateral transfers are thus construed as integrative, in that they offer a moral status to both giver and receiver (Watson 1980). In enabling strangers to adopt the moral statuses of befriender and befriended, social policy allows the members of a modern society to become integrated into a moral community based on assisting 'strangers'. Such institutions and relationships stand in direct contrast to those operating through the 'bilateral' exchanges that attach to economic relationships, in which the motives fostered are egotistical and which place in jeopardy the altruistic feelings and impulses generated by unilateral transfers.

Social policy is therefore seen by Titmuss as a force for creating solidarity in a complex society, substituting altruism for the face-to-face obligations of a simple society, as the social cement that helps bind society together. By the same token, it also increases people's propensity to give, and so helps make them morally better.

*　　*　　*　　*　　*

Plainly, however, collective provision of services and benefits has not, as Titmuss hoped, *per se* proved sufficient to secure an integrated and caring society in this modern industrial age. The developments noted above in the recent history of the Welfare State confirm that fact.

Is state acceptance of responsibility for the welfare of its citizens simply proving to have been a unique and transient outgrowth of a particular group of societies at a specific point in their history? Will the Welfare State 'wither away' before the ineluctable winds of social and economic change? Or does it

196

correspond to more profound and permanent aspects of our social life and aspirations that will survive these temporary difficulties and re-emerge in something recognisably close to its present form? The answer to those questions, it seems to me, depends in large part on our being able to provide a proper rationale and justification for welfare provision.

Part of that rationale almost certainly requires the development of more participative structures that will give people the opportunity to become involved more directly in the governance of systems designed to provide services on their behalf. Our findings point clearly to the propensity of Church members to assume an active role in organisations to which they are attached, and this may be one sphere in which a Christian influence might make itself felt.

But how, in the final analysis, do we deal with the problems raised by the apparent future of the Welfare State to match up to the vision proposed by Titmuss? Can social policy become an instrument not only for attempting to promote social justice but also for the integration of individuals into a caring society? This is perhaps the most difficult task of all.

Public provision of services alone apparently cannot be relied upon to achieve this goal. Nor does even the ethic of professionalism render individuals immune from selfish and competitive individualism when they feel their interests to be affected. The Christian vision is ultimately one of a society of caring equals who are free to express their individuality in the pursuit of Divine Grace. It is the motivation relating to that final goal that perhaps provides the only proper and lasting basis for a caring society. It is to that the Church should probably look for its most distinct, lasting and effective contribution.

REFERENCES

Crosland, A. (1956) *The Future of Socialism*. London: Jonathan Cape.
Forrester, D. B. (1985) *Christianity and the Future of Welfare*. London: Epworth Press.
Friedman, M (1982) *Capitalism and Freedom*. Chicago: Chicago University Press.
George, V. and Wilding, P. (1976) *Ideology and Social Welfare*. London: Routledge & Kegan Paul.
Ignatieff, M. (1984) *The Needs of Strangers*. London: Chatto & Windus.
Inglehart, R. (1977) *The Silent Revolution: Changing Values among Western Publics*. Princeton, New Jersey: Princeton University Press.
Legrand, J. (1982) *The Strategy of Equality: Redistribution and the Social Services*. London: Allen & Unwin.
Marshall, T. H. (1963) Citizenship and social class', in T. H. Marshall, *Sociology at the Crossroads and Other Essays*. London: Heinemann.
Mishra, R. (1984) *The Welfare State in Crisis: Social Thought and Social Change*. Brighton, Sussex: Wheatsheaf Books.
Robertson, A. and Cochrane, R. (1976a) Deviance and cultural change, *International Journal of Social Psychiatry*, **22**, pp.79–85.
Robertson, A. and Cochrane, R. (1976b) Attempted suicide and cultural change: an empirical investigation, *Human Relations*, **29**, pp.863–83.

Tawney, R. H. (1964) *Equality*. London: Allen & Unwin.

Taylor-Gooby, P. (1985) *Public Opinion, Ideology and State Welfare*. London: Routledge & Kegan Paul.

Taylor-Gooby, P. (1986) Privatism, Power and the welfare state, *Sociology*, **20**, pp.228–46.

Titmuss, R. (1970) *The Gift Relationship: from Human Blood to Social Policy*. London: Allen & Unwin.

Townsend, P. and Davidson, N. (1982) *Inequalities in Health: the Black Report*. Harmondsworth, Middlesex: Penguin.

Turner, R. (1969) The theme of contemporary social movements, *British Journal of Sociology*, **20**, pp.390–400.

Watson, D. (1980) Richard Titmuss: social policy and social life, in N. Timms (ed.) *Social Welfare: Why and How?* London: Routledge & Kegan Paul.

Weber, M. (1930) *The Protestant Ethic and the Spirit of Capitalism*. London: Allen & Unwin.

Williams, S. (1985) Welfare Politics in Western democracies, in S. Eisenstadt and O. Ahimer (eds.) *The Welfare State and its Aftermath*. London: Croom Helm.

APPENDIX 1

Facsimile Questionnaire of The Lifestyle Survey

1. Please give your year of birth .... -11-12

2. Are you —

   Male ☐ -13
   Female ☐

3. How long have you lived at your present address?

   Less than 2 years ☐ -14
   2-5 years ☐
   6-10 years ☐
   11-20 years ☐
   More than 20 years ☐

4. (a) What age were you when you left school?

   15-16

   (b) Have you attended a College /University?

   Yes ☐ -17
   No ☐

5. What is your household's total annual income before tax?

   Under £5000 ☐ -18
   £5000-£7500 ☐
   £7501-£10,000 ☐
   £10,001-£15,000 ☐
   £15,001-£20,000 ☐
   £20,001-£25,000 ☐
   £25,001 plus ☐

6. Are you —

   Married ☐ -19
   Separated ☐
   Divorced ☐
   Widow/widower ☐
   Single ☐
   Co-habiting ☐

7. How many people in your household, including children?

   .... -20

8. (a) If you are in paid employment, what is your present job?

   ....-21

   Is this work —

   Full-time ☐ -22
   Part-time ☐
   or

   (b) If you are **not** in paid employment Are you —

   Pensioner ☐ -23
   Unemployed ☐
   Self-employed ☐
   Housewife ☐
   Student ☐

9. What sort of house do you have?

   Flat (a) owner/occupier ☐ -24
   (b) rented ☐
   or
   House (c) owner/occupier ☐
   (d) rented ☐
   Other — please specify ....

10. How many cars are in your household?

    .... -25

11. With what Company have you arranged car insurance?

    .... -26

12. Do you hold public office?
    For example — Are you a member of your Local Regional or District Council or Area Health Board?

    Yes ☐ -27
    No ☐

    If yes, please specify

    .... -28

200

13. With which **one** political party do you sympathise most? Tick one only

Conservative ☐ -29
Labour ☐
Liberal ☐
SNP ☐
SDP ☐
Communist ☐
Other ☐
None ☐

14. What is your level of commitment to the Church? Tick one only

Highly Committed ☐ -30
Fairly Committed ☐
Not Very Committed ☐
No Commitment ☐

15. How often do you attend Church services?
Tick one only

Several times a week ☐ -31
Once a week ☐
Approximately once a month ☐
Once a quarter ☐
Twice a year ☐
Once a year ☐
Only for Baptisms, Weddings and Funerals ☐
Never ☐

16. Earlier in your adult life, did you attend Church more or less frequently than now?

Tick one only

More frequently ☐ -32
About the same ☐
Less frequently ☐

17. In 5 years time, do you think your attendance will be —

Tick one only

More frequent ☐ -33
About the same as now ☐
Less frequent ☐
Difficult to know ☐

18. Do you listen to or view religious programmes on radio/TV?
Tick one only

Regularly ☐ -34
Sometimes ☐
Never ☐

19. How often do you read the Bible?
Tick one only

Every day ☐ -35
2-3 times a week ☐
Once a week ☐
Seldom ☐
Never or hardly ever ☐

20. Where would you say you gain your knowledge of Church events from?
Indicate three in order of importance 1, 2, 3 — 1 being the most important.

(a) Newspapers ☐ -36
(b) Radio ☐ -37
(c) Television ☐ -38
(d) Life and Work Magazine ☐ -39
(e) Other Church Literature ☐ -40
(f) Minister or Priest ☐ -41
(g) Not interested in Church events ☐ -42

21. (a) What daily newspaper(s) do you read?
.... -43

(b) What Sunday newspaper(s) do you read?
.... -44

(c) What religious newspaper(s) or magazine(s) do you read?
.... -45

(d) What weekly magazine(s) do you read?
.... -46

If the answer to any one of these is none, please write "none"

201

22. About how often do you pray?
Tick one only

Every day ☐ -47
2-3 times a week ☐
Once a week ☐
Seldom ☐
Never or hardly ever ☐

23. Do your family pray together?
Tick one only

Every day ☐ -48
2-3 times a week ☐
Once a week ☐
Seldom ☐
Never or hardly ever ☐
On special occasions only ☐
At times of special need only ☐

24. Was a devotional life, (praying, Bible reading), the rule in your childhood?
Tick one only

Yes ☐ -49
No ☐
Doubtful, don't know ☐

25. (a) Are you a member of the Church of Scotland?

Yes ☐ -50
No ☐

(b) If "no" — are you a member of another Church?

Yes ☐ -51
No ☐

If "yes", please specify

.... -52

(c) If you are a member of a Church, please indicate which are the three most important reasons for your Church membership

Please give your three reasons in order of importance 1, 2, 3 — 1 being the most important.

Wish to support the Church and Christian values ☐ -53
Opportunity for baptism, marriage, funerals ☐ -54
Participate in services/ Communion ☐ -55
Fellowship and contact with others ☐ -56

Support missionary work ☐ -57
Support everyday Christian life ☐ -58
Want to strive for justice and Christian solidarity ☐ -59
Natural for me to be member of the Church ☐ -60
Family expectations ☐ -61
Don't want to upset a relative/friend by leaving ☐ -62
Other reasons ☐ -63
Never thought of leaving ☐ -64
Nothing special ☐ -65

26. Of which of the following organisations within the Church of Scotland are you a member?
Tick all of those which apply to you

Uniformed organisations eg. Boys Brigade or Girls Brigade ☐ -66
Bible Class ☐ -67
Youth Fellowship ☐ -68
Woman's Guild ☐ -69
Other women's organisations ☐ -70
Men's organisations ☐ -71
House groups and Bible Study Groups ☐ -72
Prayer Groups ☐ -73

2

27. Do you hold any of the following positions of responsibility in the Church?
Tick all of those which apply to you.

Kirk Session member ☐ -11
Congregational Board Member ☐ -12
BB/GB Officer ☐ -13
Sunday School Teacher or Bible Class Leader ☐ -14
Guild Committee member ☐ -15
No ☐ -16
Does not apply ☐ -17

28. If you are married, is your spouse a member of:

The Church of Scotland ☐ -18
Another Church ☐
No Church ☐
Does not apply ☐

29. Do you regard yourself as a Christian?

Yes ☐ -19

No ☐

Doubtful, don't know ☐

30. Are you —

Baptised in the Church of
Scotland ☐ -20

Baptised in another Church ☐

Not baptised ☐

31. If you attended Sunday School at what age did
you stop?

.... 21-22

32. Is/was your mother a regular Church attender?
Tick one only

Yes ☐ -23

No ☐

Don't know ☐

33. Is/was your father a regular Church attender?
Tick one only

Yes ☐ -24

No ☐

Don't know ☐

34. Do you attend services in other denominations?
Tick one only

Every week ☐ -25

Every month ☐

Every few months ☐

Seldom ☐

Never ☐

35. Are you a member of any ecumenical group?

Yes ☐ -26

No ☐

36. Do you believe in God?
Tick one only

Yes ☐ -27

No ☐

Don't know what to believe ☐

37. Do you believe that God controls our lives
here and now?
Tick one only

Yes ☐ -29

No ☐

Don't know what to believe ☐

38. Which one of the following corresponds most
closely with your own opinion of God?
Tick one only

All powerful judge who sees
and judges our sins and
virtues ☐ -30

Loving, he hears our prayers
and controls our lives ☐

A father whose concern is to
save and to help ☐

A sort of distant, impersonal
power or force ☐

No opinion ☐

39. Do you believe Jesus died for your sins?
Tick one only

Yes ☐ -31

No ☐

Don't know what to believe ☐

40. Do you believe Jesus is risen from the dead?
Tick one only

Yes ☐ -32

No ☐

Don't know what to believe ☐

41. Do you believe in eternal life?
Tick one only

Yes ☐ -33

No ☐

Don't know what to believe ☐

42. Do you believe in the individual's life after
death?
Tick one only

Yes ☐ -34

No ☐

Don't know what to believe ☐

203

56. Is it consistent with Christianity to be a member of:

(a) The Orange Order:

Yes ☐ -70

No ☐

Don't know ☐

(b) Freemasons:

Yes ☐ -71

No ☐

Don't know ☐

(c) Knights of St. Columba

Yes ☐ -72

No ☐

Don't know ☐

57. Do you think that abortion is:
Tick one only.

(a) A matter entirely for the persons concerned ☐ -73

(b) Justifiable in certain circumstances ☐

(c) Always wrong ☐

(d) Don't know ☐

58. Do you think that it is ever right to have sexual intercourse before marriage?
Tick one only

Yes ☐ -74

Yes, but only if couple intend to marry ☐

Not under any circumstances ☐

Don't know ☐

59. Which of the following corresponds to your attitude towards homosexuality?
Tick one only

(a) An unnatural act ☐ -75

(b) Sexual love between members of the same sex is acceptable. ☐

(c) A personal matter — up to the individual ☐

(d) Don't know ☐

60. Please give your view on each of the following: (Answer these quickly — do not spend time agonising over your answers)

3

	Agree	Disagree	
In order to work more efficiently, I cut down on social life and pleasure	☐	☐	-11
Compared with other people of my age, I've made a lot of foolish decisions in my life	☐	☐	-12
Our family do many things together	☐	☐	-13
Regular exercise is important for me	☐	☐	-14
When I think back over my life I didn't get most of the important things I wanted	☐	☐	-15
I like to discuss politics and community questions	☐	☐	-16
I've got pretty much what I expected out of life	☐	☐	-17
I have to a great extent the things that make life really pleasant and satisfying for people my age	☐	☐	-18
I like simple things and a natural way of life	☐	☐	-19
I am just as happy now as when I was younger	☐	☐	-20
I am attracted by new religious groups outside the Christian Church	☐	☐	-21
Solidarity with the weak is important to me	☐	☐	-22
My life could be happier than it is now	☐	☐	-23

204

	Agree	Disagree	
Religion is important in my life	☐	☐	-24
When I join a club or society I engage myself fully in its work	☐	☐	-25
Compared with other people I get down in the dumps too often	☐	☐	-26
If I had a teenage daughter I would let her go on holiday with her boyfriend	☐	☐	-27
I feel just miserable most of the time	☐	☐	-28
I want to change society	☐	☐	-29
The only way to get something valuable is to save for it	☐	☐	-30
I am just as happy now as when I was younger	☐	☐	-31
I prefer to pay cash even if I have to wait for larger purchases	☐	☐	-32
I restrict my circle of friends to a few	☐	☐	-33
I like new exciting experiences even if they are a bit frightening or unconventional	☐	☐	-34
It would be useful for me to reduce my material standards	☐	☐	-35
I am not specially fashion conscious	☐	☐	-36
I think that private motoring has more disadvantages than advantages	☐	☐	-37
These are the best years of my life	☐	☐	-38
If I had a teenage son I would let him go on holiday with his girlfriend	☐	☐	-39
In an election I would always vote for a party with a strong defence policy	☐	☐	-40
I would not change my past life even if I could	☐	☐	-41
One shouldn't show one's feelings at work	☐	☐	-42
It is best to live in an area where all the neighbours have a similar standard	☐	☐	-43
I never felt better in my life	☐	☐	44
I would like to change society so that material things matter less	☐	☐	-45

During the past few weeks I have felt:

	Agree	Disagree	
Particularly excited or interested in something	☐	☐	-46
Proud because someone complimented me on something I had done	☐	☐	-47
Pleased about having accomplished something	☐	☐	-48
On top of the world	☐	☐	-49

43. Which **one** of the following most closely reflects your opinion of the Bible?

Tick one only

God's word — true in every detail ☐ -35

Written by men who were inspired by God and therefore must be interpreted ☐

Contains much vision but God has not affected it specially. ☐

A normal book ☐

No opinion ☐

44. There are different opinions about what happens after death. Which **one** of the following is nearest to your own?

Tick one only

After death man stands before God and His judgment ☐ -36

Man's soul lives forever without judgment ☐

Man's soul goes to another existence ☐

Death is the end — man ceases to exist ☐

We don't know what happens after death ☐

No opinion ☐

45. There are different opinions about heaven and hell. Which **one** of the following is nearest to your own?

Tick one only

Heaven and hell are places with eternal bliss or suffering where man must live after God's judgment ☐ -37

The expressions 'heaven' and 'hell' mean that after death, man may live near or far from God, but otherwise there are no possibilities. ☐

As such, heaven and hell do not exist — everything is related to man's life here and now. ☐

No heaven or hell now or in the future ☐

No opinion ☐

46. Which **one** of the following is nearest to your own opinion of humanity?

Tick one only

There is good and bad in everyone ☐ -38

Everybody is basically good ☐

Everybody is basically bad ☐

47. Looking again at the last eleven questions, would you say that these are questions which you think about?

Tick one only

Often ☐ -39

Seldom ☐

Never ☐

48. What do you think about each of the following things?

	Very Important	Important	Unimportant	Completely Unimportant	
Joint services for Church of Scotland and other denominations	☐	☐	☐	☐	-40
Improved co-operation between the Church of Scotland and other Protestant churches	☐	☐	☐	☐	-41
Joint Communion for Church of Scotland and other denominations	☐	☐	☐	☐	-42
Local Bible Study and prayer groups including Church of Scotland members and members of other churches	☐	☐	☐	☐	-43
Joint effort, eg. information campaigns about the under-developed countries	☐	☐	☐	☐	-44
Church of Scotland and other churches should have a common view on Bible translation	☐	☐	☐	☐	-45
Improved co-operation with the Roman Catholic Church	☐	☐	☐	☐	-46
Improved co-operation on inter-church marriage	☐	☐	☐	☐	-47

49. Indicate the degree of importance you think the following activities will have for the Church's future by ranking the three "most important" and the three "least important" in the columns below. Rank the three "most important" activities 1 - 3 in the first column, 1 being the most important. Similarly, rank the three "least important," 1 - 3 in the second column, 1 being the least important.

		Most Important	Least Important	
(a)	Political awareness	☐	☐	-48
(b)	Evangelisation	☐	☐	-49
(c)	Social Work	☐	☐	-50
(d)	Help to developing countries	☐	☐	-51
(e)	Work with pensioners and the sick	☐	☐	-52
(f)	Personal renewal	☐	☐	-53
(g)	Increased awareness of economic and social justice	☐	☐	-54
(h)	The position of women in the Church	☐	☐	-55
(i)	Efficient organisation and good financial management	☐	☐	-56
(j)	More spiritual leadership	☐	☐	-57
(k)	Christian Education	☐	☐	-58

50. Would you welcome greater control over the amount of sex and violence shown on television?

Tick one only

Yes ☐ -59
No ☐
Don't know ☐

51. Do you think there should be classification of home videos?

Tick one only

Yes ☐ -60
No ☐
Don't know ☐

52. Please rank the following jobs in order of importance in the life of the community.

Please number 1-6, 1 being the most important

Doctor ☐ -61
Policeman ☐ -62
Social worker ☐ -63
Minister ☐ -64
School teacher ☐ -65
Lawyer ☐ -66

53. If you are employed, would you ever go on strike?

Tick one only

Yes ☐ -67
No ☐
Don't know ☐
Does not apply ☐

54. What is your opinion of the present level of unemployment?

Tick one only

(a) Helpful for putting the unions in right perspective ☐ -68
(b) Necessary to get the country back on its feet economically ☐
(c) Unacceptable because of waste of human resources ☐
(d) No opinion ☐

55. What is your opinion of nuclear weapons?

Tick one only.

(a) An effective deterrent against war ☐ -69
(b) Morally unacceptable ☐
(c) No opinion ☐

61. During your free time do you prefer to be —
    Tick one only

    Alone ☐ -50
    With the family ☐
    With friends ☐
    In a crowd ☐

62. Do you like being with people whose ideas and values vary from your own?
    Tick one only

    Yes ☐ -51
    Don't mind ☐
    Prefer not to be ☐
    Not at all ☐

63. Do you ever feel lonely?
    Tick one only

    Yes often ☐ -52
    Yes sometimes ☐
    Seldom ☐
    Never ☐

64. Generally speaking, would you describe yourself as —
    Tick one only

    Very happy ☐ -53
    Quite happy ☐
    Not particularly happy ☐
    Not at all happy ☐

65. (a) How would you describe your present consumption of alcohol?
    Tick one only

    Never drink alcohol ☐ -54
    Very occasionally drink alcohol ☐
    Occasionally drink alcohol ☐
    Regularly drink alcohol ☐

    (b) How often do you drink each of the following:
    Tick as appropriate.

	Every day	Most days	Every week	Most weeks	Mthly	S'ldom	Never	
Beer	☐	☐	☐	☐	☐	☐	☐	-55
Wine	☐	☐	☐	☐	☐	☐	☐	-56
Fortified wine (port, sherry, etc.)	☐	☐	☐	☐	☐	☐	☐	-57
Spirits	☐	☐	☐	☐	☐	☐	☐	-58

66. (a) Do you make your own wine?

    Yes ☐ -59
    No ☐

    (b) Do you make your own beer?

    Yes ☐
    No ☐

67. If wine was served at a function, how would you react?
    Tick one only.

    Drink it ☐ -60
    Allow it to be poured and only sip it ☐ -61
    Say that you want something non-alcoholic ☐ -62
    Say that you don't want anything to drink ☐ -63
    Don't know — it depends on the situation ☐ -64

68. If you drink at all, what are your main reasons for drinking?

    Indicate three in order of importance, 1, 2, 3 — 1 being the most important

    Easier social contact ☐ -65
    Easier to relax ☐ -66
    In order not to appear self-righteous ☐ -67
    Abstinence is out of date ☐ -68
    Atmosphere is better with a little alcohol ☐ -69
    Increase the value of a good meal ☐ -70
    Difficult to be TT in my job ☐ -71
    Don't believe that I would be damaged ☐ -72
    Want to use Christian freedom ☐ -73
    Don't want to be different from friends ☐ -74
    Medicinal ☐ -75
    Other reasons ☐ -76

69. If you **do** drink, why do you not drink more? 〔4〕

Indicate three in order of importance, 1, 2, 3 — 1 being the most important.

Damaging to my health ☐ -11
To avoid a hangover the following day ☐ -12
I am resisting social pressure ☐ -13
Drinking in pregnancy damages the foetus ☐ -14
Don't want to get drunk ☐ -15
Don't want to risk becoming dependent ☐ -16
I drank too much in earlier life ☐ -17
For the sake of those damaged by alcohol ☐ -18
Drinking and driving is dangerous and against the law ☐ -19
Don't want to be a danger in traffic ☐ -20
Don't like the taste ☐ -21
Don't want to lose control ☐ -22
Don't want to gain weight ☐ -23
Example for my children ☐ -24
Example for others ☐ -25
Can't afford it ☐ -26
Have seen what alcohol has done to others ☐ -27
Solidarity with friends ☐ -28
Other reasons ☐ -29

(b) If you do **not** drink, why not?

Indicate three in order of importance 1, 2, 3 — 1 being the most important.

Damaging to my health ☐ -30
To avoid a hang-over the following day ☐ -31
Christian conviction leads me to abstain ☐ -32
Drinking in pregnancy damages the foetus ☐ -33
To resist social pressure ☐ -34
Don't want to risk becoming dependent ☐ -35
Drank too much in earlier life ☐ -36
For the sake of those damaged by alcohol ☐ -37

Want insurance and other financial advantages available to abstainer ☐ -38
Don't want to be a danger in traffic ☐ -39
Don't like the taste ☐ -40
No need of alcohol ☐ -41
Don't want to gain weight ☐ -42
Example for my children ☐ -43
Example for others ☐ -44
Have taken the pledge ☐ -45
Have seen what alcohol has done to others ☐ -46
Can't afford it ☐ -47
Solidarity with friends ☐ -48
Other reasons ☐ -49

70. Do you think a Christian should be a total abstainer?
Tick one only.

Yes ☐ -50
No ☐
Don't know ☐

71. Do you think that communion wine should be —
Tick one only.

Alcoholic ☐ -51
Non-Alcoholic ☐
Doesn't matter ☐
Don't know ☐

72. Do you smoke?
Tick one only.

Yes ☐ -52
No ☐

73. Do you think people should be allowed to use cannabis freely?
Tick one only.

Yes ☐ -53
No ☐
Don't know ☐

Thank you for completing this form. Please post it as soon as possible using the envelope supplied.

Dr. A. Robertson,
Lifestyle Survey Unit,
University of Edinburgh
Department of Social Administration,
Adam Ferguson Building,
George Square,
Edinburgh.